Robert L. Chapman's Ireland

Photographs from the Chapman Collection 1907–1957

Compiled by Christiaan Corlett

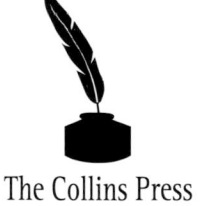

The Collins Press

First published 2008 by
The Collins Press,
West Link Park,
Doughcloyne,
Wilton,
Cork

British Library Cataloguing in Publication Data
Chapman, Robert L., 1891-1965
Robert L. Chapman's Ireland : photographs from the Chapman
Collection 1907-1957
1. Chapman, Robert L., 1891-1965 - Photograph collections
2. Ireland - History - 20th century - Pictorial works
3. Ireland - Social life and customs - 20th century -
Pictorial works
    I. Title
    779.9'9417
    ISBN-13: 9781905172771

Design and typesetting (inc. cover): Burns Design
Font: Bembo
Printed in Singapore by Tien Wah Press Pte. Ltd.

CONTENTS

Contents

CHRISTIAAN CORLETT, archaeologist
with the Department of Environment,
Heritage & Local Government, has
researched the Chapman collection
of photographs for some time.
Honorary Librarian of the Royal
Society of Antiquaries of Ireland, he
has an extensive knowledge of early
photographs and photographers.

Cover:
Robert L. Chapman

Frontispiece:
Cycling in snow at Glencree,
County Wicklow (F 161)
3 p.m., 2 April 1922
Imperial Non-filter Orthochromatic, f13, 1/50 sec

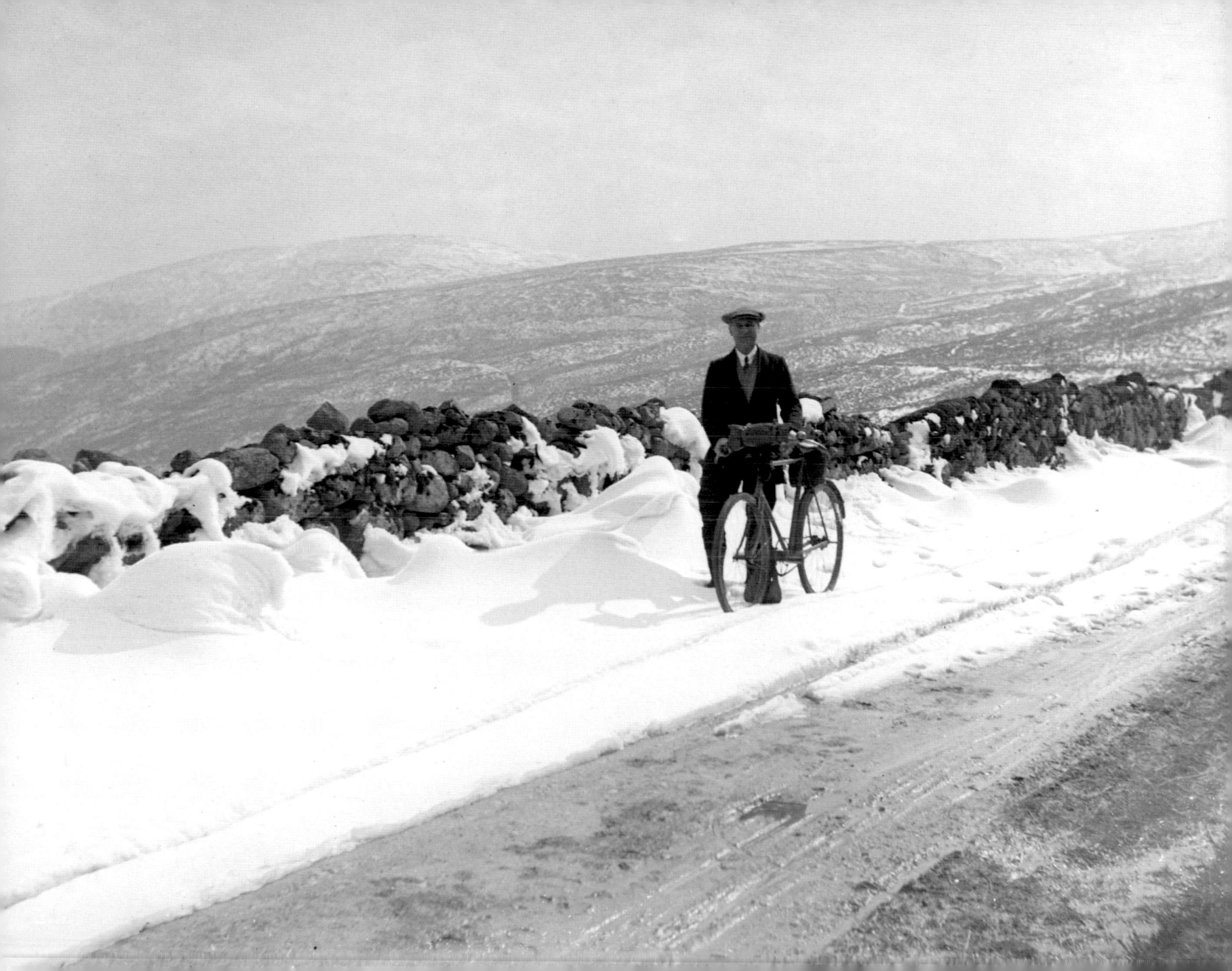

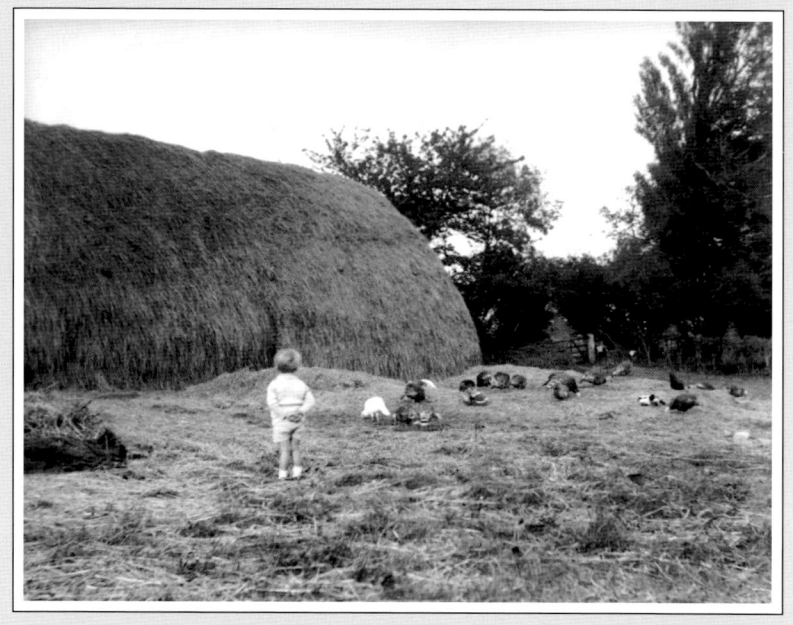

Eric Chapman in front of haystack at Ballyman Cottage, Old Connaught, County Dublin (E 1260)

2 p.m., 23 October 1927

Wellington Anti Screen, f8, 1/25 sec

PREFACE

The introduction by Christiaan Corlett covers many aspects of my late father's interest in cycling tours and photography. His membership of various cycling clubs is likewise recorded.

From my point of view, interest in Father's diaries and photographs did not come to the fore until I was married in 1958. In due course I inherited my father's home, Cloragh. My brother, who was five years older than I, had married and settled in the USA. He, like our father, took an interest in cycling and photography. Sadly, he died some years ago while still living in America.

I was six years old when I came to live in Cloragh in 1930 and at that age I had no interest in where my father's photographic items were stored. When the time came to find them I was at a loss.

My first find was some 2,900 old glass negatives in the somewhat damp garage at Cloragh. Then twenty old photo albums came to light under the stairs. Nine diaries were discovered in a garden shed, and finally a rather scruffy catalogue turned up, but where I can't recall. This was, perhaps, the most important item, which listed nearly all the photographs taken by my father from 1907.

In 2002, a Mr J.V. Kennedy, who had taken an interest in my findings, made prints for me of some negatives of trains and old crosses.

In 2003, by chance, I made contact with Davison & Associates Ltd., and entered into an agreement with them. They repaired some damaged negatives, made prints of interesting items, and established the Chapman/Livingston Collection. These now form part of their very valuable Irish Picture Library, where they are accessible to researchers.

It is an honour to see my father's photographs so tenderly respected and treated in this book, and I sincerely hope that they will bring much pleasure to the reader.

Eric H. Chapman

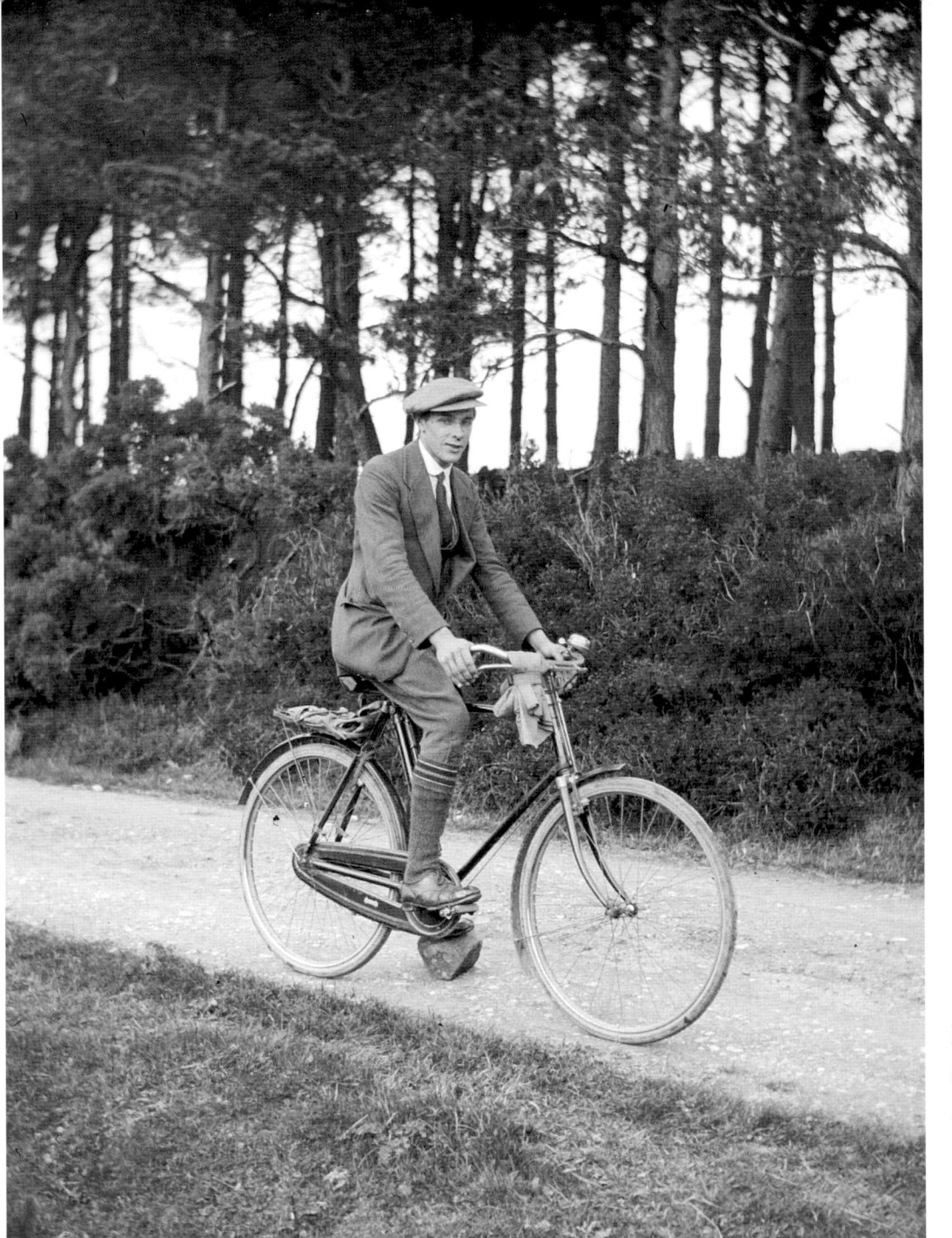

Robert L. Chapman (F 95)

6 p.m., 29 September 1918

Imperial Non-filter Orthochromatic, f8, 1 sec

IT IS EXTRAORDINARY TO THINK, at the turn of the twenty-first century, that extensive collections of Irish photographs, particularly those of amateur photographers, are still held privately and have never seen the light of day. A fine example of this is the collection of photographs taken by Robert L. Chapman, spanning the years 1907 to 1957. For many years these photographs have been held by RLC's son Eric Chapman, and, in more recent years, some have been available through the Irish Picture Library. Despite this, the collection remained unstudied and under-utilised as a historical resource. Here, a selection of photographs from this remarkable collection is reproduced in order to both acknowledge the photographic achievements of RLC himself and to draw attention to the existence of this wonderful visual record.

Born on 8 May 1891, Robert L. Chapman was the eldest son of William Henry Chapman and Amelia Beatrice Livingston. The Chapmans were a Quaker family, with roots that can be traced back to the seventeenth century in Carlow. RLC not only took his name from his mother's father, Robert R. Livingston, but he also appears to have acquired his interest in photography from his grandfather. RLC's brother Henry Harbourn was born in May 1892, and was always known as Harry. The family lived at Moyne Road, Ranelagh in Dublin, but RLC was educated at Newtown School, Waterford. Some of his earliest memories recorded in his diaries date from his

final years there. It was during this period that he developed a keen interest in both photography and cycling.

In 1918, RLC married Ethel Margaret Partridge and they subsequently had two sons, Ronnie and Eric. RLC recorded the arrival of Ronnie in his diary on 6 March 1919 – '*Arrival of R[obert] S[tuart] C. our future "Boss"*.' Eric was born on 4 April 1924. In the autumn of 1927 RLC and his family moved to Ballyman Cottage in the south of County Dublin, near Bray, where they lived for a number of years before finally settling down at Cloragh, Foxrock.

RLC began taking photographs in 1907 at the age of sixteen. By this time photography was a well-established profession and hobby. It is not clear where RLC got his training but like many photographers of that period he was most likely self-taught, though he was probably introduced to photography by his maternal grandfather. RLC was not a professional photographer – he took photographs for his own interest. However, he was certainly as skilled with the camera as many professional photographers of his time. A certain degree of his success must also be related to his use of a superior quality camera, although, it is not clear what type or make of camera he used in the early years. All we can say with certainty is that he used quarter-plate-sized glass negatives and that from 1926 many of his photographs were taken with a Goerz Box Tengor that used nitrate-based film negatives.

Many of the photographs appear in a variety of albums. Many more survive as negatives, and it would appear that he processed the prints from these himself. Perhaps what makes this collection stand out from many others of the period is that he maintained a meticulous catalogue of his photographs, in which each photograph was attributed a unique reference number, under which the image was identified. The catalogue also contains information regarding the time and date each photograph was taken, as well as the make of plate used, the exposure and f stop in each instance. (The f stop is the focal length of the camera divided by the diameter of the lens.)

In total there are 2,926 photographs listed in the catalogue. The catalogue is divided into seven sections. Sections A, B and C list photographs of railway subjects, mostly taken from 1907 to 1913. Section D lists photographs of boats and ships, and were mostly taken between 1908 and 1913. Clearly railway and shipping scenes were important subjects during his formative years as a photographer but RLC did not maintain a continued photographic interest in these subjects later in life. Section E is the largest section and lists some 1,370 photographs of landscapes and buildings. Another large number of photographs, 1,082 in total, are listed in Section G. These are photographs, also of landscapes and buildings, taken from 1926 to 1957 with a Goerz Box Tengor. Section F lists 251 portrait and group photographs, dating from 1908 to 1933. These are typically photographs of family, friends and members of the Irish Road Club or the Irish Cyclists Old Timers Fellowship.

The photographs are complemented by a collection of nine diaries covering the period from March 1909 to February 1931, though the first diary begins with some recollections of earlier years. The photographs are frequently referenced at the end of an entry, but the photographs themselves are rarely described in the diary entries. One of the few diary accounts of taking a photograph was recorded on 23 January 1927:

> *Near Calary tried a photo of Glencree with the snow on mtns. Stand trembled like an aspen leaf in the breeze. Hands did ditto in the cold. Put in slide crooked & dished the plate.*

Unfortunately, the diaries provide no insight into RLC's initial interest in photography nor, indeed, into how that interest developed over time. Instead, the diaries are primarily a record of cycling trips and the road and weather conditions encountered on these trips. There are accounts of other family trips, usually in and around Dublin, but also some longer cycling holidays around the country as well as descriptions of cycling trips to England, Wales, Scotland and the Isle of Man. However, and perhaps, inevitably, the entries reflect the changing political events during this period and provide a useful contemporary record of travelling, and in particular cycling, the roads of Ireland at the time.

For the most part RLC was dependent on his bicycle for transport. In 1918, the year he got married, he bought a tandem, which enabled him to travel by bicycle with his wife.

The subsequent addition to the family of two sons, Ronnie and Eric, meant that, in 1924, RLC was forced to acquire a motorcycle and sidecar, which was not his preferred choice of transport. At the end of that year he wrote:

Did some Motor cycling on Ariel sidecar outfit but don't like it, though it is useful for bringing family about. Too much time has to be spent overhauling while it is dangerous compared to cycling.

The first diary is entitled 'Cycling & other Notes', and begins with some early recollections of cycling while still attending Newtown School, Waterford:

My first cycling experiences are mostly obscured by the years which have passed, but one or two experiences are still fresh in my memory. I learnt to ride on a variety of machines. Some had fixed others freewheels … In those far-away days the freewheel was not by any means universal. Well do I remember a school fellow 'Skins' who had an old fixed wheel bike which he had not yet converted. I met him on his first run on the freewheel just emerging from the School Gates. That picture of flying pedals, waving legs & bad language will live long in my memory.

One day, wishing to ride to Dunmore, I managed to get the loan of a bike. The machine was fitted with a freewheel but both brakes were out of order so I had some exciting experiences descending a steep hill near Waterford. I saw in front of me 2 priests who completely blocked the road & paid no heed to my frantic bell ringing. I was in a desperate fright as I thought the penalty for running down a priest would be something appalling.

I managed to pass between the reverend gentlemen with about an inch to spare. They were both somewhat surprised & said their prayers hurriedly, at least I suppose it was prayers. On the return journey I had a somewhat similar experience. This time it was a herd of cattle so I steered for the middle of the fattest one. Fortunately my intended buffer stop moved in time & I got by leaving the drover to set fire to the hedgerows with his remarks.

On 24 March 1909, he recorded in his diary the purchase of what may have been his first bicycle:

Invested in a second-hand Rover bicycle. 26" frame. 28" wheels. Dunlop 28x1½" tyres. Gear about 59. Leather gearcase. Pull up front brake & wire rear brake. Weight about 38lbs. Cost £3.5.0.

Perhaps it was this bicycle that he used in 1910 for the qualifying membership of the Irish Road Club. The main requirement to join was to cycle 100 miles in 12 hours or 150 miles in 24 hours. On 4 May 1910 he cycled 206 miles in 24 hours, thereby qualifying for membership. Over the years he invested in other bicycles, including a tandem in 1919:

Bought Raleigh Cross-Frame Tandem (second-hand) 3 speed Sturmey Archer Gear old model, Normal 75. 2 Wire brakes, new front saddle. Cost £10.0.0

On 28 March 1925 he bought a 'new' Peugeot bicycle:

Frame, chain, wheel, cranks etc almost new. BSA North Road Drop Handlebars of good but ancient vintage, they having passed

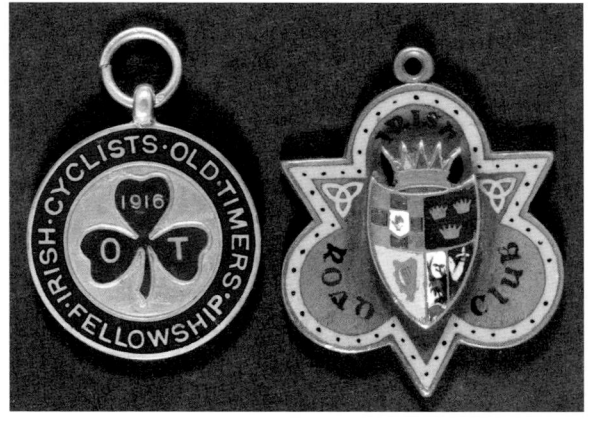

Above: Irish Cyclists Old Timers Fellowship medal (left) and Irish Road Club medal recording his 206-mile cycle ride in 24 hours.

Right: Certificate of Honorary Life Membership of the Irish Road Club.

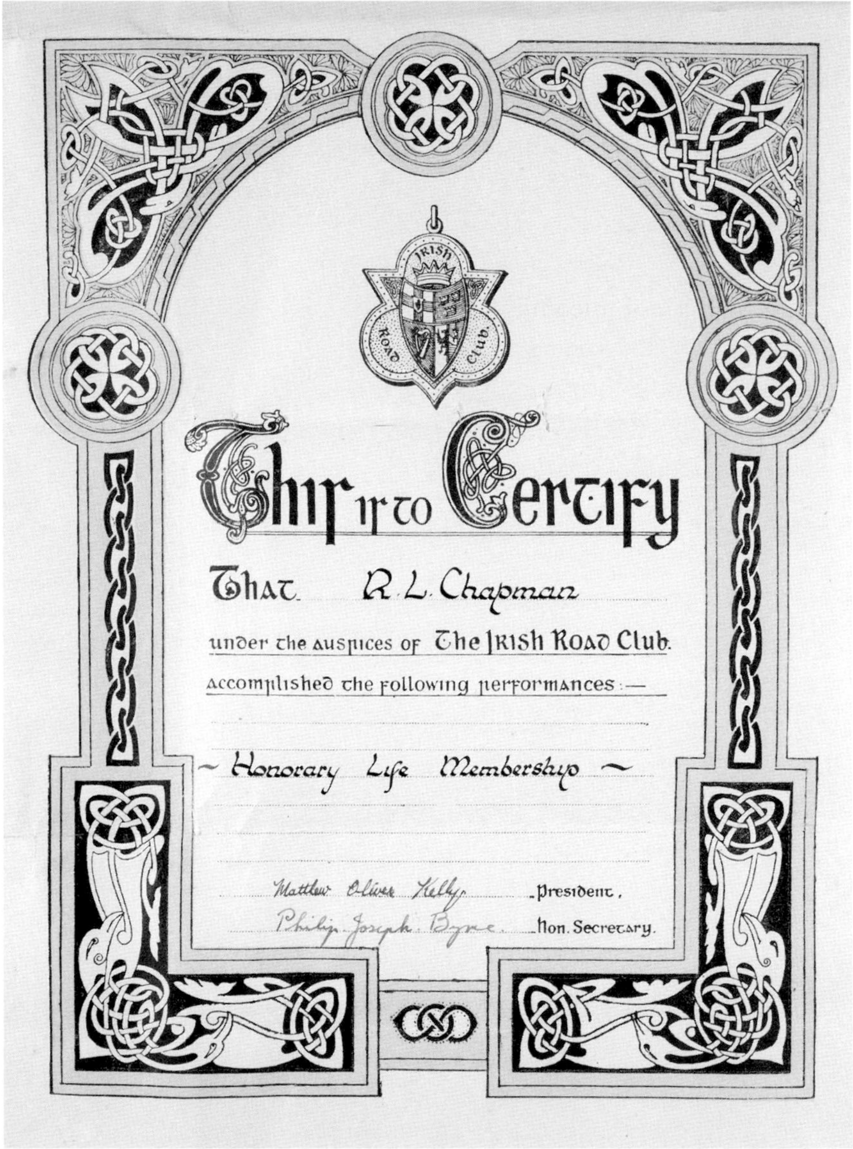

This to Certify

That R. L. Chapman

under the auspices of The Irish Road Club.

accomplished the following performances :—

~ Honorary Life Membership ~

Matthew Oliver Kelly ___President.

Philip Joseph Byrne ___Hon. Secretary.

through hands of many Irish Road Club members. 2 Peugôt Toggle Calliper Brakes. New British Hubs, Endrick Rims 28" x 1 3/8" & Meredith Tyres (full hand-made roadsters). Double cog back hub giving 64 & 72, both fixed with wing nuts. Victoreuse Springless Saddle. Cost £5.12.0 cash.

Today, it is not uncommon for road conditions to form one of the most frequent topics of an Irish conversation. While cyclists today may complain of potholes and inferior road surfaces, these are rather minor compared to hazards and obstacles faced by RLC on Irish roads. RLC had a version of a well-known saying – *'one magpie evidently means "bad road", two, an "unmentionable road".'* At this time very few roads had a tarmac surface. For the most part the roads were little better than dirt tracks. RLC frequently records the road conditions he encounters while cycling. On 7 December 1913, after cycling in Glencree in County Wicklow he wrote:

Ruts over a foot deep & mud enough to bury all the politicians in Ireland. All this due to cutting down of woods on Lord Powerscourt's estate.

After cycling through the muddy roads near Dolphin's Barn on 4 January 1920 he wrote, *'Must start potatoe planting on bike.'* Apart from the condition of road surfaces, there were nails and thorns that caused all too regular punctures. Little Bray, on the Dublin side of Bray in County Wicklow, appears to have been notoriously hazardous for broken glass:

At Little Bray the usual collection of broken bottles & old saucepans on the road was augmented by the addition of some pieces of barbed wire. **26 MARCH 1922**

Another hazard is still a problem for some cyclists today:

Mischievous young ruffians in Howth amusing themselves throwing bottles & hoops in front of the 'Ould Fellers'. **5 APRIL 1919**

The diaries also frequently document the results of some all too frequent breakdowns:

While on way out to Ballycorus on borrowed machine something went wrong with 2 speed gear. Back wheel suddenly locked nearly throwing me. Walked for about a mile wheeling bike, at last hill up, wheel refused to revolve except when machine was wheeled backwards. Needless to say the sight of a cyclist wheeling his machine backwards up a steep hill caused some strong & not favourable comments from passers by. **7 MAY 1911**

One of the interesting aspects of the diaries is the evidence they provide of the attitudes of other road users to cyclists. During this period the numbers of motor cars and motorcycles, relatively new additions to Irish roads, were very gradually increasing, and it is clear that the attitude of motorists to cyclists, still prevalent today, has its origins during this formative period of the motor car. At Lawless's Hotel in Aughrim on 1 February 1925, a drunken motorist informed RLC that he *'dishn't like bishicles'.* As motorised traffic became more frequent on Irish roads, travel became increasingly dangerous for cyclists. Following an incident with a motorbike and sidecar RLC wrote:

> *Really it is not safe to be on the road these days unless in a Tank or a Steam Roller.* 22 FEBRUARY 1920

While repairing a puncture to a tyre of his tandem outside Dunshaughlin, County Meath:

> *Several motor cyclists offered assistance which was rather decent of them. Perhaps a tandem is not in the same category as the despised push-bike.* 20 MAY 1922

While today few cyclists, whatever about motorists, would venture out at night without a light, on 23 September 1922 RLC recorded his surprise to see a cyclist with a rear light on his bicycle:

> *Was greatly surprised to see a cyclist on a racing machine with a good head-lamp & a 'Rear Light' & it no tiny twinkle either. Whatever is happening in Ireland. Think of it! A rear light! & yet passed dozens of lightless cyclists, in fact rarely saw any with even a pretence of a lamp. Even motors & motor cyclists were offenders too. One of the latter passed lampless under the nose of a policeman at a crossing in Kilmainham, & the bobby didn't even wink.*

Of course, one of the best known Irish traits is the inability to give clear road directions. While travelling through Limerick in August 1917 RLC documented a fine example of the frustrations of local directions:

> *Seemed to have travelled a great distance without coming to Kilmallock. Stopped several times to ask how far on it was. First person said 6 miles. Rode 4 miles & asked again, still 6. Another 2 miles & it was 2 miles. Further again it had become 4.*

While travelling through Wicklow the directions provided by one woman were slightly more precise:

> *On enquiring of a countrywoman if I was going right for Glenealy she answered 'Straight on. Take neither turn nor twist till ye come to Glenaily.* 9 JUNE 1919

Occasionally RLC provides a brief picture of the people he encountered on his travels as he noted on one trip while cycling from Aughrim to Aughavanagh, County Wicklow:

> *Met many little donkey carts jogging along with old men driving, who called out a cheery 'Good Day' or 'Fine day, thank God'. If it was raining cats & dogs they would have said the same thing rather than contradict you.* 4 OCTOBER 1914

During a solo cycle trip through Kerry in May 1915 he noted:

> *At every village & farm the colleens were out dressed in their best & perched up on the mud walls which are the boundaries of the fields. They were not at all bashful about giving you 'The Time of Day'.*

He briefly recorded an amusing incident while cycling through Trim, County Meath:

Going by a house saw a woman hard at work washing & without looking up passing compliments across the street to a man on the opposite side, also working but completely indifferent to remarks. 'You're a liar! A low ruffian! A scoundrel! A cur! Etc.'
25 SEPTEMBER 1917

In recent years most shops, garages, pubs and hotels cater for the hungry passer-by. Throughout his diaries RLC documents a persistent difficulty in trying to obtain refreshments. While cycling through Fermanagh in May 1914 RLC and a friend stopped at a hotel in Newtownbutler:

An old woman answered our ring & after hearing we wanted tea, disappeared, but no tea appeared. After hanging round the hall for half an hour & nearly pulling the bell out, a girl appeared & asked, 'Did yiz want anything?' We explained politely that we were consumed with starvation. Apparently the old woman had got frightened & cleared off to warn the shopkeepers that two hungry cyclists were knocking the house down.

The next day in an unnamed rural part of Fermanagh RLC and his companion had a more positive experience.

Just when we were giving up all hope & looking round for quiet place to die in, met man who in response to our enquiries told us he would give us tea if didn't mind waiting until kettle boiled … tucked into excellent tea of home-made bread with honey & delicious butter. When came to settling up our preserver refused to take more than 1/6 though the honey alone was worth more than that.

On another occasion, at Shannonbridge, County Offaly, RLC experienced further difficulties:

Could not get tea at Hotel so had to be content with lemonade & biscuits at one of the local pubs. Biscuits were discovered after long search among ironmongery. **25 AUGUST 1917**

After stopping on his return from a cycle trip to County Meath RLC wrote:

Pushed on to Summerhill which reached after dark. Knocked up old lady whom was informed gives teas but she said it was too late. However, told her if she didn't give me some, would lie down on her doorstep & die of starvation. She took me in! Long wait! Tea & bread & butter 1/6! **25 SEPTEMBER 1917**

With a long tradition of tourism the hotels of County Wicklow were more prepared than most for hungry cyclists and other travellers through the county:

[At Aughrim] Got an excellent lunch of bacon, 2 eggs with plenty of tea, toast, home-made bread & jam. A real cyclist's meal & only 2/6. Had always heard this little Hotel the 'Ardee' well spoken of. The proprietess Miss Coyle is one of the few who really work on the right lines. Would that there were many more like her in Ireland. **3 JANUARY 1922**

The period of RLC's diaries was a politically turbulent one in Ireland that saw the outbreak of the First World War, the Easter Rising of 1916, the War of Independence and the subsequent Civil War. RLC himself was not directly involved in any of the

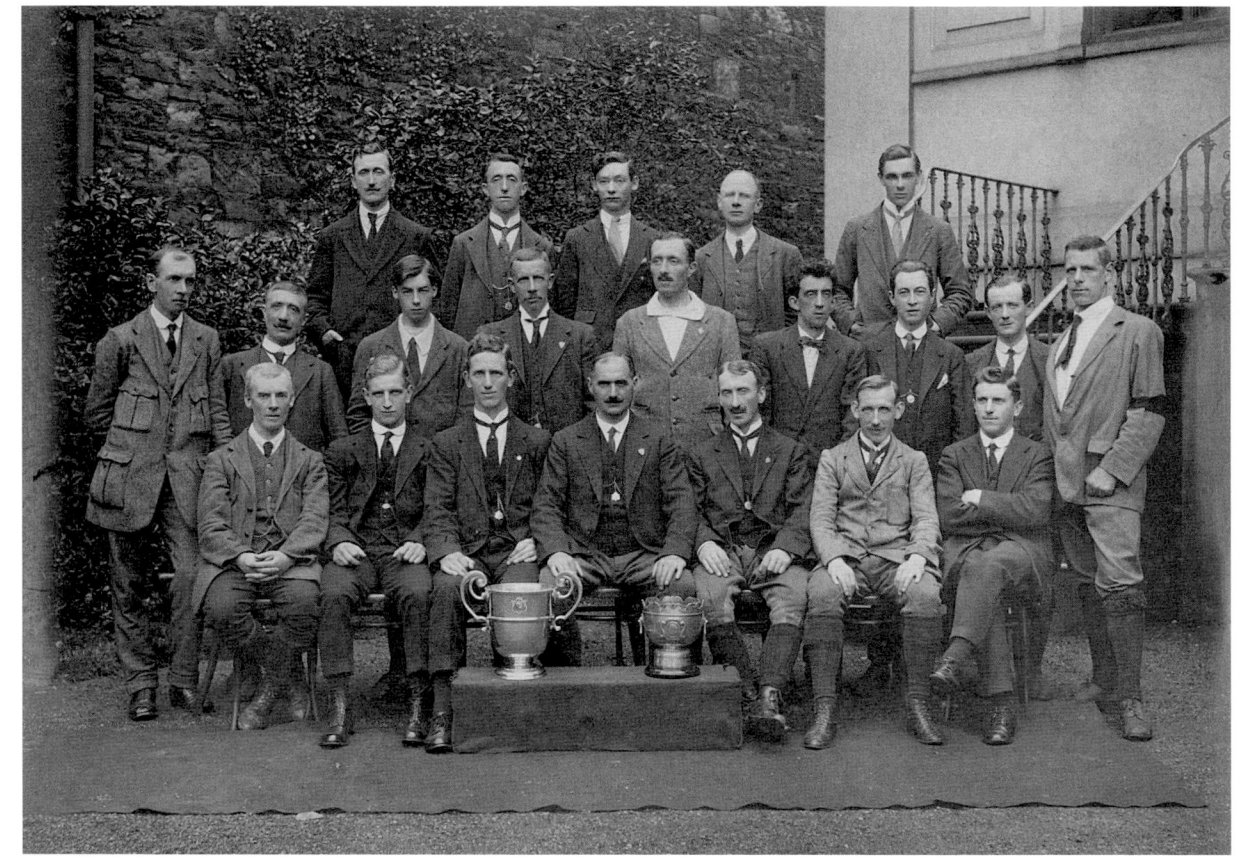

Group photograph of Irish Road Club, taken at the Mansion House on 25 August 1918

(Photo by Keogh Brothers Photographic Studios, Dublin)

Back row (l–r): J. Walker, M.J. Healy, J.F. Fagan, F.S. Ganter & R.L. Chapman

Middle row: D.J. Nugent, J.W. Kenny, W.J. Finn, R. Galway, M.J. Rohan, W.J. Taaffe, T.J. Tyndall, W. O'Neill & L.P. Ganter

Front row: M. McDonald, E.T. Galway, R.E. Galway, E.P. Monks, M. Walker, R. Walker & P.G. Dardis

political events of the period, but like anyone else he was not divorced from them, and his causal observations provide an equally interesting insight into the effects of these events on everyday life. With the outbreak of the First World War came an immediate paranoia that German spies had infiltrated Ireland, and police (Royal Irish Constabulary) checkpoints were commonplace. As a cyclist, RLC encountered many of these on his travels. While cycling home at night from Woodenbridge, County Wicklow he was stopped at a checkpoint at the Glen of the Downs:

At Glen o the Downs heard 'Halt' so halted & found RIC man with Carbine presented at me. "Where's your light?" Explanations followed by conversation about rumoured destruction of German pork shops in Dublin … Stopped by policeman on Bray Road but was allowed to proceed after half hours conversation.
16 AUGUST 1914

During a trip around County Kerry in May 1915, he awoke early one morning in a Tralee hotel:

Was awakened by sounds of a vigorous cross-examination under my bedroom window. The rich Kerry brogue of an RIC. man trying to find out all about the 'stranger' & the proprietess's answers which were to say the least of them, not lacking in imagination, were highly amusing. 9 MAY 1915

RLC provides a more detailed account of a checkpoint at Waterville two days later:

Road ran through barbed wire enclosure with soldiers in guard at each end. On reaching far end was stopped by an RIC. man with a Kerry brogue. 'Where do you come from & where are you goin?' 'What is your name?' 'Where do you live?' 'What is your business?' 'What are you doing down here?' 'You are on a cycling tour?' 'So you are cycling for pleasure!' 'And why are you doing it now?' 'So you have to take your holidays when you get them!' Having answered all these questions to his satisfaction, the sergeant informed me that I might proceed. 'I must apologise for stopping you & asking you so many questions, but we have to do it, because you might be a German spy. However I wish you Good Day & a pleasant journey.' Assured the worthy man that it was a pleasure to answer his questions, & went on. Wonder does it ever occur to the authorities that German spies are hardly likely to walk into a barbed wire enclosure visible a mile off, without being able to satisfy the police that they are alright. 11 MAY 1915

Later on the same day he was stopped again at Adrigole:

Here two stalwart members of the RIC. compelled a halt & wanted all sorts of information. Informed them that it seemed great carelessness that the RIC should have allowed me into Castletown without any questions. For all they knew I might have been a German spy. They were so perturbed at this that they bade me 'Good Evening' & allowed me to depart without getting an answer to any of their questions.

Introduction

On Monday 11 November 1918, RLC wrote:

Armistice declared at 11 a.m.. Great rejoicing. Flags everywhere. Huge crowds in town all night. Soldiers dancing in streets like children. Went into town on top of tram with Ethel to see fun.

The first indication in RLC's diaries of the changing political scene in Ireland after the Easter Rebellion of 1916 is recorded following a cycling tour through Wexford in 1917:

Saw many Sinn Fein flags tied to topmost branches of trees. The lower branches had been cut or broken away to prevent anyone reaching them. However, the elements were fast reducing them to faded rags. 20 AUGUST 1917

A few days later he was cycling through Scariff, County Clare:

Scariff is small village some distance inland. It was festooned with Sinn Fein flags & the walls had appropriate inscriptions in letters 2ft high, for the celebrated election had taken place only a week or so ago. Got some tea in a little cottage, where the people were fearfully bitter against the soldiers. The tea however was none the worse for that. 24 AUGUST 1917

Political tensions increased throughout the country during the local elections of 1919. RLC recorded one occasion cycling near Aghavannagh in County Wicklow how he and his companions were mistaken for Sinn Féin activists:

As we struggled along the level & bare bog road we were mistaken by some men working nearby for Sinn Feiners out campaigning & a tremendous cheer went up which was returned. 9 JUNE 1919

Despite the fact that the situation in Ireland became increasingly violent during the War of Independence, RLC and his cycling companions do not seem to have been prevented from taking to the road. However, as during the years of the First World War, checkpoints were once again a regular occurrence, though now they were carried out by the army rather than the police. The perceived threat was now not an external one, but an internal one, and travellers were subjected to more formal searches rather than a few casual questions:

Returning from Moyne Rd on bike abt 10.30 p.m. found a big crowd in Rathmines Rd. Couple of seconds later soldiers with rifles & bayonets loomed up apparently from nowhere. Was surrounded & ordered Hands Up! Which complied with as quickly as possible, while pockets were felt. Soldiers had the 'Wind up' badly. Self ditto as was kept covered all the time by 2 soldiers a few feet distant. After a few minutes was allowed to proceed home. Expected more trouble as had a turnip in one pocket & jam jar in other. Two likely bombs & a nice yarn to tell to the soldier. Perhaps he was afraid to take them out & look at them.
22 MARCH 1920

On Sunday 20 February 1921, he cycled to Balbriggan, County Dublin to see the results of the Black and Tan burning of the village as a reprisal for the killing by the IRA of two members of the RIC. Two members of the IRA were killed in what became known as the Sack of Balbriggan:

Rather quaint to see a row of horses & cars tethered to rings in the wall outside the chapel. Had a look at the burnt out houses of which there seem to be about 6 or 7, though nothing like the destruction which the papers would lead one to expect. The burnt-out factory of Deeds Templar & Co. presents an extraordinary sight being chock full of machinery.

RLC also records an amusing incident, though it must have been an equally frightening one, after he had been stopped by the Black and Tans:

Near Dundrum [County Dublin] came on wall built across road with barbed wire on top. About a dozen men busy throwing stones into the fields, under the surveillance of the Black & Tans. Was politely but firmly requested to set to & do likewise. Being at wrong end of the revolvers, no use arguing. Don't like wall unbuilding. At the job for ½ hr & ½ hr waiting while B & T were collecting further batch. All able bodied men stoppped & made work. Searching only carried out in some cases. Had a big bundle of cycle tools in pocket which ought to have attracted attention but did not. Machine gun posted on corner wall facing us, while an Auxiliary played pitch & toss with an egg bomb a few yards away. No place for anyone with nerves. Very careless watch kept by the B & T. Would have been very easy for a few well armed men to have captured the lot … Returned home same way. Wall gone. Would have been some joke if the Sinn Feiners had held me up to rebuild it. 3 APRIL 1921

While cycling through Wicklow, RLC captures the end of an era in a fleeting reference:

Pushed on south for Kiltimon getting occasional glimpses of the sea where a few transports were bearing away the last British Military from Southern Ireland. 17 DECEMBER 1922

During the Civil War that followed the signing of the Treaty, checkpoints were maintained by the Irish Free State troops. RLC records being stopped, albeit belatedly, at one such checkpoint while cycling with some companions through Blessington, County Wicklow:

Were proceeding slowly into the town when cries of halt sounded from somewhere. At first could see no one, but after a minute or two a crowd of soldiers dashed out of a house & surrounded us. After a very perfunctory search they apologised for troubling us & let us go on. Evidently they had not been keeping a proper look out, for we had passed by the house they were in before they saw us. Had we been Republicans we could easily have rushed it. As Blessington has recently been several times raided this carelessness was foolish. 11 MARCH 1923

On 1 June 1918 RLC married Ethel Margaret Partridge. The event, and their subsequent journey to Killarney for their honeymoon, are recorded briefly in his diaries:

Up at 5.15 a.m.. Glorious sunny morning. J.N. arrived about 7.30 a.m. & acted as escort to Rathmines Church. No escape. Feeling a bit nervous. Got spliced at 8 a.m. Heavy showers of confettti, which fell out of taxi at Kingsbridge much to amusement of Porters. Train left at 9.15 a.m. & reached Killarney at 4.45 p.m. Long & very hot journey … At Headford Junction, red-haired

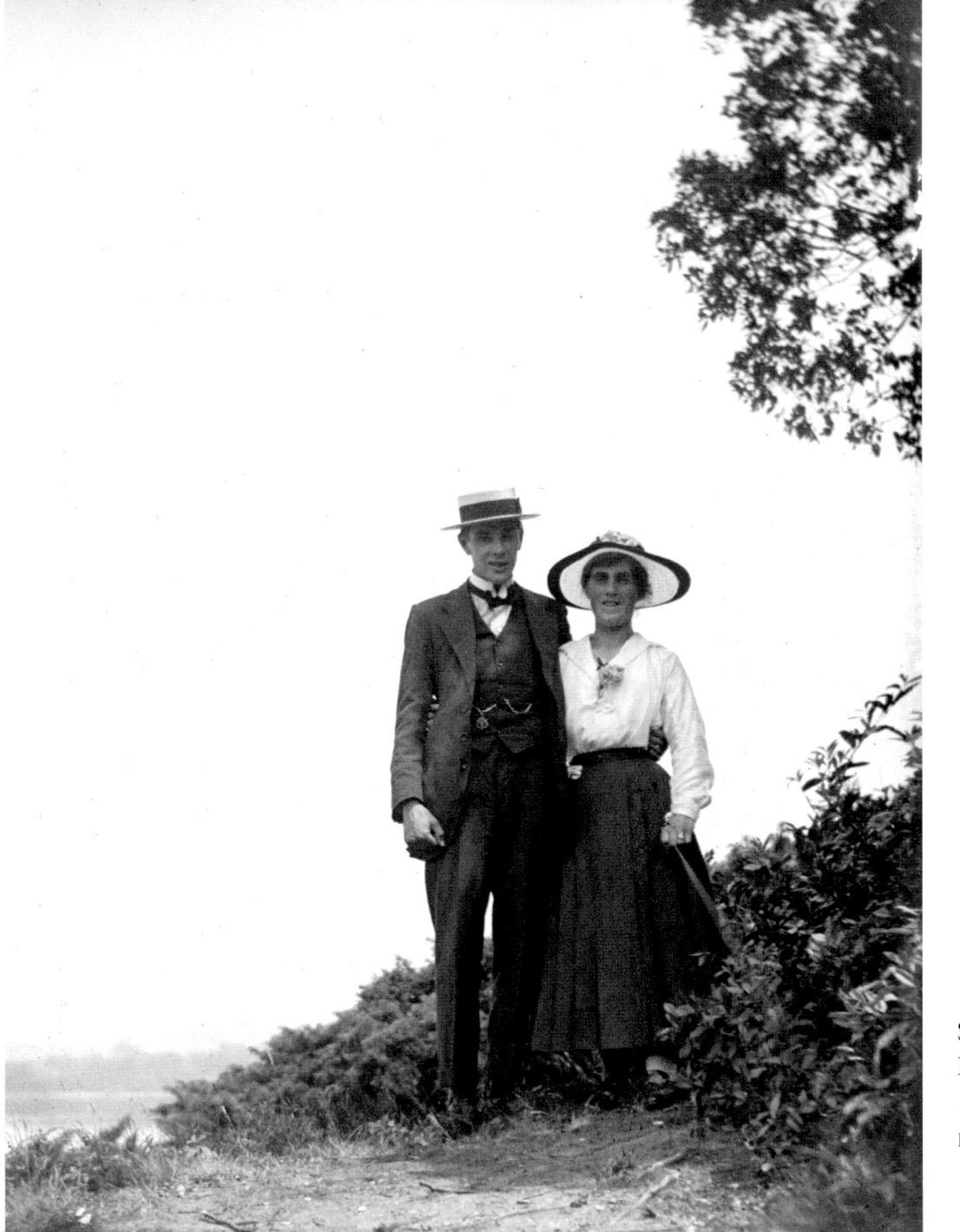

Selves at Lakeside, Muckross,
Killarney, County Kerry (F 90)

1 p.m., 2 June 1918
Imperial Non-filter Orthochromatic, f9, 1/25 sec

individual got in & made himself very affable. Recognised him as Hotel Tout who had waylaid me on previous occasion in Killarney, so took wind out of his sails first before he could get started on his rigmarole. 1 JUNE 1918

During their honeymoon in Kerry they stayed at O'Sullivan's Hotel near Muckross. The morning after they arrived RLC took a photograph of himself and his wife, with the aid of a piece of thread attached to the camera, standing at the lakeshore at Muckross. The following day they took a trip to the Gap of Dunloe, where he himself had visited on a solo trip only three years earlier. His diary account provides a useful insight into the well-established tourism industry flourishing in Kerry at that time:

Large group of pony boys mounted on horses! Waiting to waylay the unwary. Wanted 10/- to the top. Nothing doing, so pushed on to Kate Kearney's Cottage where had a cup of tea & some bread & butter for 2/6. More extortion. Arranged with donkey man to take Ethel to top for 2/6 … Heard serenade on bugle by old friend of previous visit, now apparently from force of circumstances much thirstier … Had another encounter with a native determined to sell us some Kerry cows milk. 3 JUNE 1918

Later that week they took the train to Killorglin; from there they cycled to Glenbeigh. They then waited at Carragh Lake station for a train back to Killarney:

When train came in sight, there were some ducks on the line, so the man who acts as Station Master, Porter, Ticket Collector &

Guard all rolled into one, got down on the line & in a leisurely manner speeded up the leisurely progress of the trespassers with a small switch which he had cut from the hedge. It was a picture of "No hurry" … On reaching Killorglin it waited for 20 minutes while the engine did a bit of local shunting. Meanwhile we admired certain ancient barefooted dames who made themselves comfortable in the 1st Class Waiting Room … The same performance was repeated at every station so it took 2 ½ hrs to cover the 24 miles. The direct road is only 13 miles so it would have been quicker to cycle. 7 JUNE 1918

RLC's diaries and photographs provide an eyewitness account of a relatively short but momentous and defining period of Irish history. While RLC was not directly involved in any of the events, the diaries provide a fascinating perspective from a distance, and occasionally the consequences of these events appear in his photographs. RLC's interests in trains and shipping, as reflected by his early photographs, were soon overshadowed by a more long-term interest in cycling and the landscape in which he travelled, particularly that of County Wicklow. It is RLC's photography which is the main focus of this book. He was clearly a gifted photographer, not just in terms of his technical ability, but also his composition, and how best to use the technology to capture the subject matter. RLC was, without doubt, as able with the camera as any professional photographer of his time.

Selection of
Robert L. Chapman's Photographs

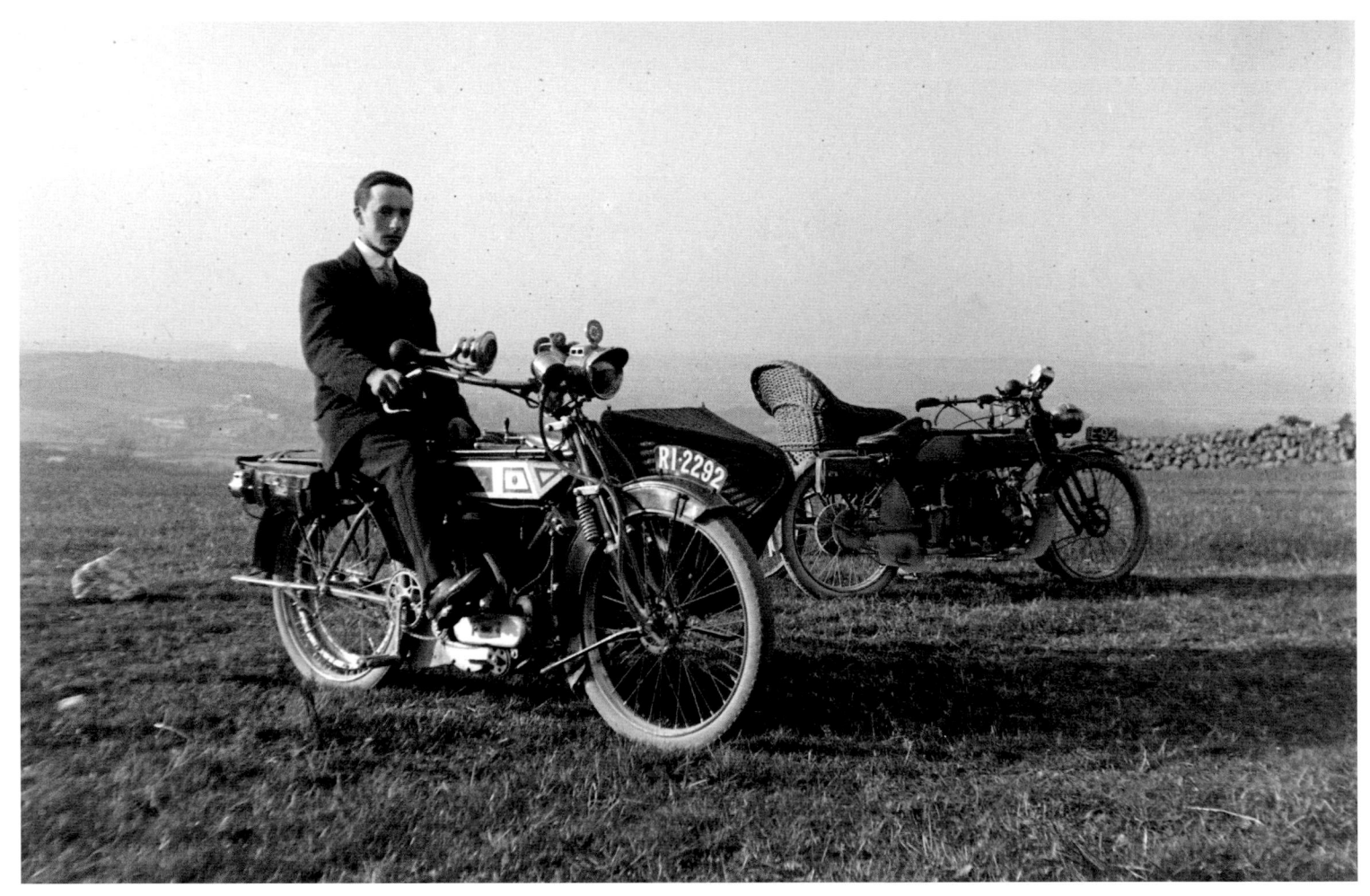

Harry Chapman on motorbike (F 58)

5.15 p.m., 19 April 1914

Edwards Isochromatic Auto Screen, f16, 1/5 sec

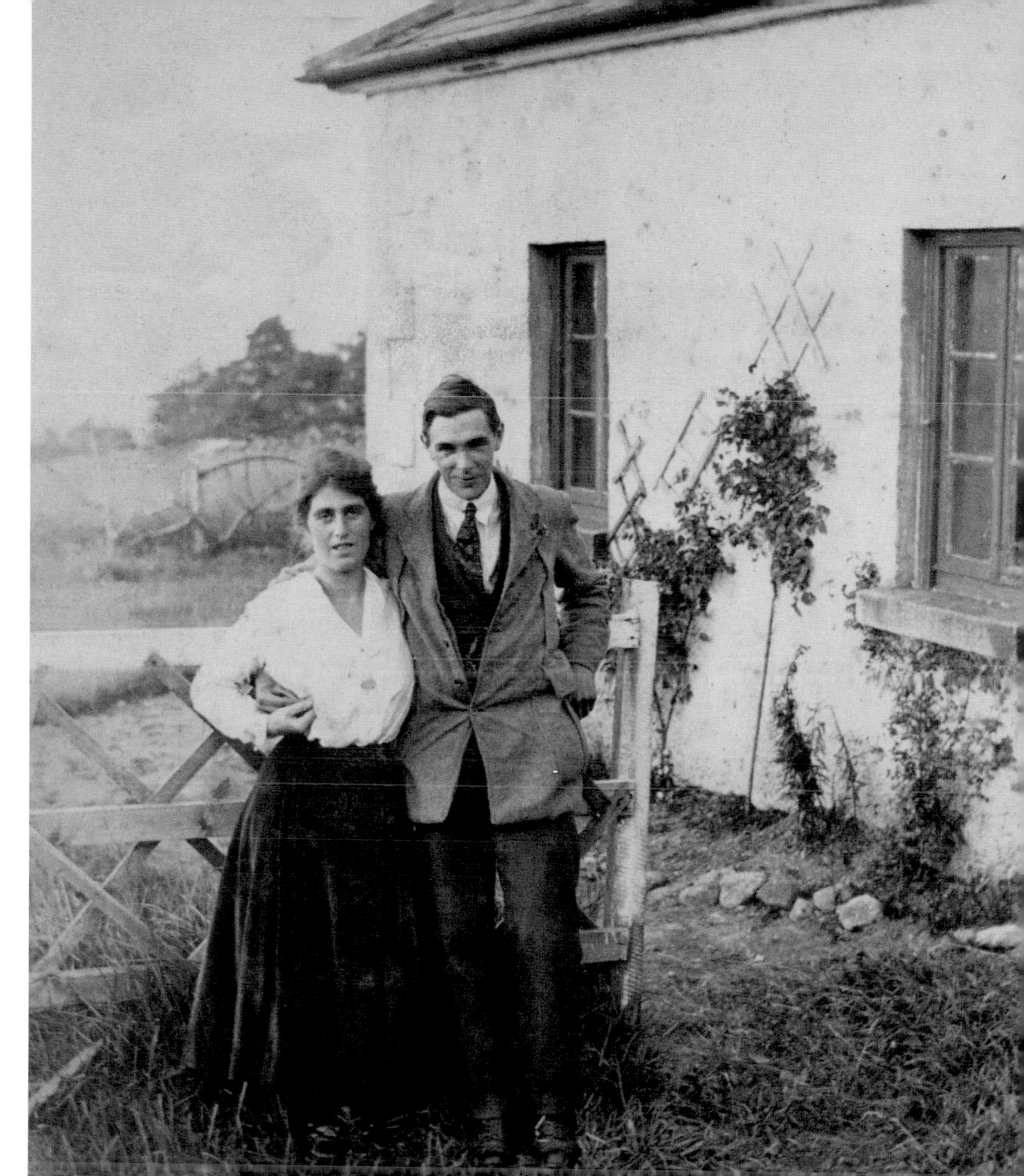

Robert L. Chapman and his wife
Ethel M. Partridge (F 92)

7.30 p.m., 11 August 1918

Imperial Non-filter Orthochromatic, f8, 1/5 sec

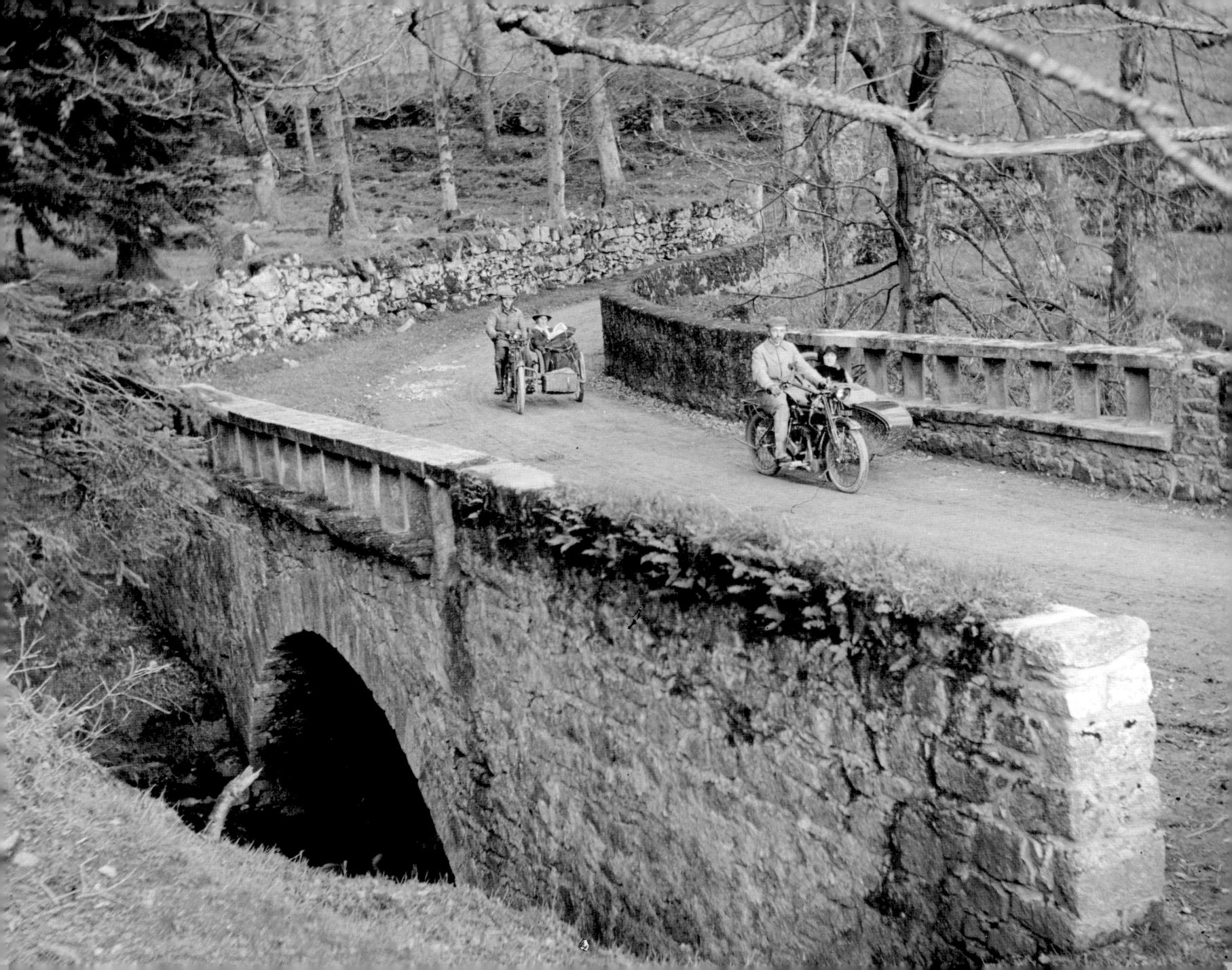

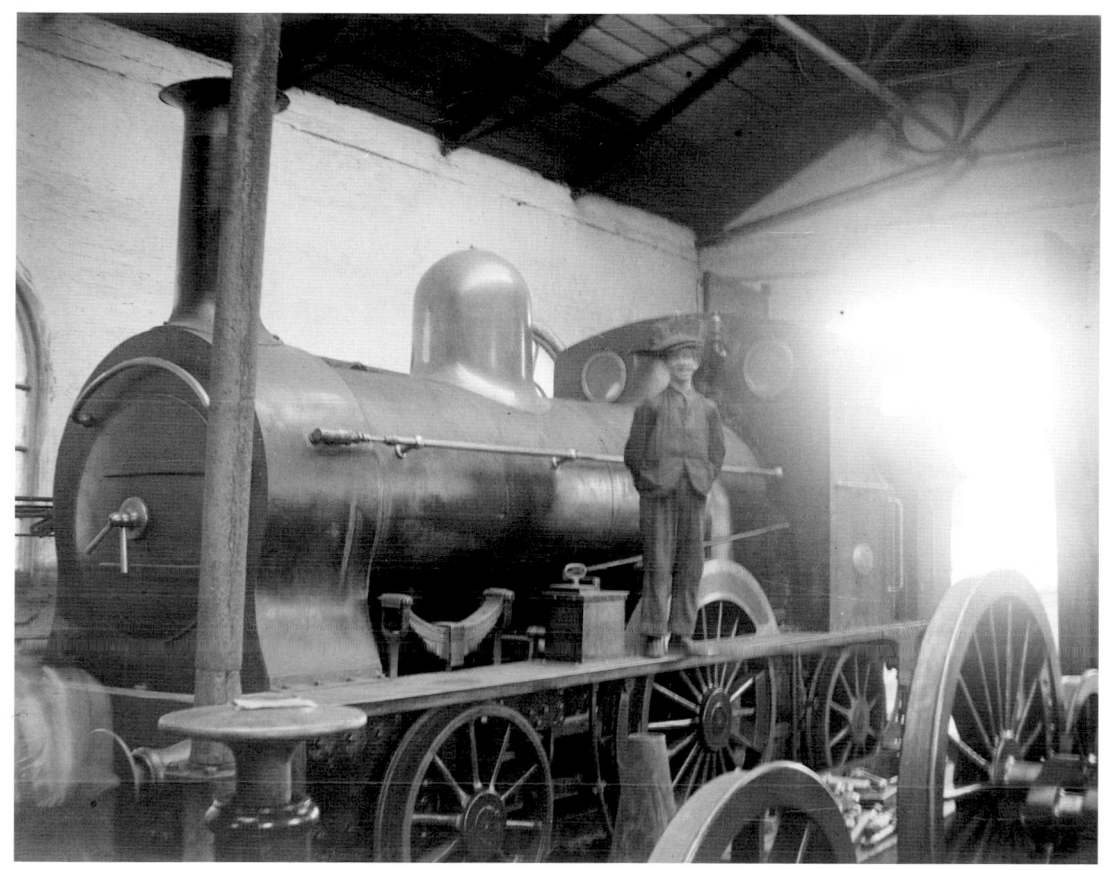

Waterford & Tramore
Railway engine in
locomotive shop, Waterford
(B 17)

2 p.m., 2 August 1909

Ilford Special Rapid, f16, 10 sec

RLC PROVIDED THE FOLLOWING
ACCOUNT IN HIS DIARY:

*Bank Holiday. Went on Excursion
per Rail to Waterford & back. Took
bicycle. Cycled out to Railway bridge
over R. Suir about 2 miles above the
town. Went to Station of Waterford
and Tramore Railway where was
shown over the engine shed & repairing
shop. Saw an old single driver of very
early date with large copper dome over
firebox. Same had been in use until
quite recently.*

Facing page:
Father and Mother in front on Matchless, and Harry, Ethel and baby
Ronnie on Brad in rear, Cloghleagh Bridge, Manor Kilbride (E 614)

7.30 p.m., 4 May 1919

Imperial Non-filter Orthochromatic, f8, ½ sec

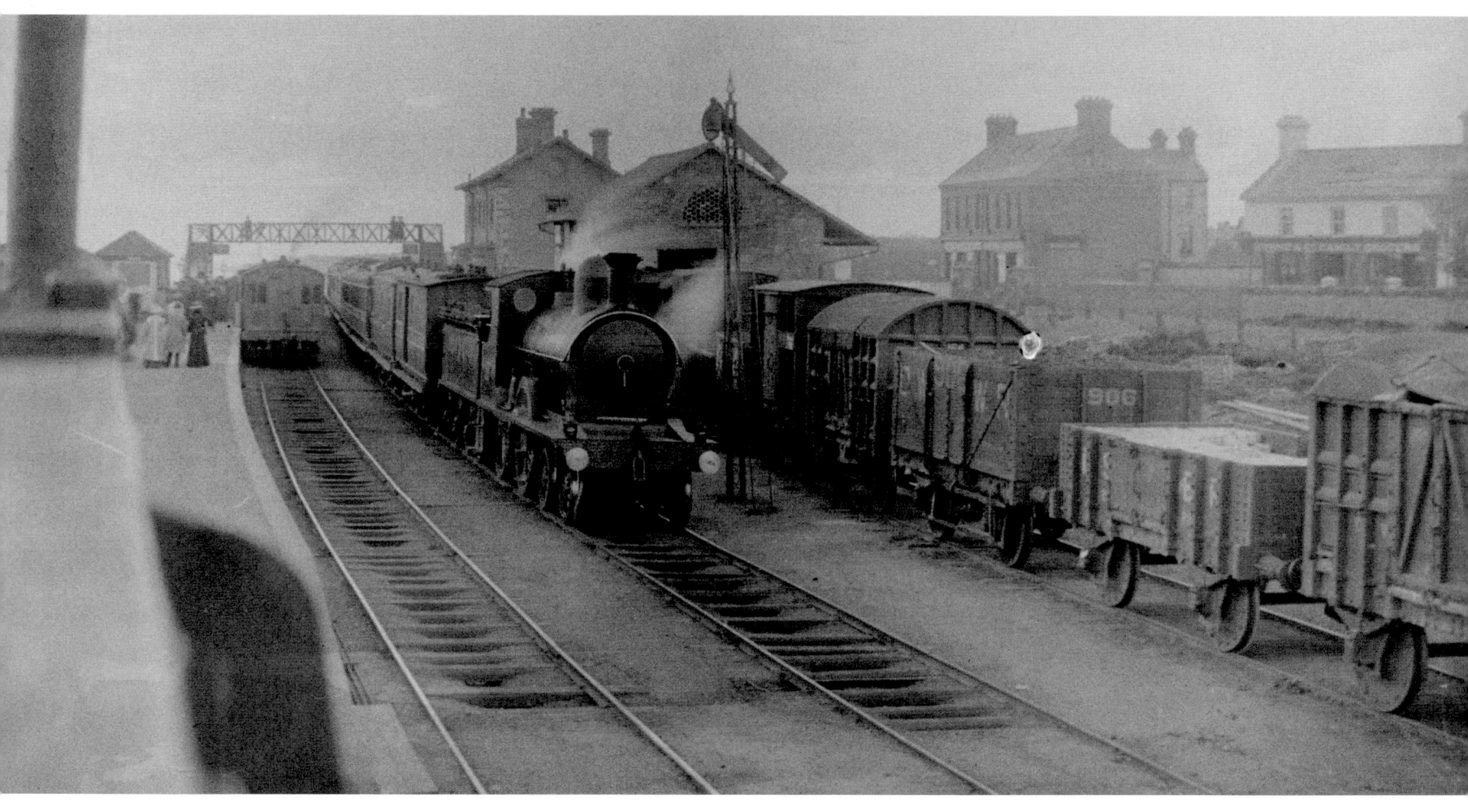

Limited Mail (Engine No. 27, Rathmore) and 6.15 p.m. down at Greystones Station, County Wicklow (C 8)

6.45 p.m., 15 September 1909

Paget Extra Special Rapid, f22, 4 sec

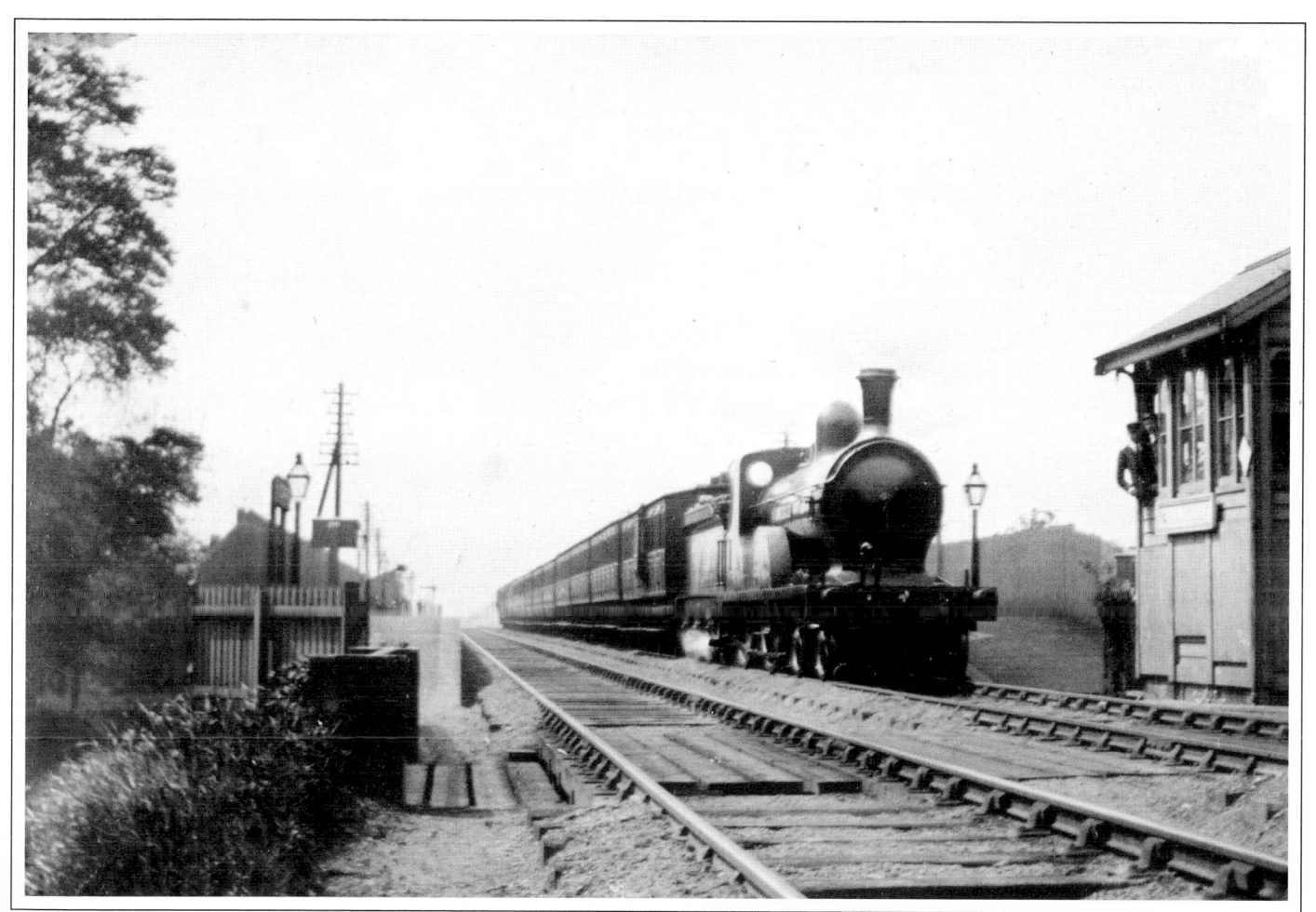

Great Northern Railway engine No. 132, Mercury, passing Clontarf, County Dublin (A 10)

June 1908

Edwards Snapshot Isochromatic, f9, 1/30 sec

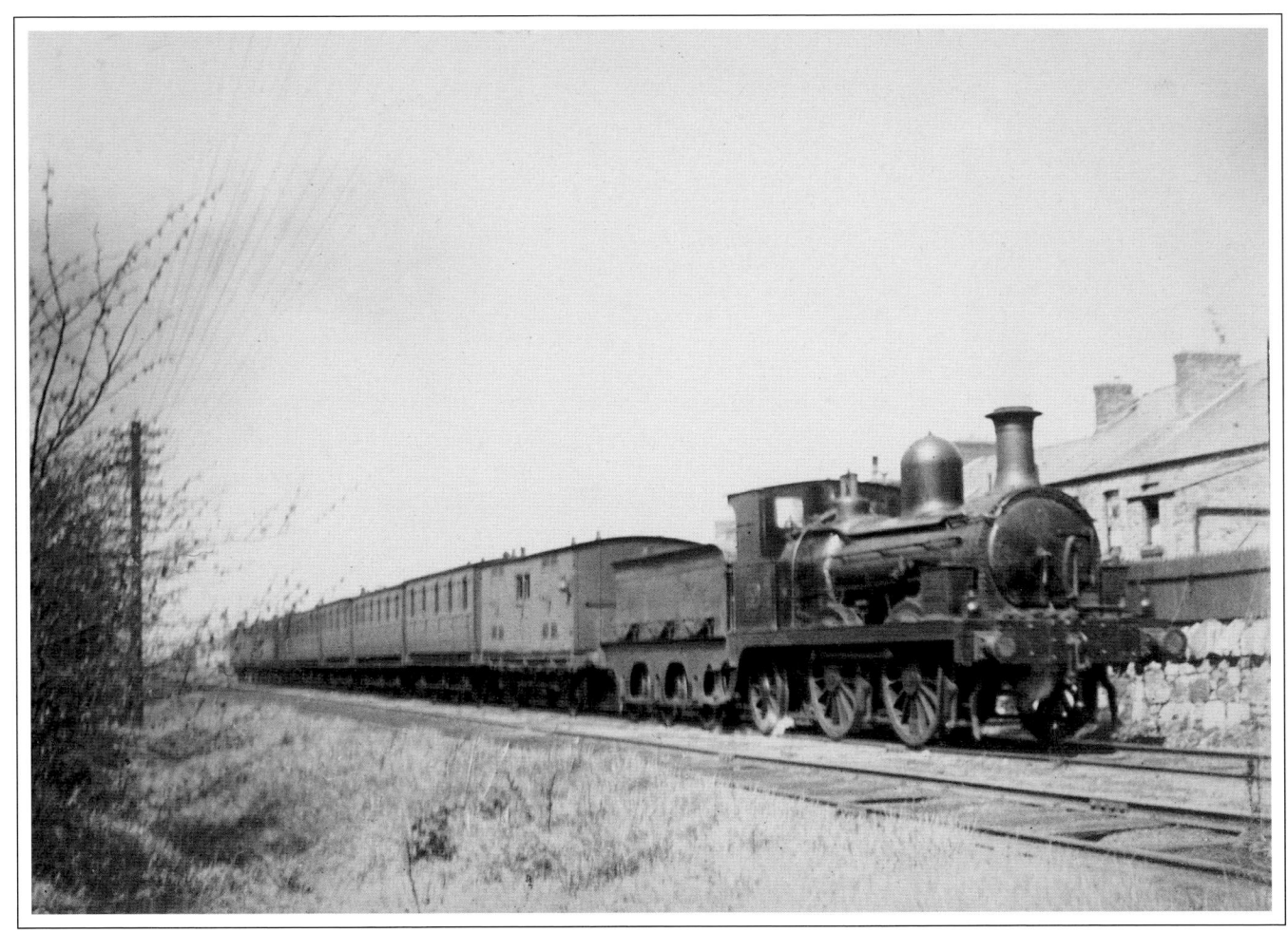

Dublin & South Eastern Railway engine No. 22, 12.30 p.m. Leopardstown Race Special leaving Ranelagh, County Dublin (A 4)

1 May 1908

Edwards Snapshot Isochromatic, f9, 1/100 sec

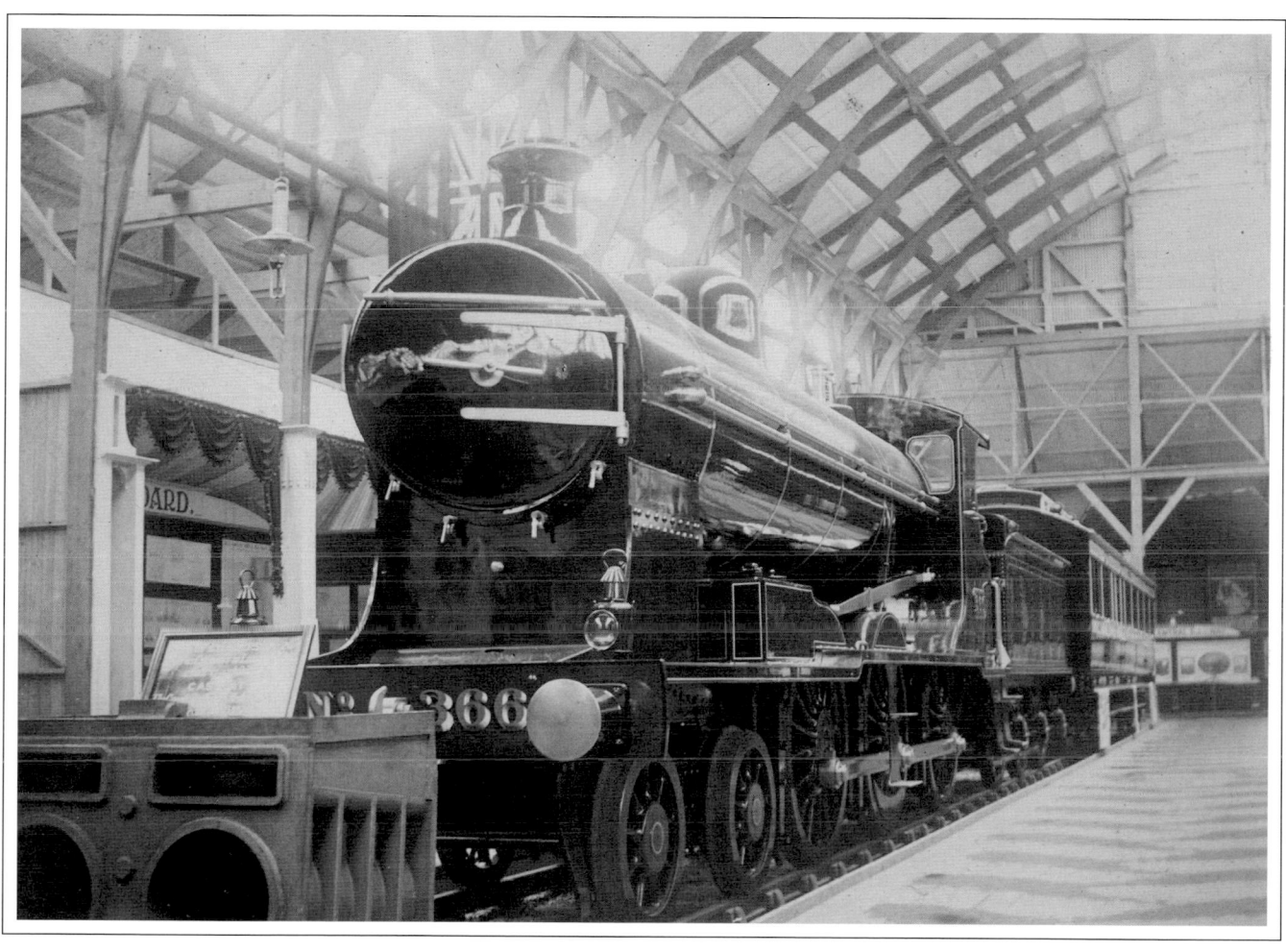

Great Southern & Western Railway Engine No. 366 in the Machinery Hall, Irish International Exhibition, Dublin (B 1)

August 1907

Ilford Special Rapid, F9, 1 sec

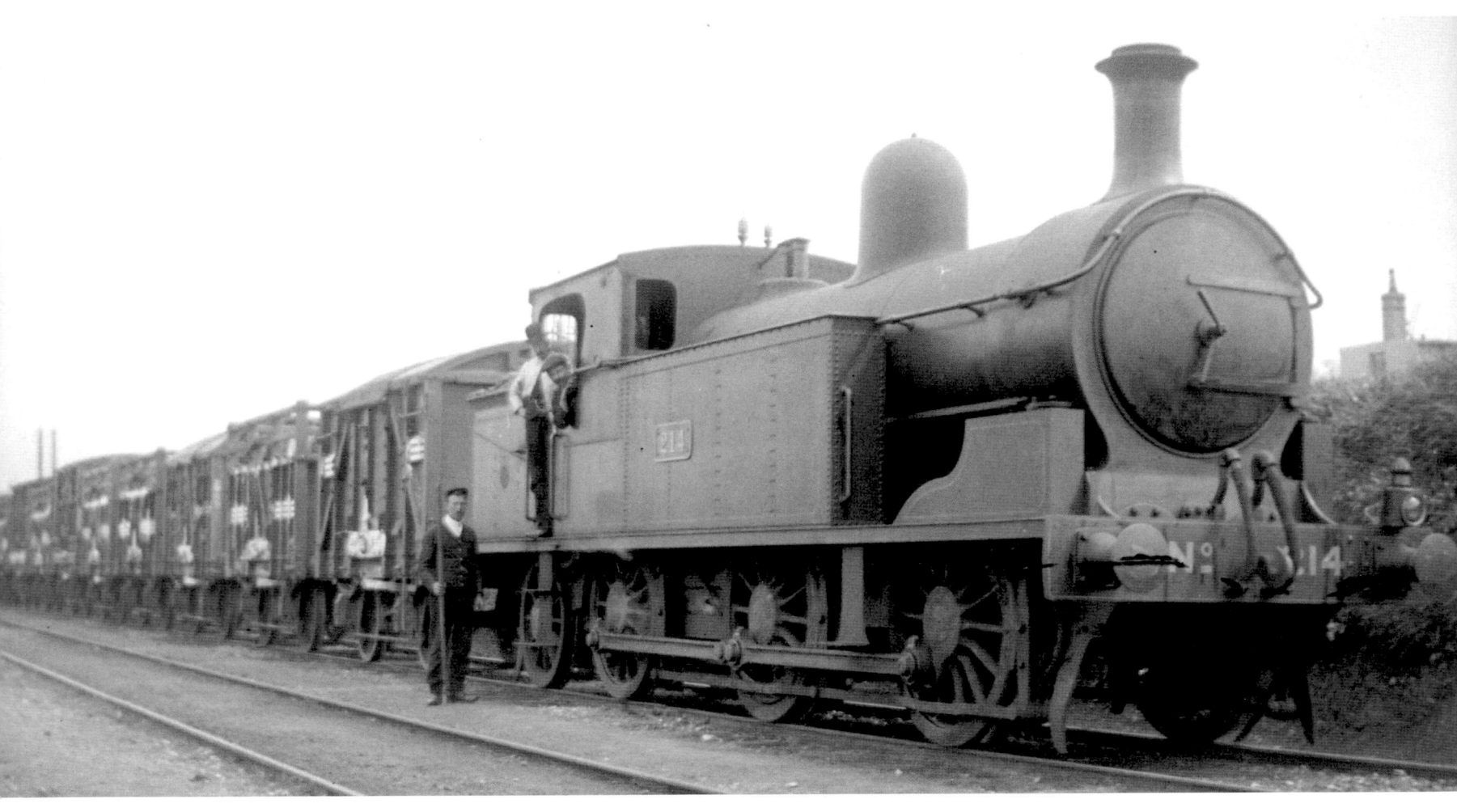

Great Southern & Western Railway engine No. 214, at Kingsbridge [now Heuston Station], Dublin (B 6)

May 1908

Edwards Snapshot Isochromatic, f9, 1/20 sec

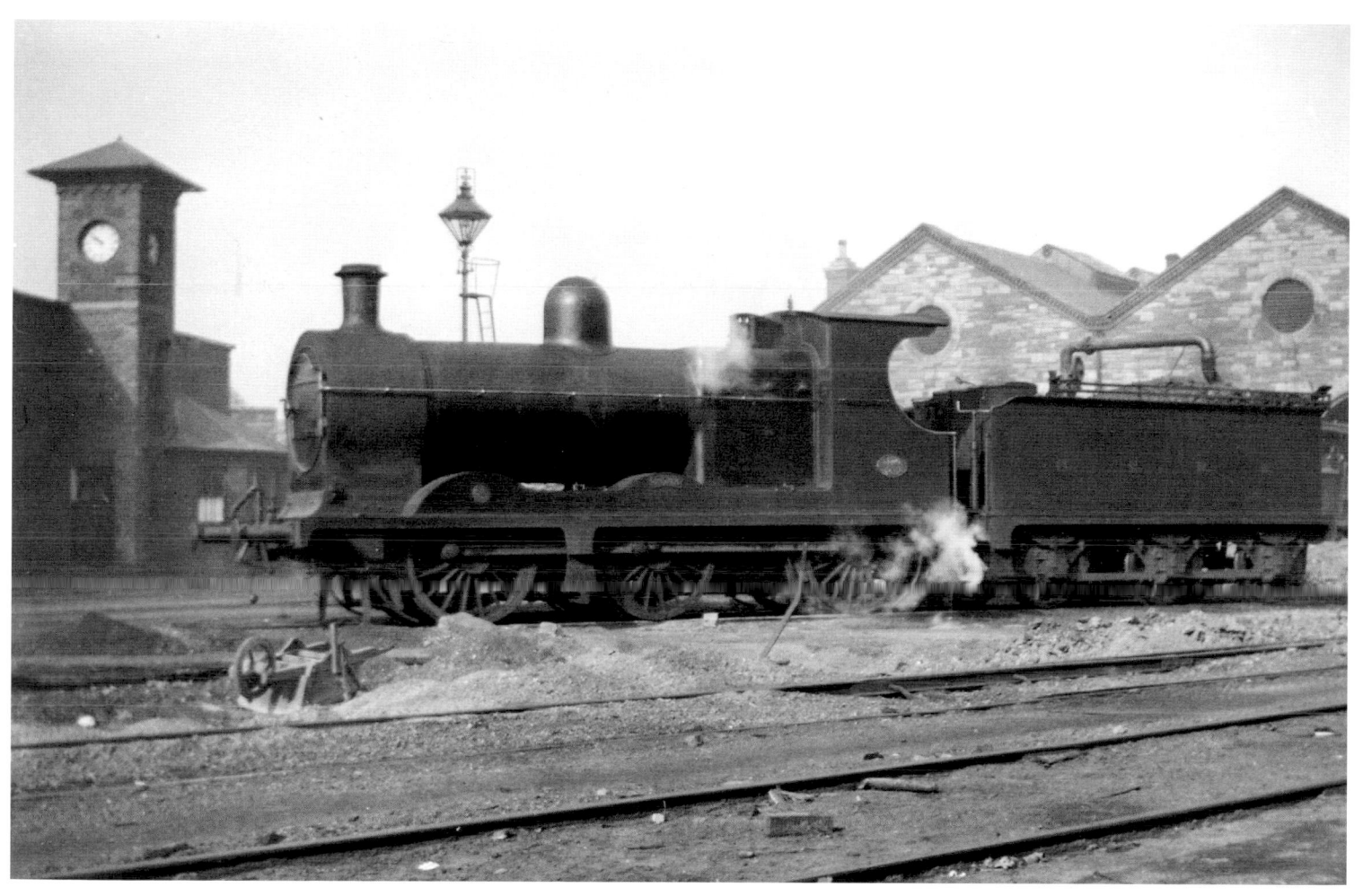

Midland Great Western Railway *India* at Broadstone, Dublin (B 11)

October 1908

Ilford Empress, f9, ½ sec

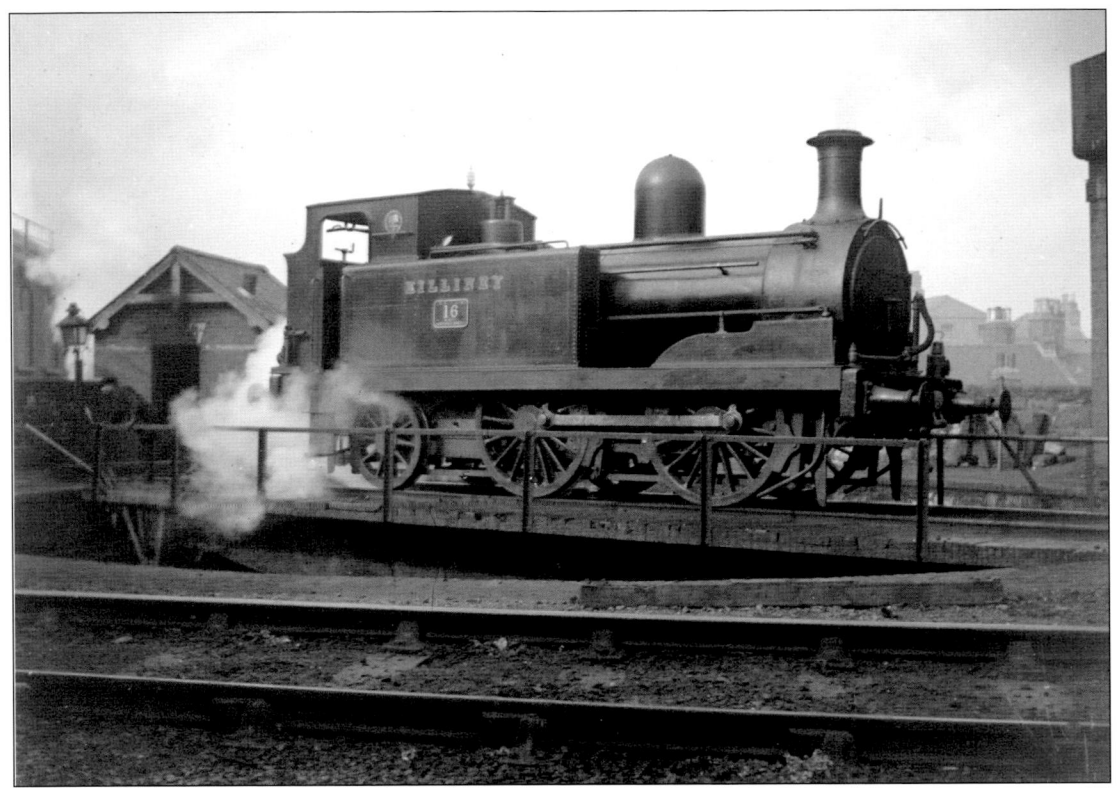

Above: Dublin & South Eastern Railway engine No. 16 *Killiney* at Amiens Street (now Connolly Station), Dublin (B 12)

October 1908

Ilford Empress, f9, ½ sec

Facing page: Dublin & South Eastern Railway engine No. 31 *Glen o the Downs* at Amiens Street (now Connolly Station), Dublin (B 13)

2.15 p.m., 10 April 1909

Edwards Snapshot Isochromatic, f16, 1 sec

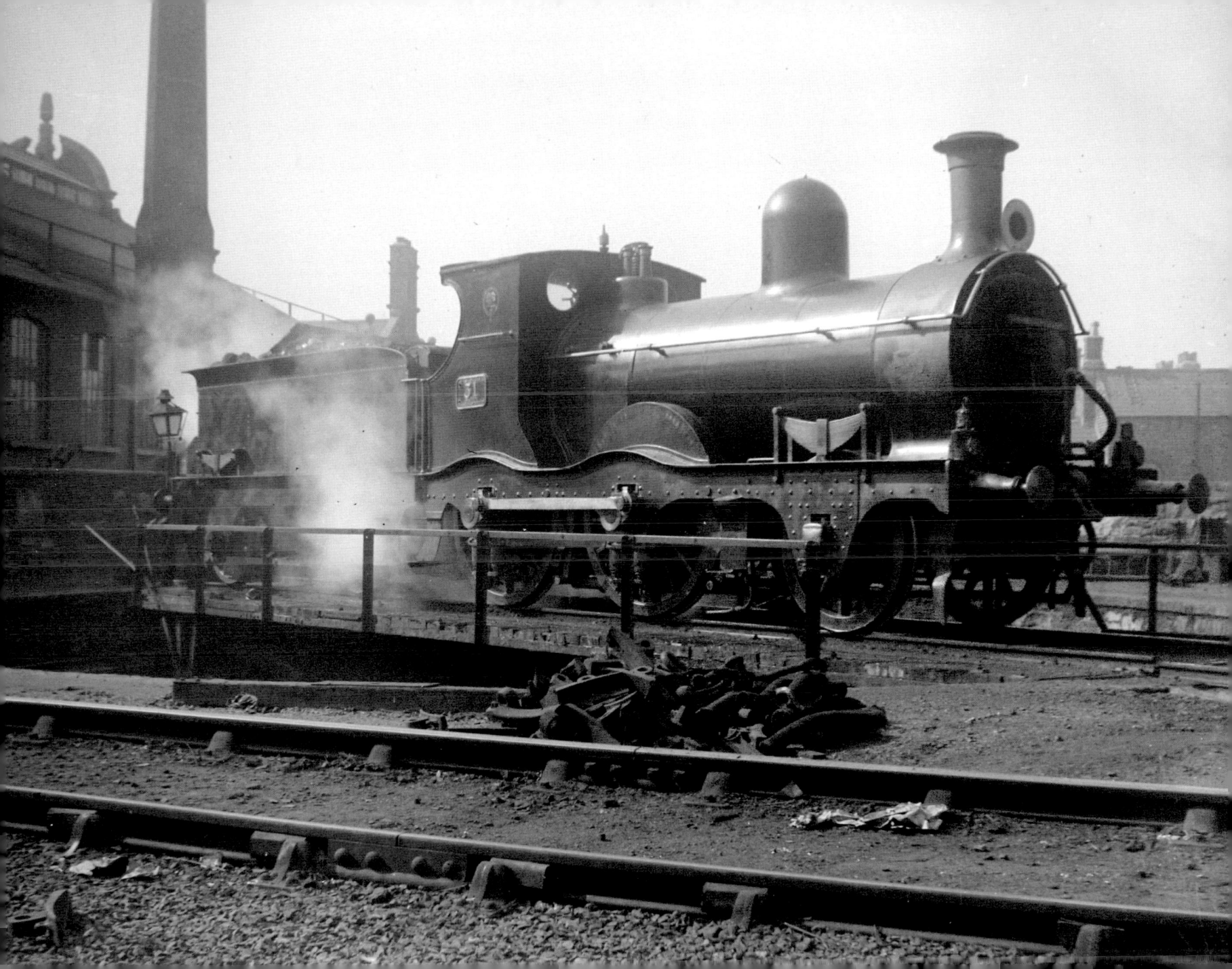

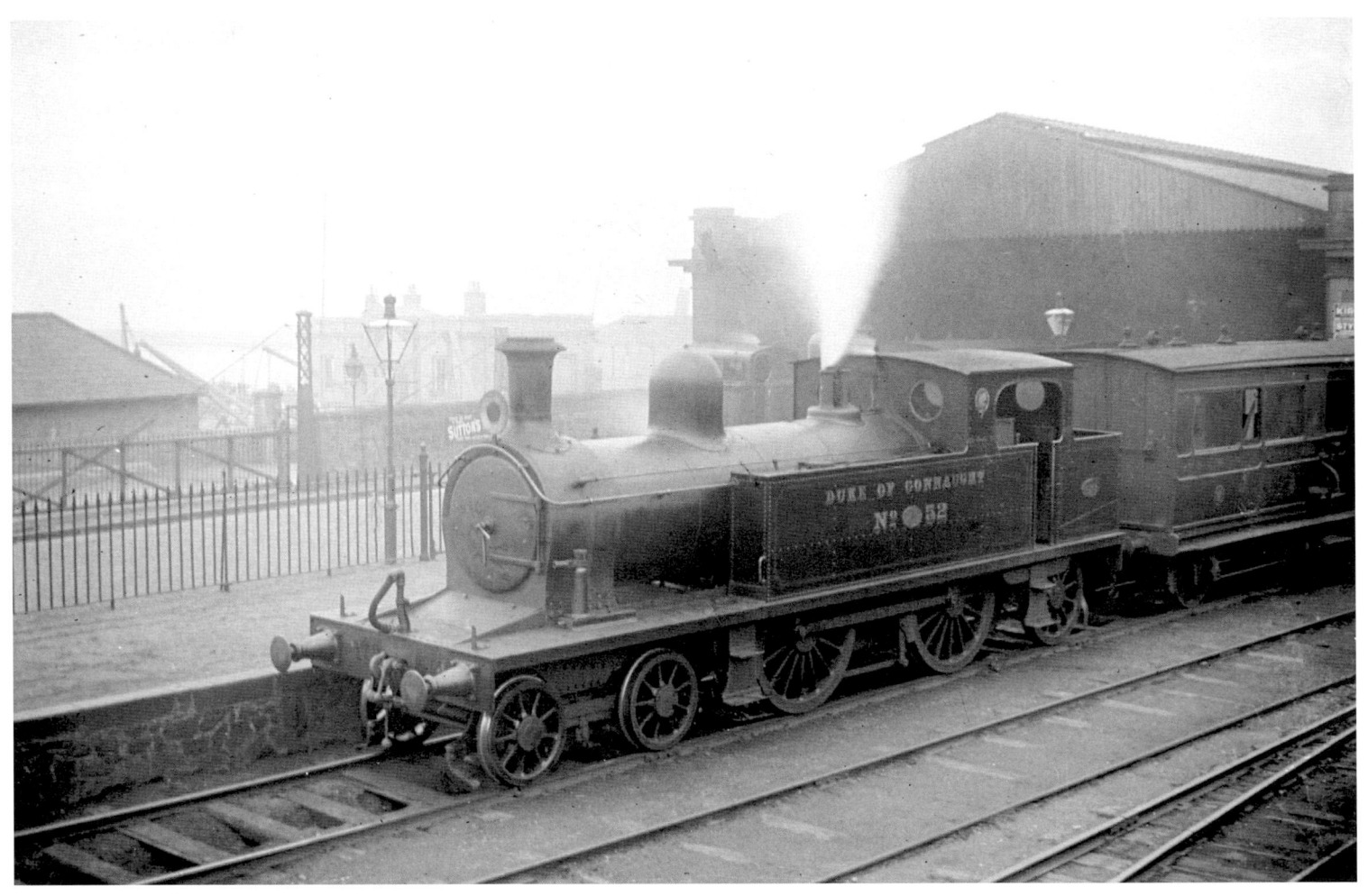

Dublin & South Eastern Railway 52 *Duke of Connaught* at Dun Laoghaire [formerly known as Kingstown],
County Dublin (B 16)

7.15 p.m., 31 July 1909

Ilford Special Rapid, f16, 16 sec

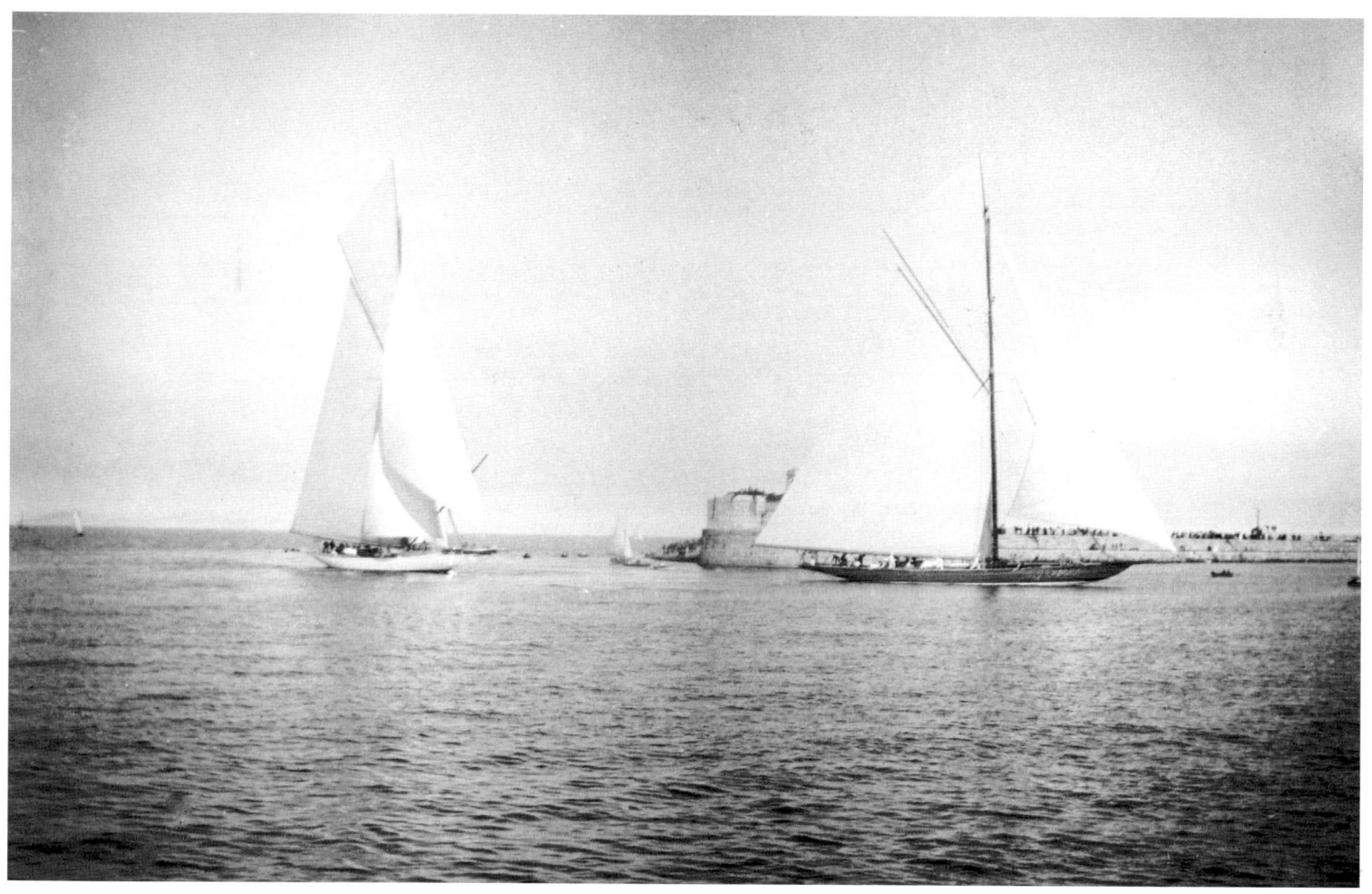

The *Shamrock* and *Brynhild* [both 23-metre Class Cutters], entering Dun Laoghaire Harbour during
Royal St George Yacht Club Regatta (D 12)

June 1908

Edwards Snapshot Isochromatic, f9, 1/50 sec

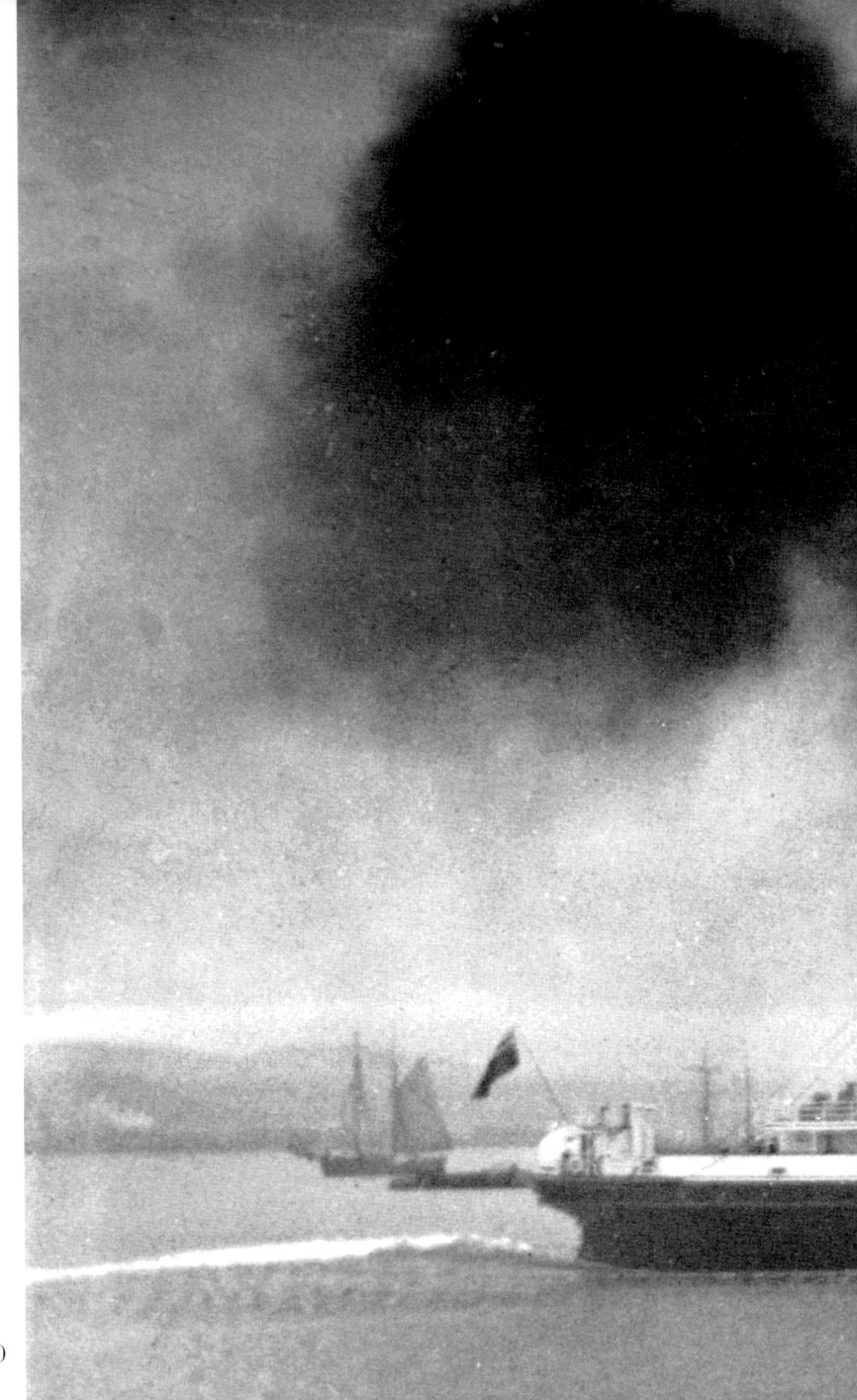

SS *Anglia* leaving Dun Laoghaire Harbour on
1st run of 1.40 p.m. services (D 5)

1.45 p.m., 1 April 1908

Edwards Snapshot Isochromatic, f9, 1/20 sec

30

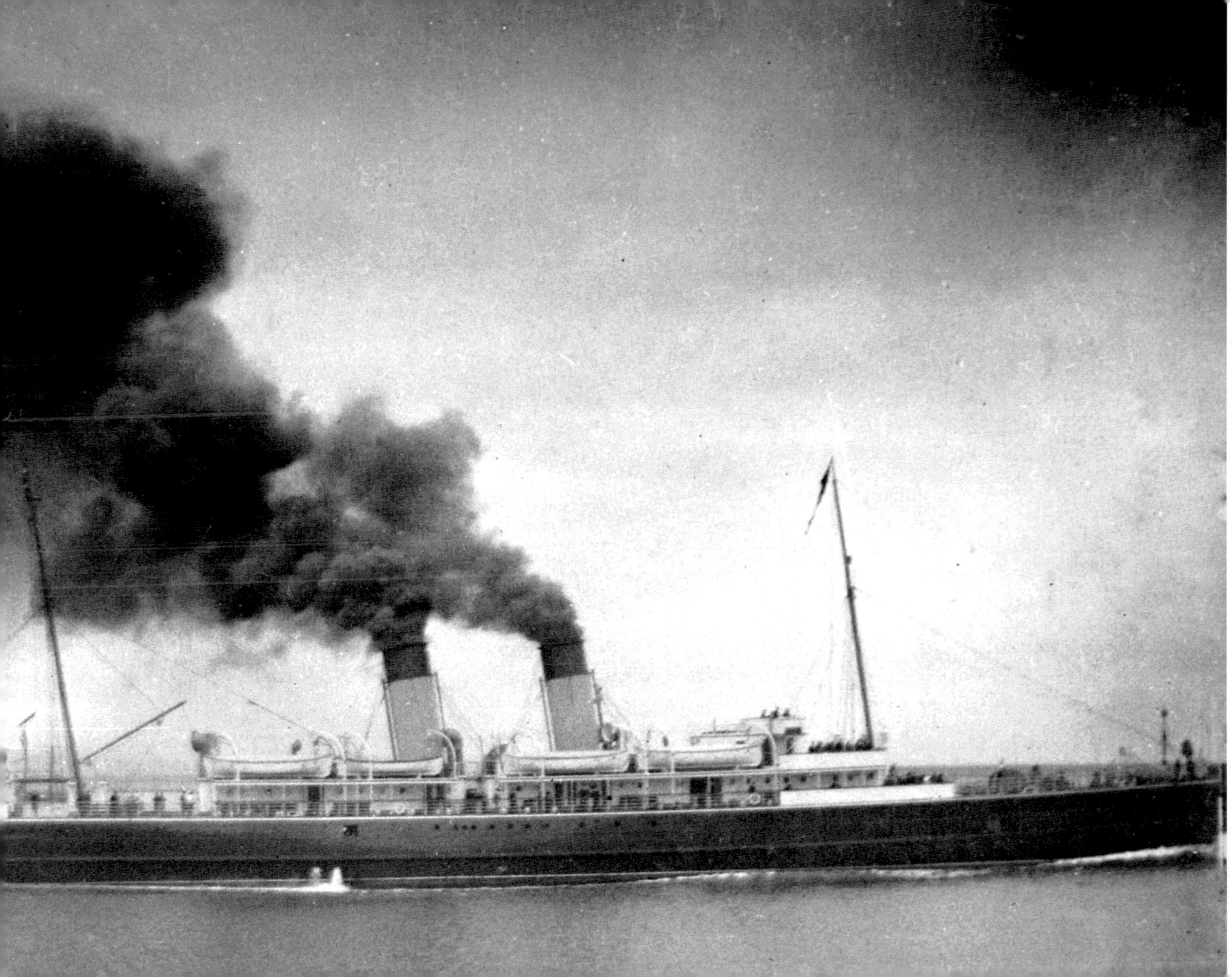

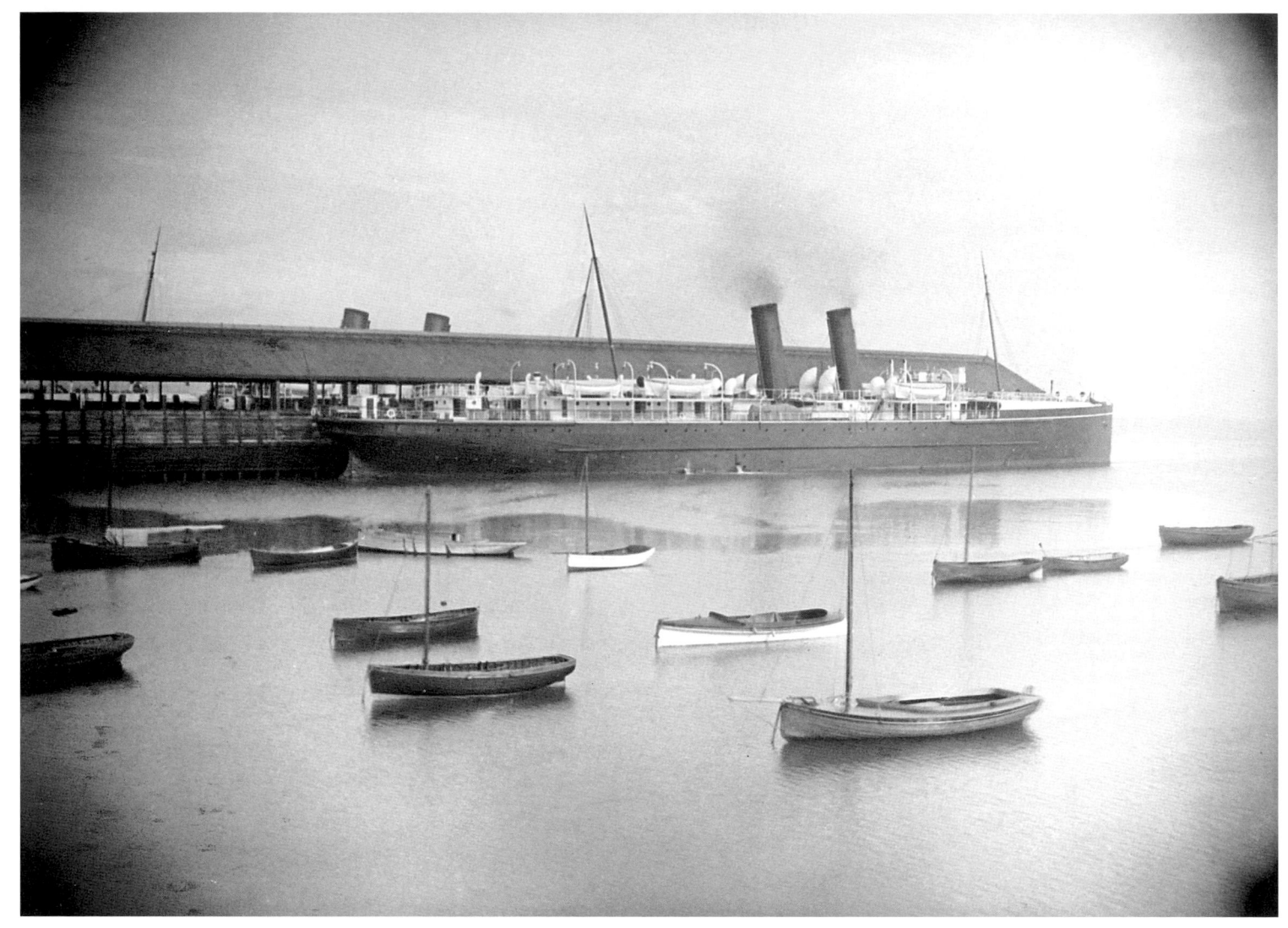

RMS *Ulster* at Packet Pier, Dun Laoghaire Harbour (D 19)

8 a.m., 25 April 1909

Paget Extra Special Rapid, f22, 3 sec

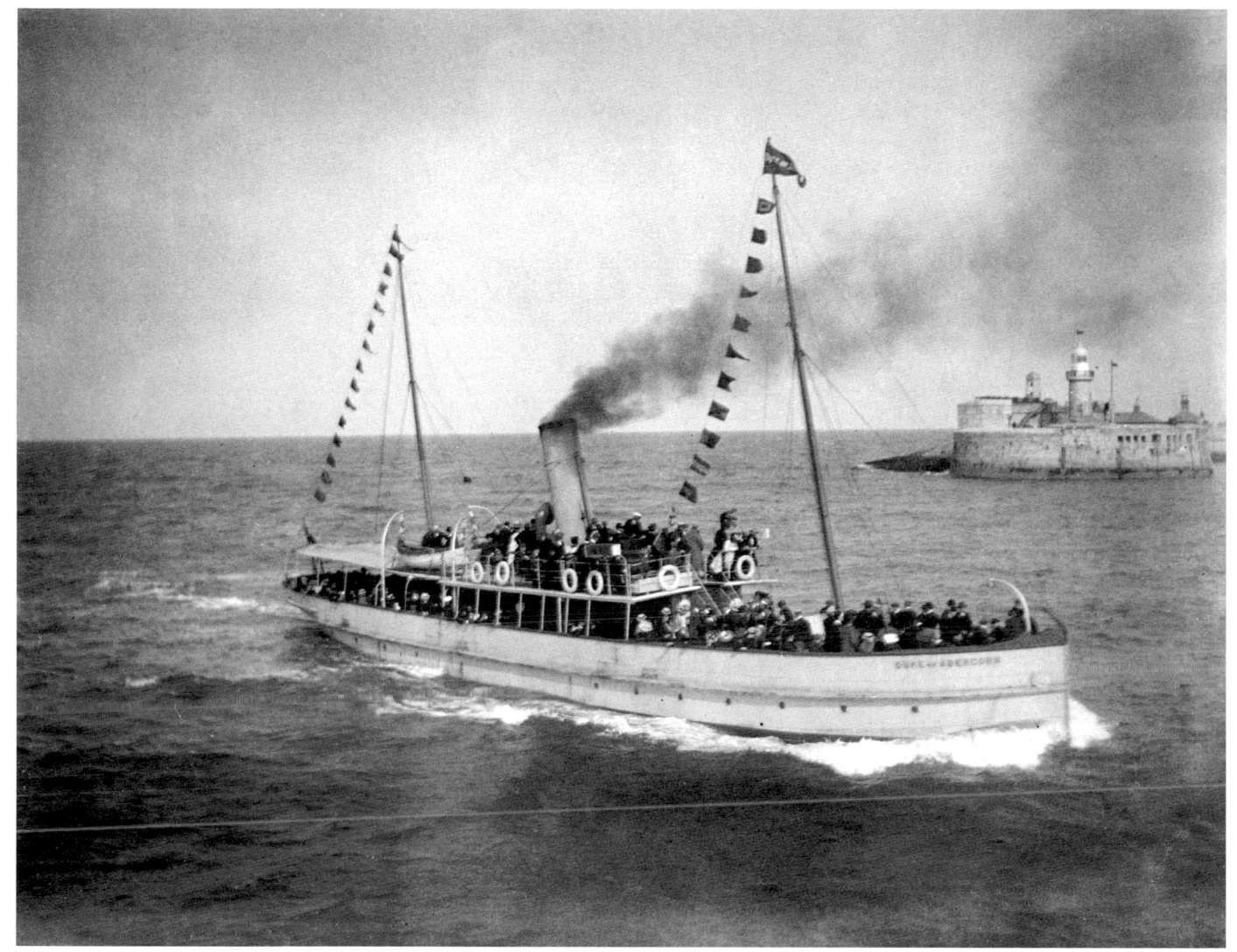

SS *Duke of Abercorn* entering Dun Laoghaire Harbour (D 22)

4 p.m., 6 June 1909

Edwards Snapshot Isochromatic, f9, 1/30 sec

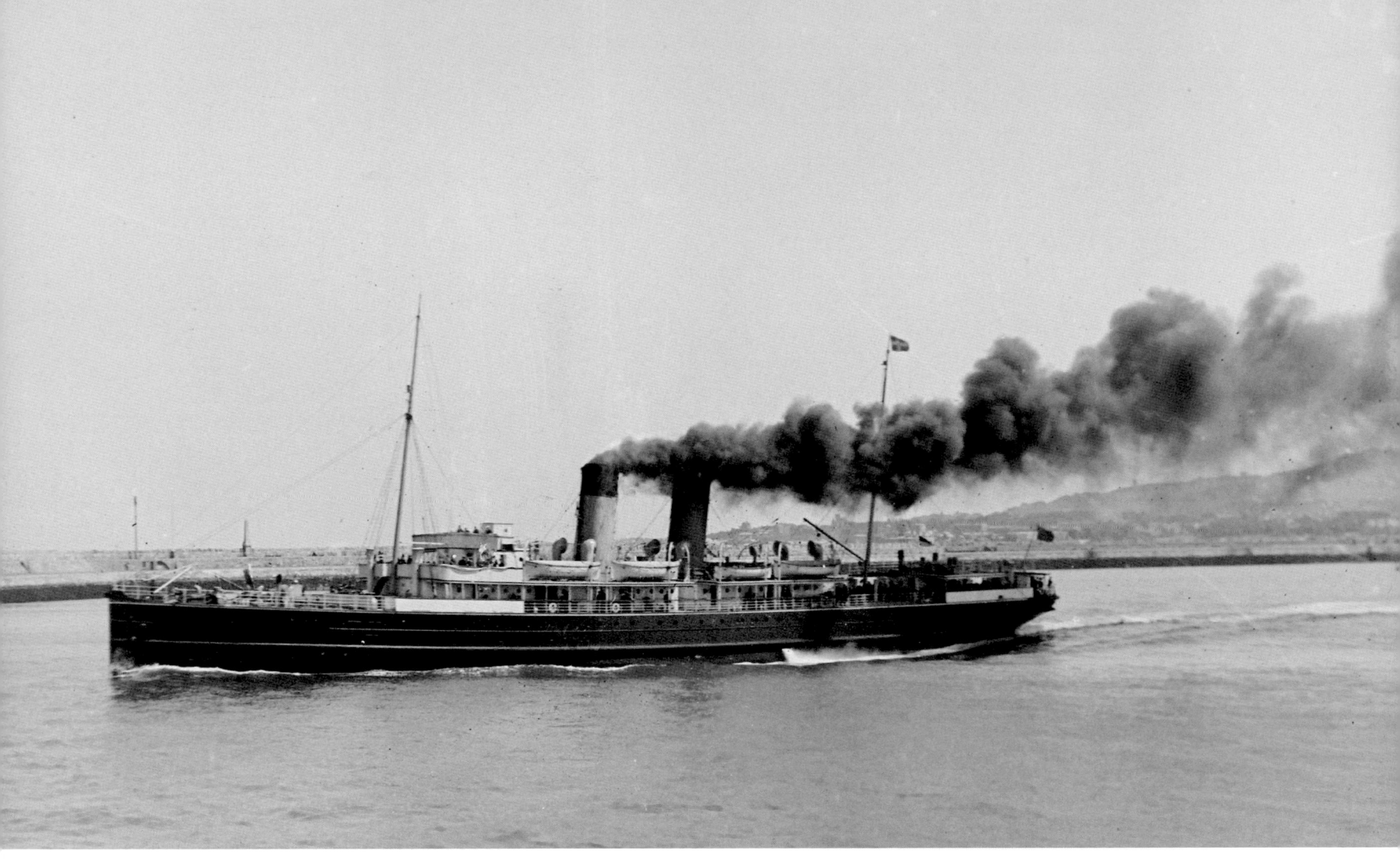

Above: SS *Hibernia* leaving Dun Laoghaire Harbour (D 66)

2 p.m., 6 June 1911

Edwards Isochromatic Auto Screen, f6, 1/100 sec

Facing page: Packet Pier, Dun Laoghaire Harbour (E 17)

6.35 a.m., 8 May 1909

Edwards Snapshot Isochromatic, f22, 2 sec

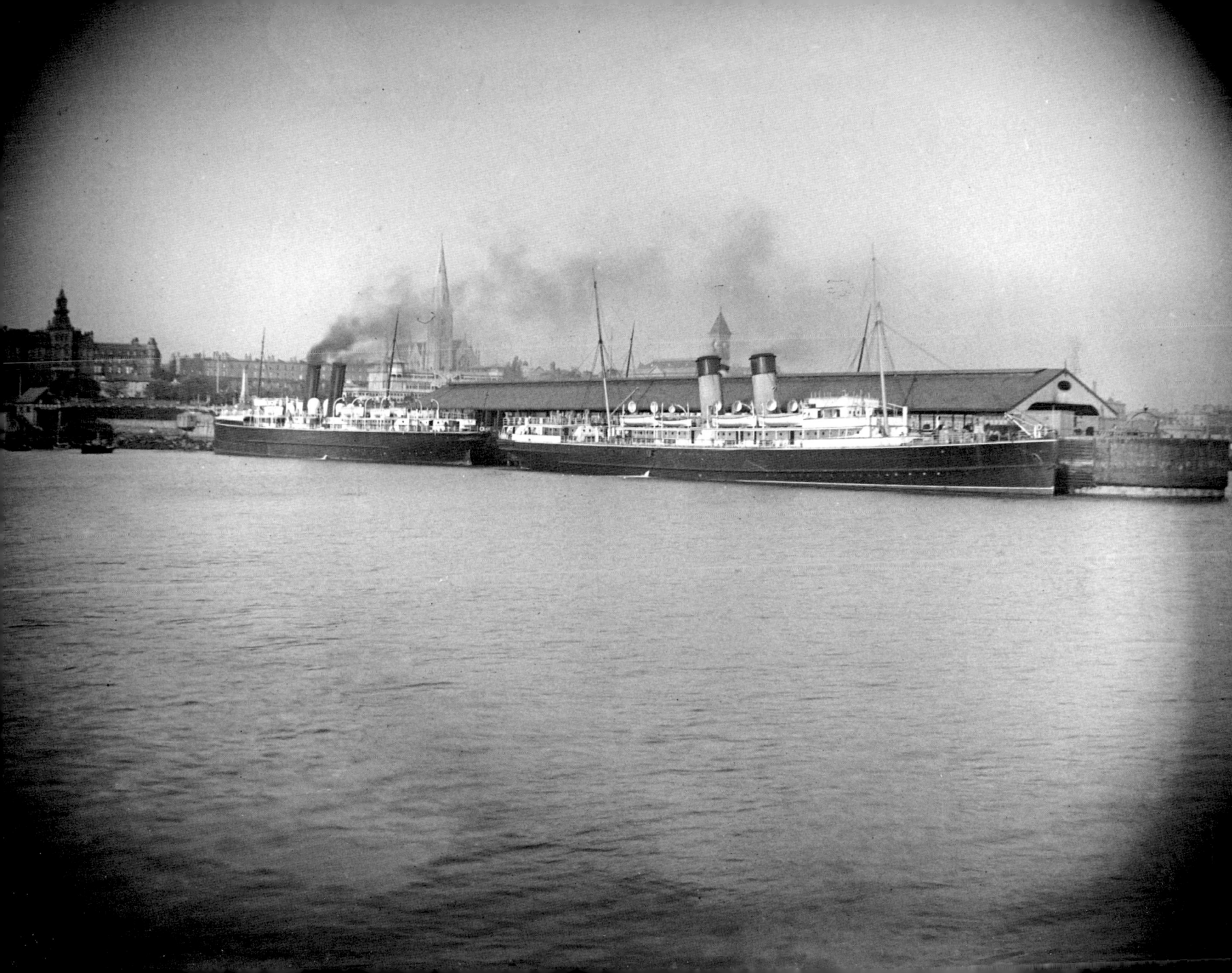

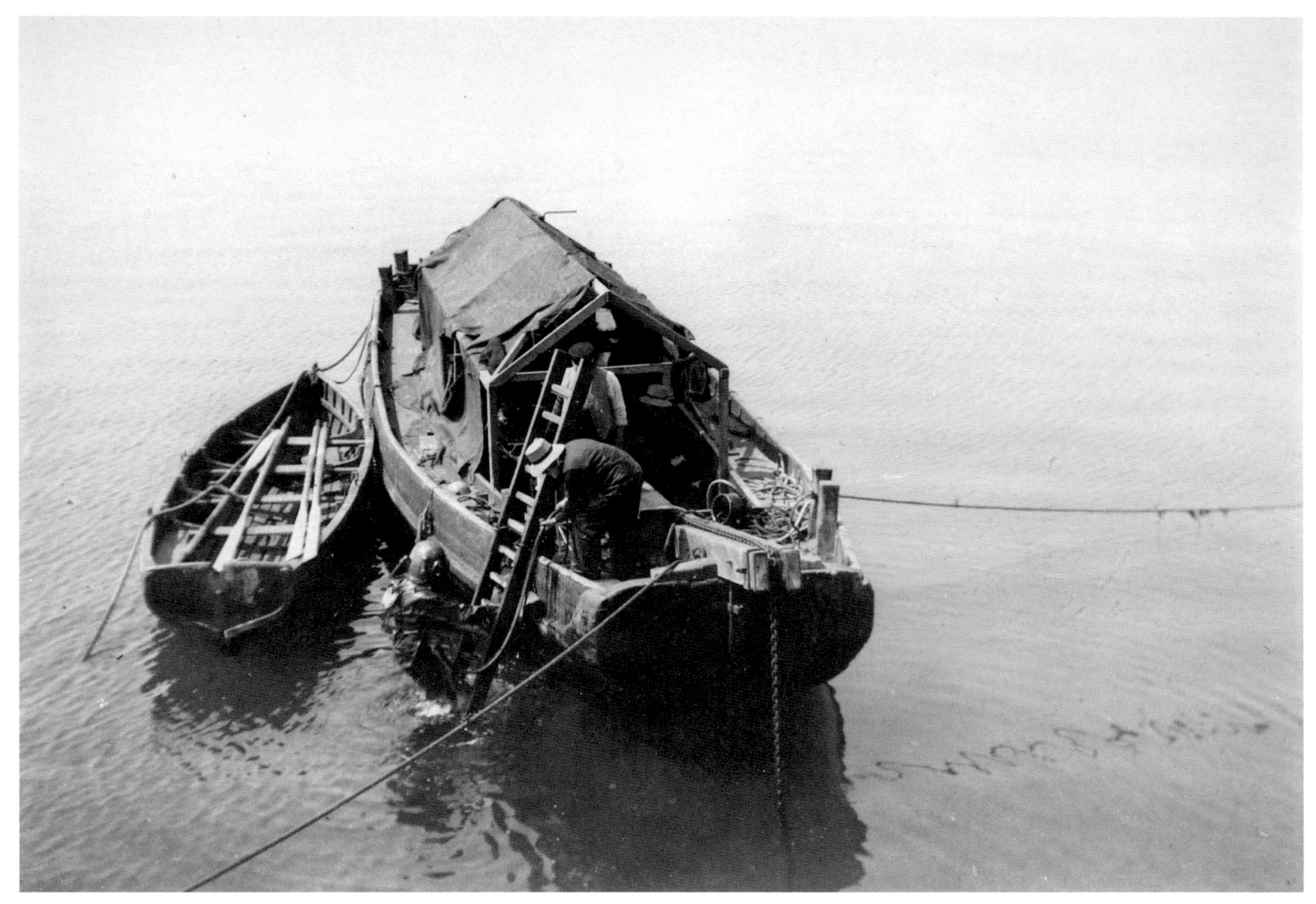

Diver, Dun Laoghaire Harbour (E 83)

1.30 p.m., 16 June 1910

Imperial Non-filter Orthochromatic, f11, 1/50 sec

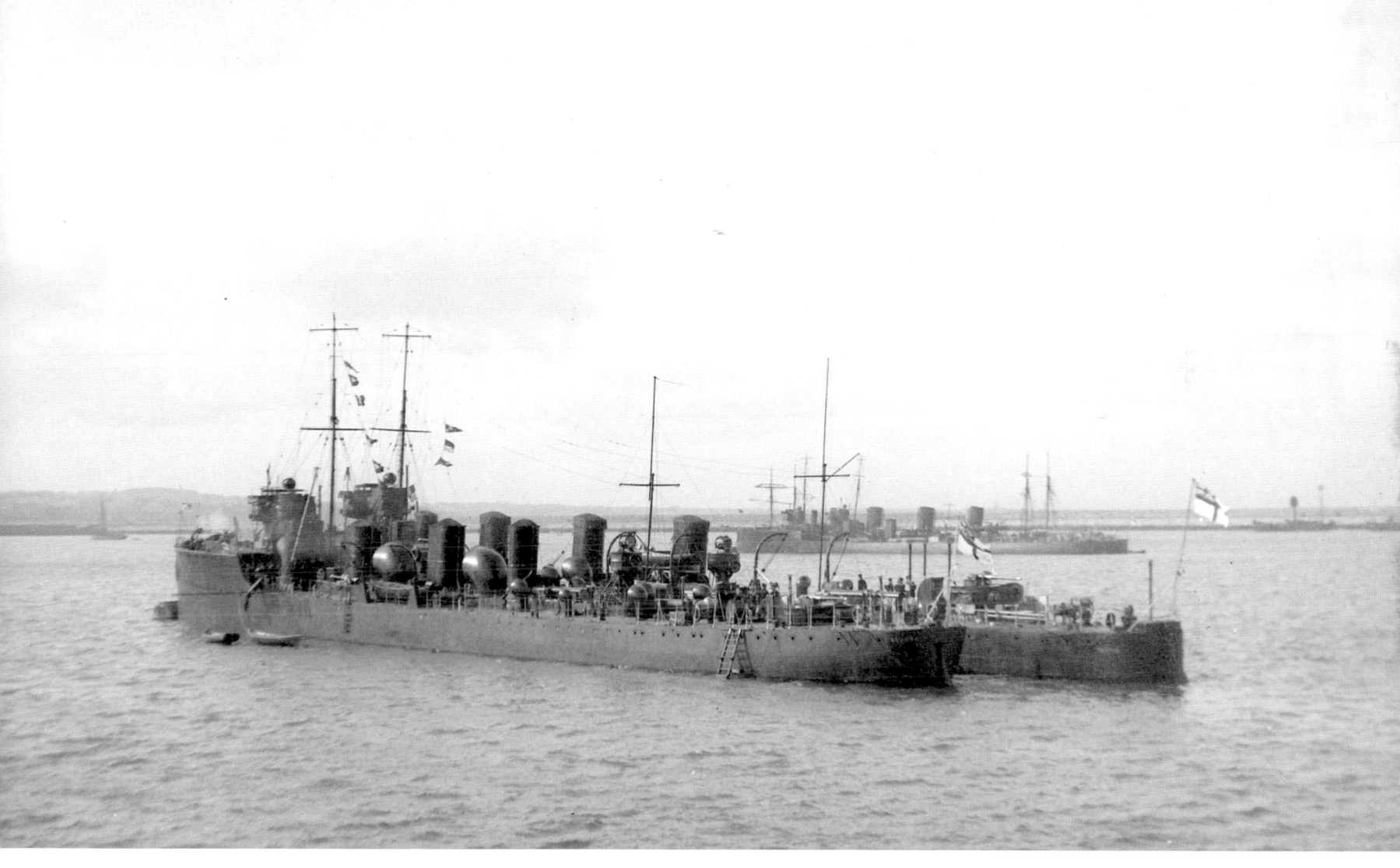

Torpedo Boat Destroyers, Dun Laoghaire Harbour (D 75)

1 p.m., 2 March 1913

Edwards Isochromatic Auto Screen, f14, 1/50 sec

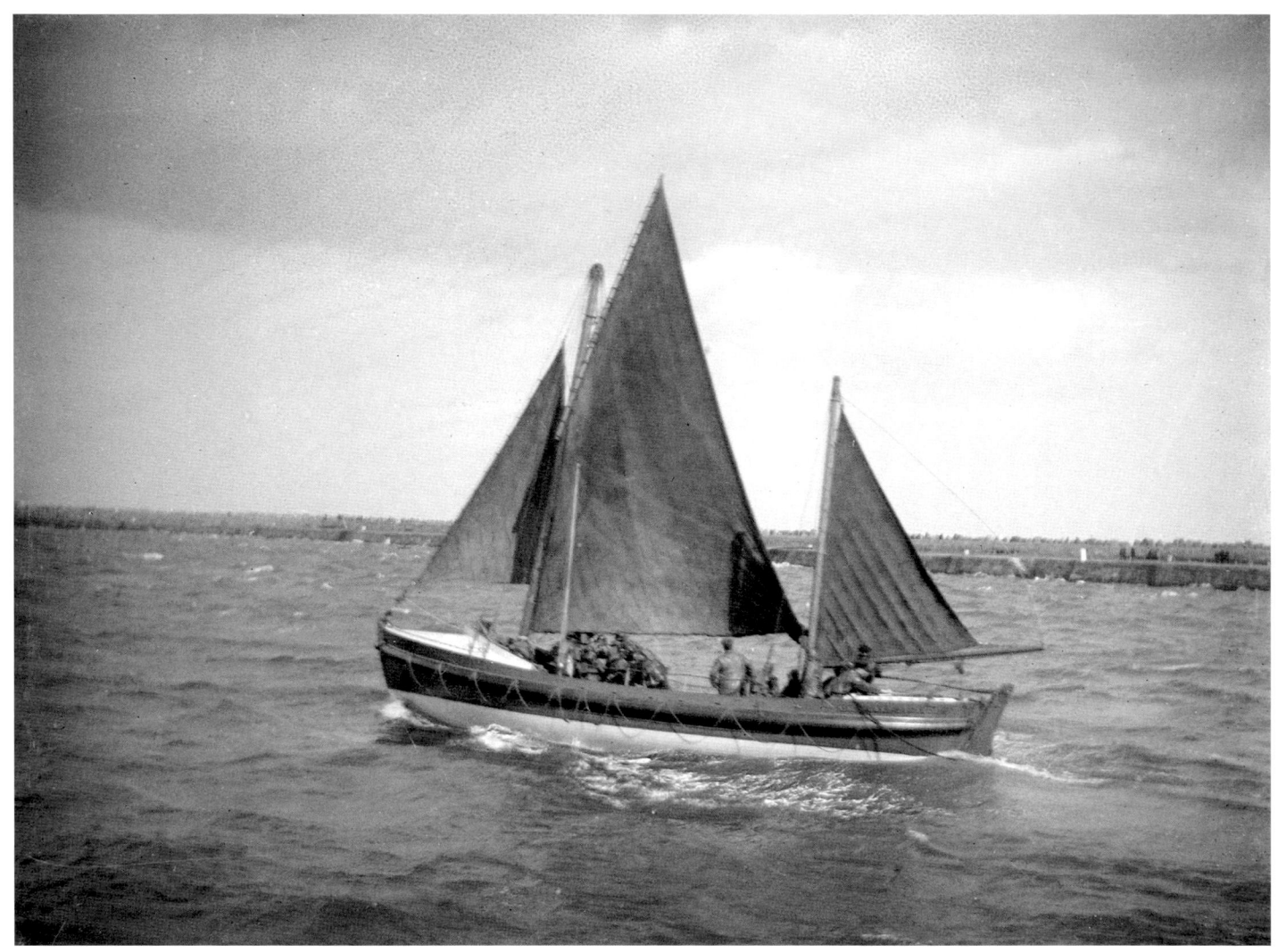

Lifeboat *Dunleary* in Dun Laoghaire Harbour (D 16)

2.25 p.m., 12 April 1909

Edwards Snapshot Isochromatic, f9, 1/20 sec

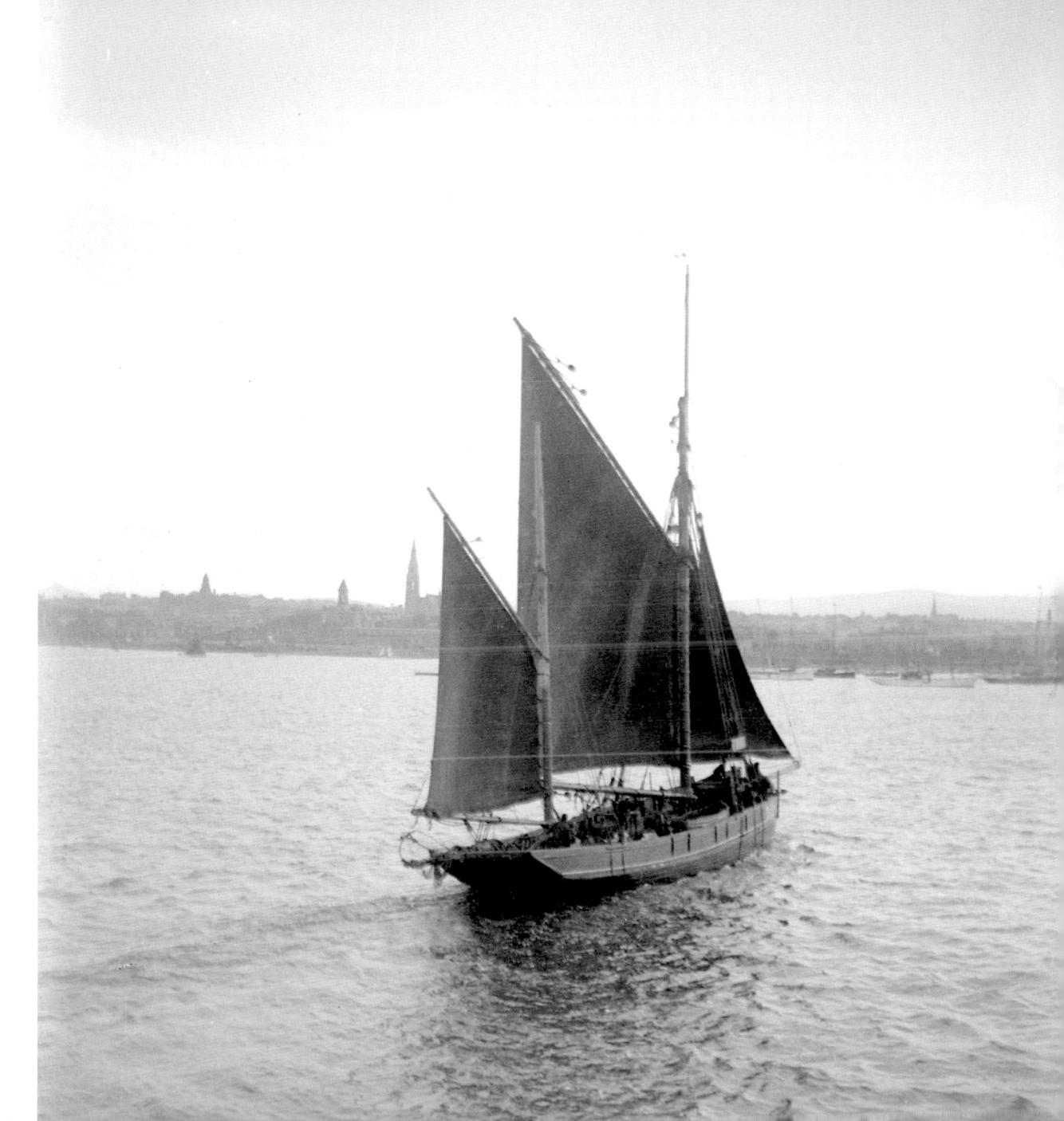

Fishing boat in
Dun Laoghaire Harbour
(D 28)

5.15 p.m., 23 July 1909

Ilford Special Rapid, f9, 1/20 sec

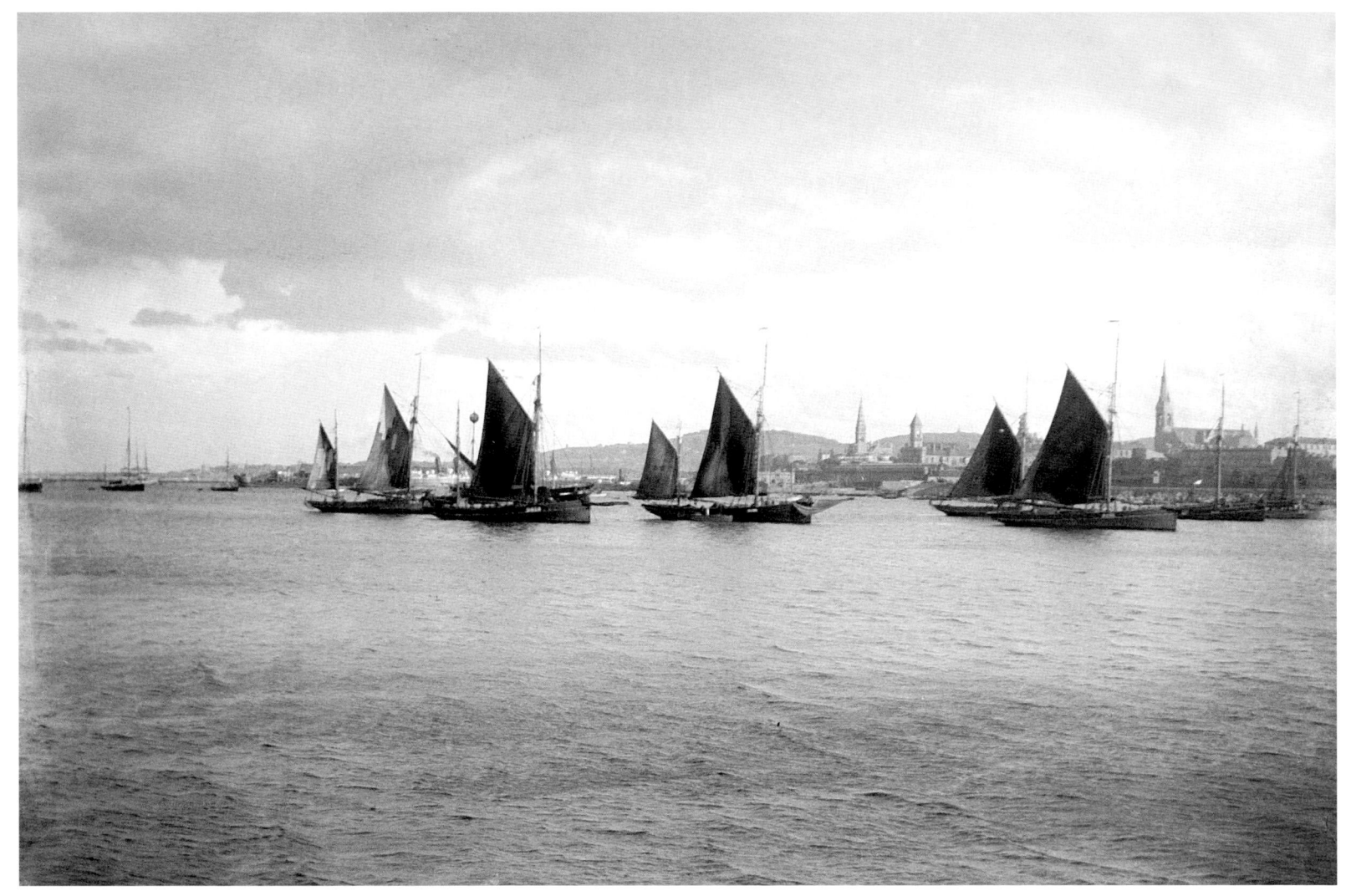

Fishing fleet at anchor, Dun Laoghaire Harbour (D 30)

5.30 p.m., 23 July 1909

Edwards Snapshot Isochromatic, f13, 1 sec

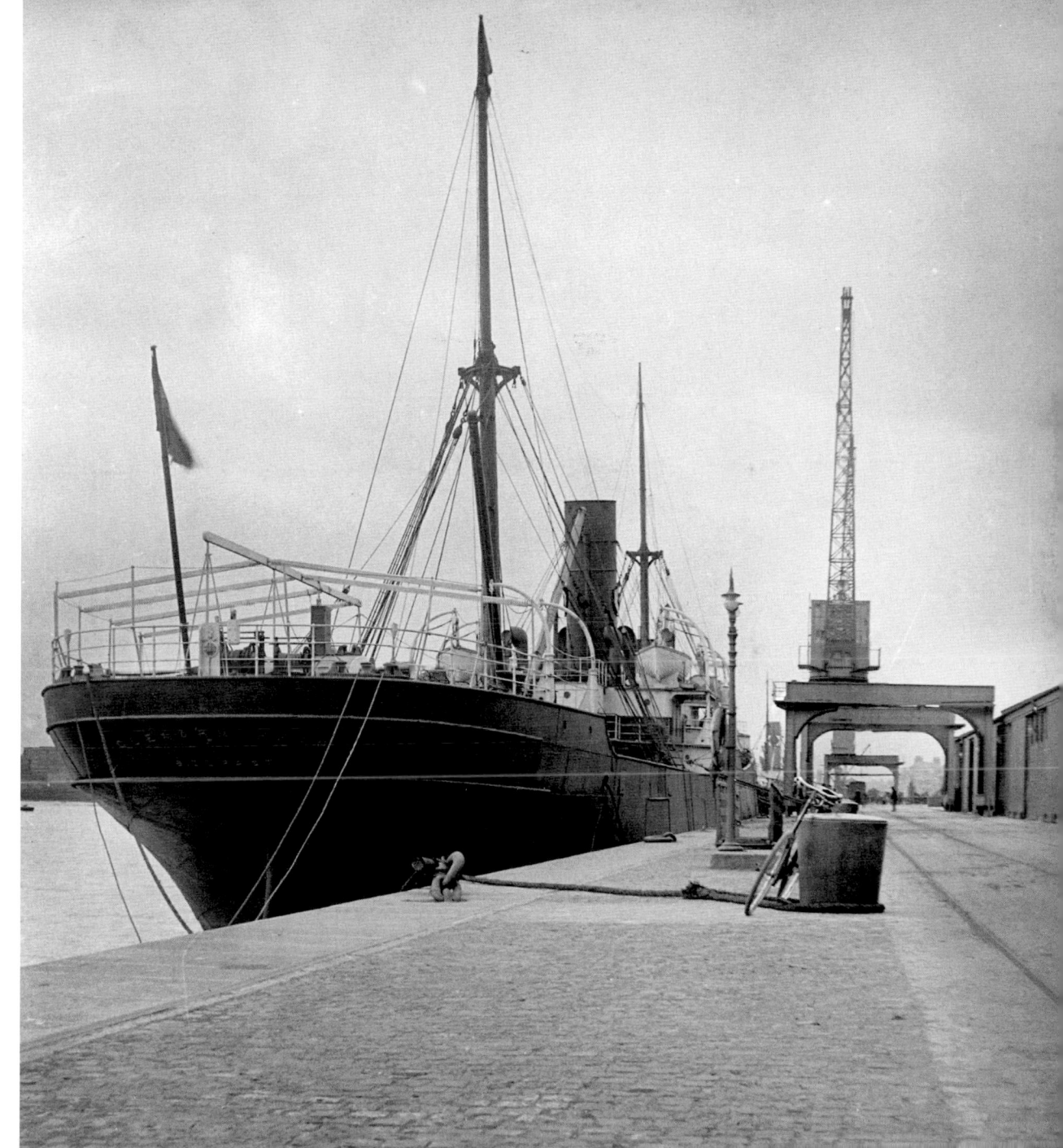

North Wall quays,
Dublin (E 21)

1.30 p.m., 15 May 1909

*Paget Extra Special Rapid,
f22, 2 sec*

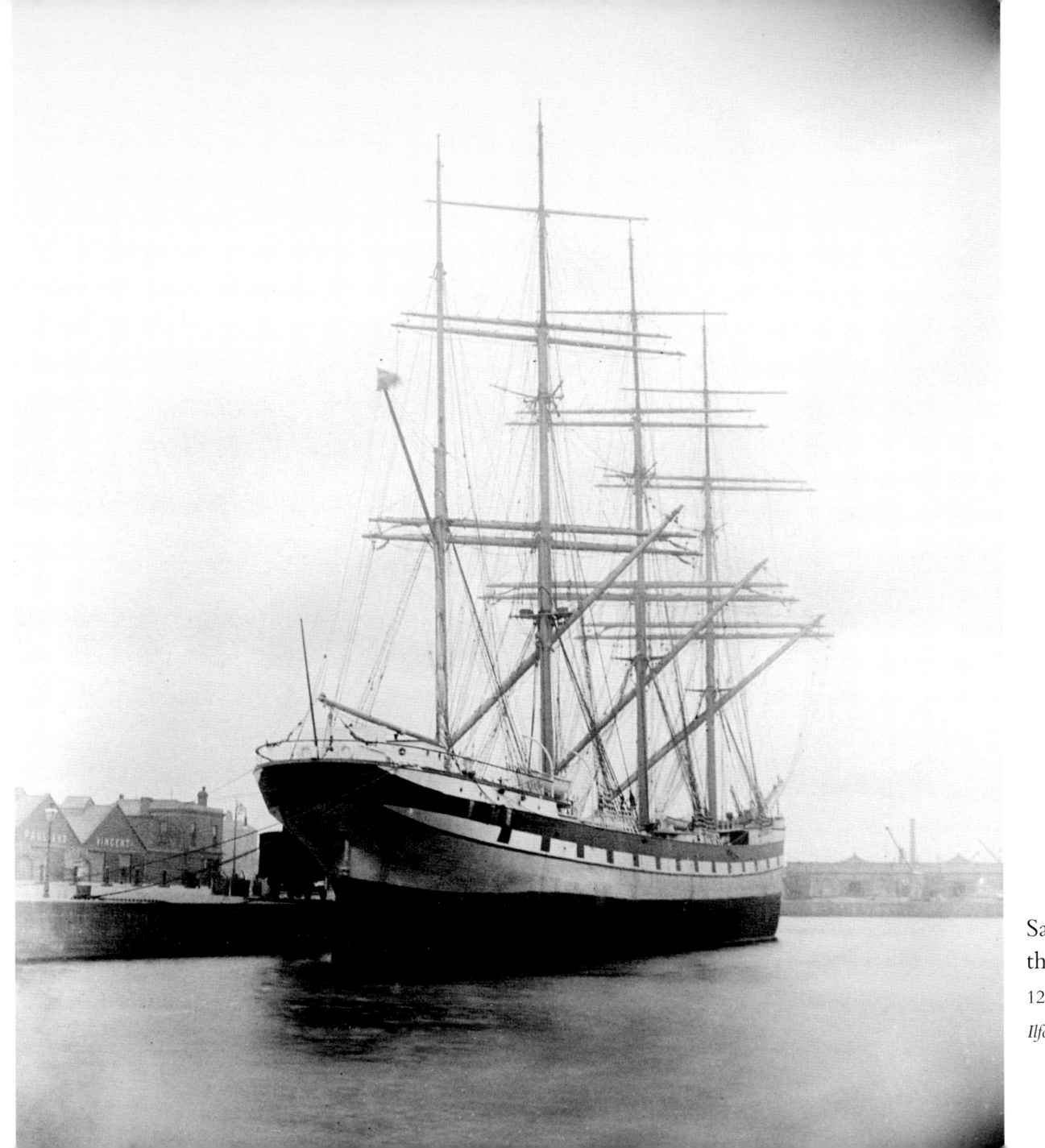

Sailing ship *Archibald Russell* on the River Liffey, Dublin (D 37)

12.30 p.m., 3 August 1909

Ilford Special Rapid, f9, 1/8 sec

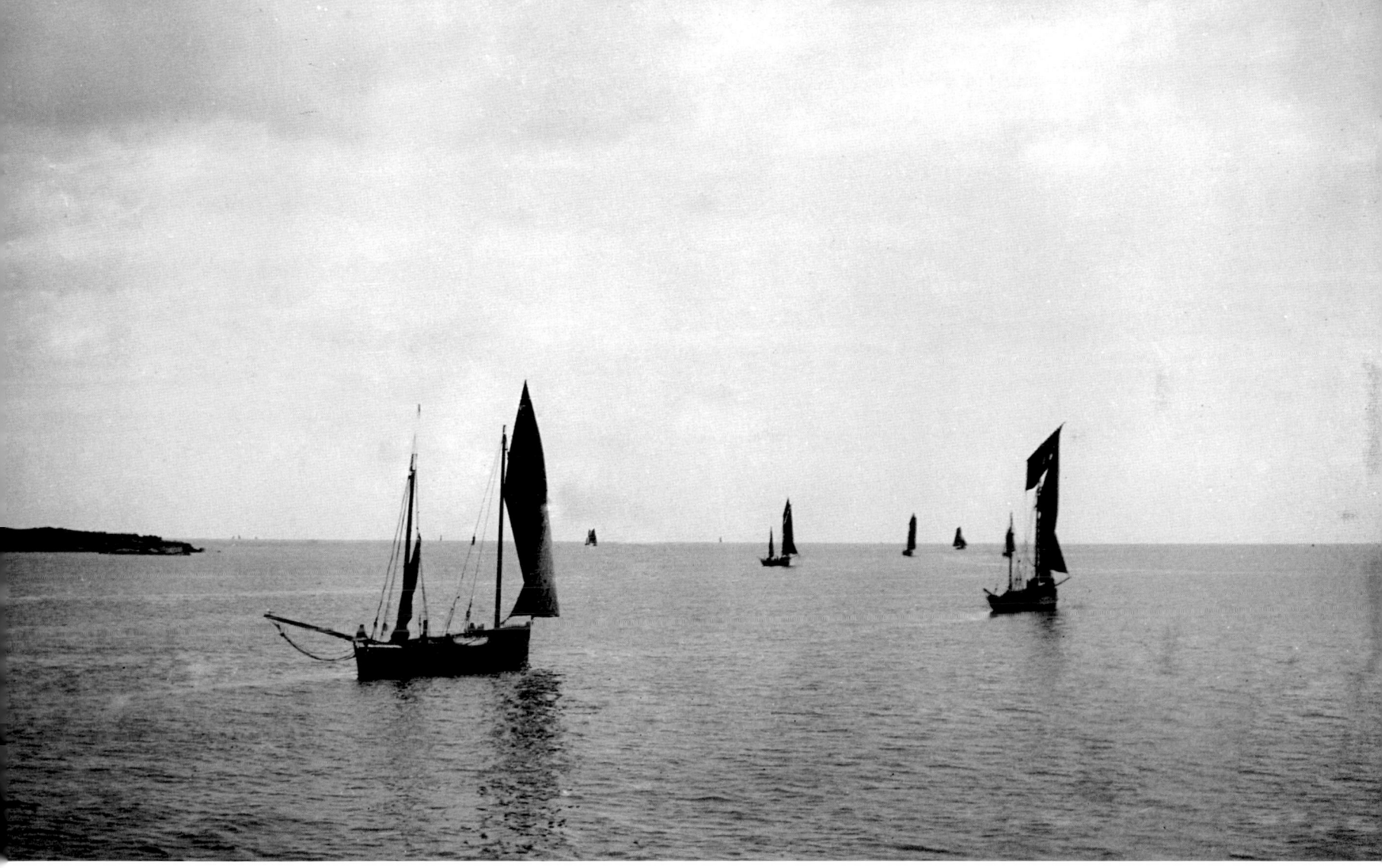

Fishing fleet off Howth, County Dublin (D 36)

12.00 p.m., 28 July 1909

Ilford Special Rapid, f16, 1 sec

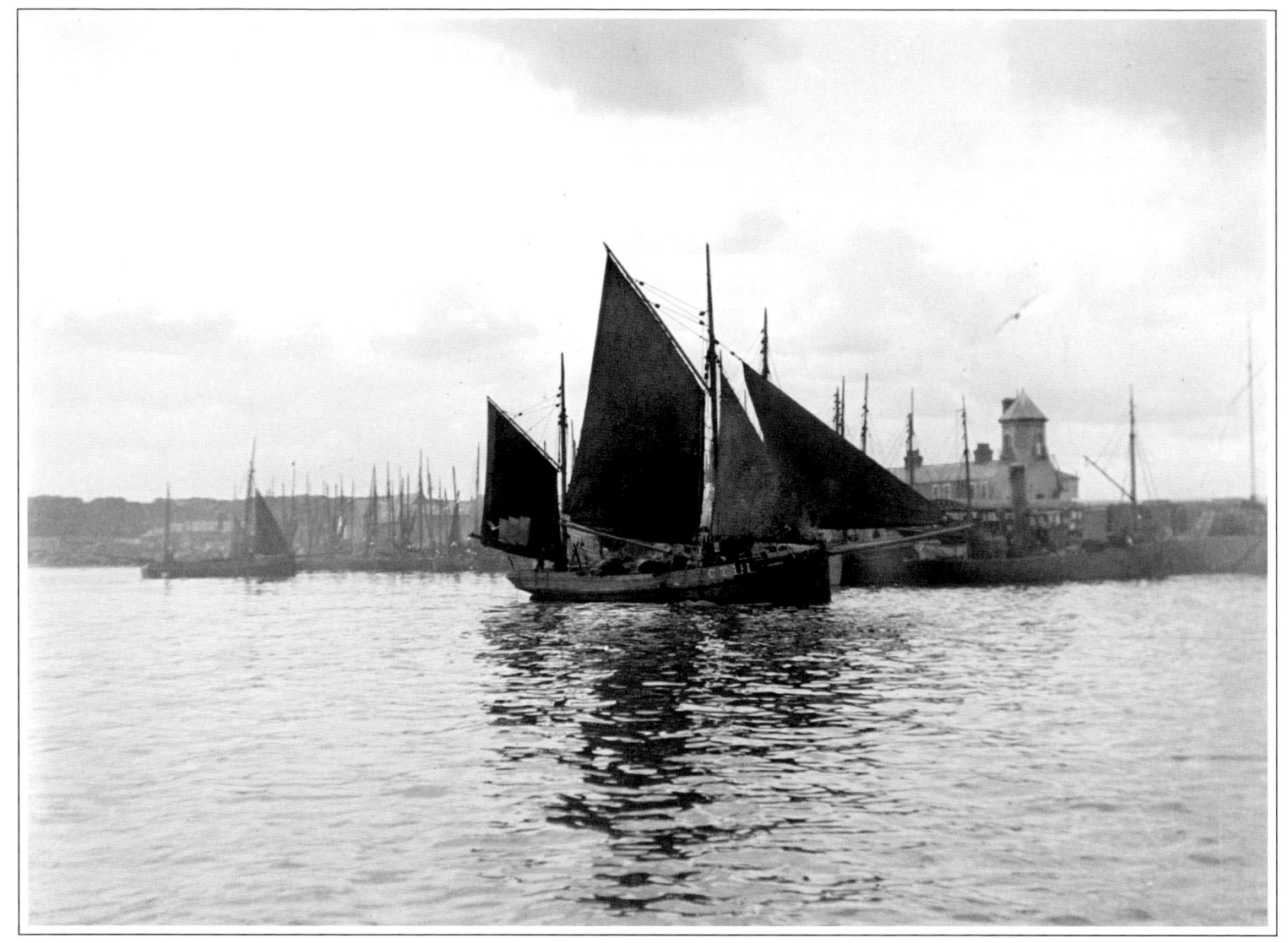

Fishing boat leaving Howth Harbour (D 70)

12 noon, 2 August 1912

Edwards Isochromatic Auto Screen, f11, 1/50 sec

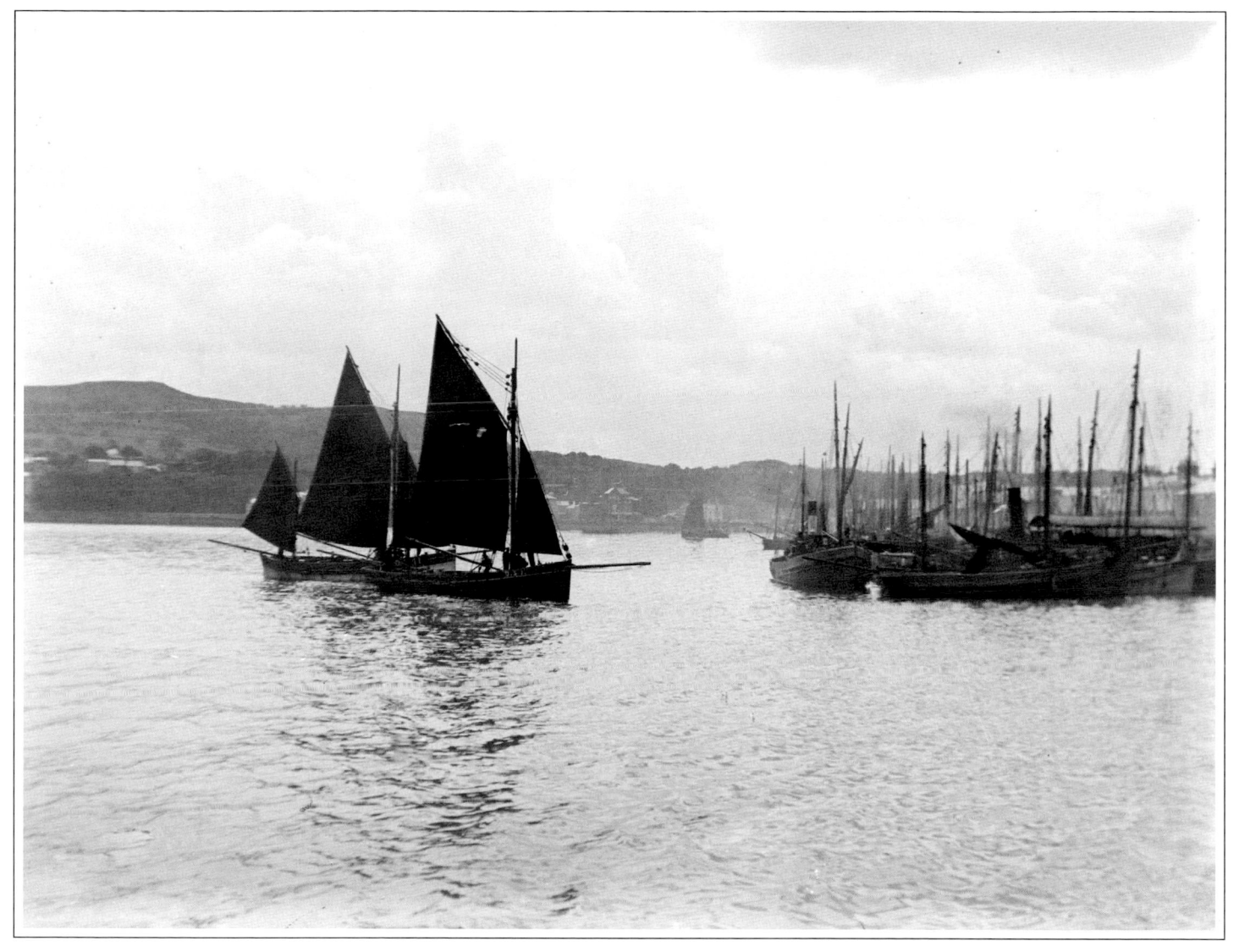

Fishing boats in Howth Harbour (D 73)

1 p.m., 2 August 1912

Edwards Isochromatic Auto Screen, f14, 1/50 sec

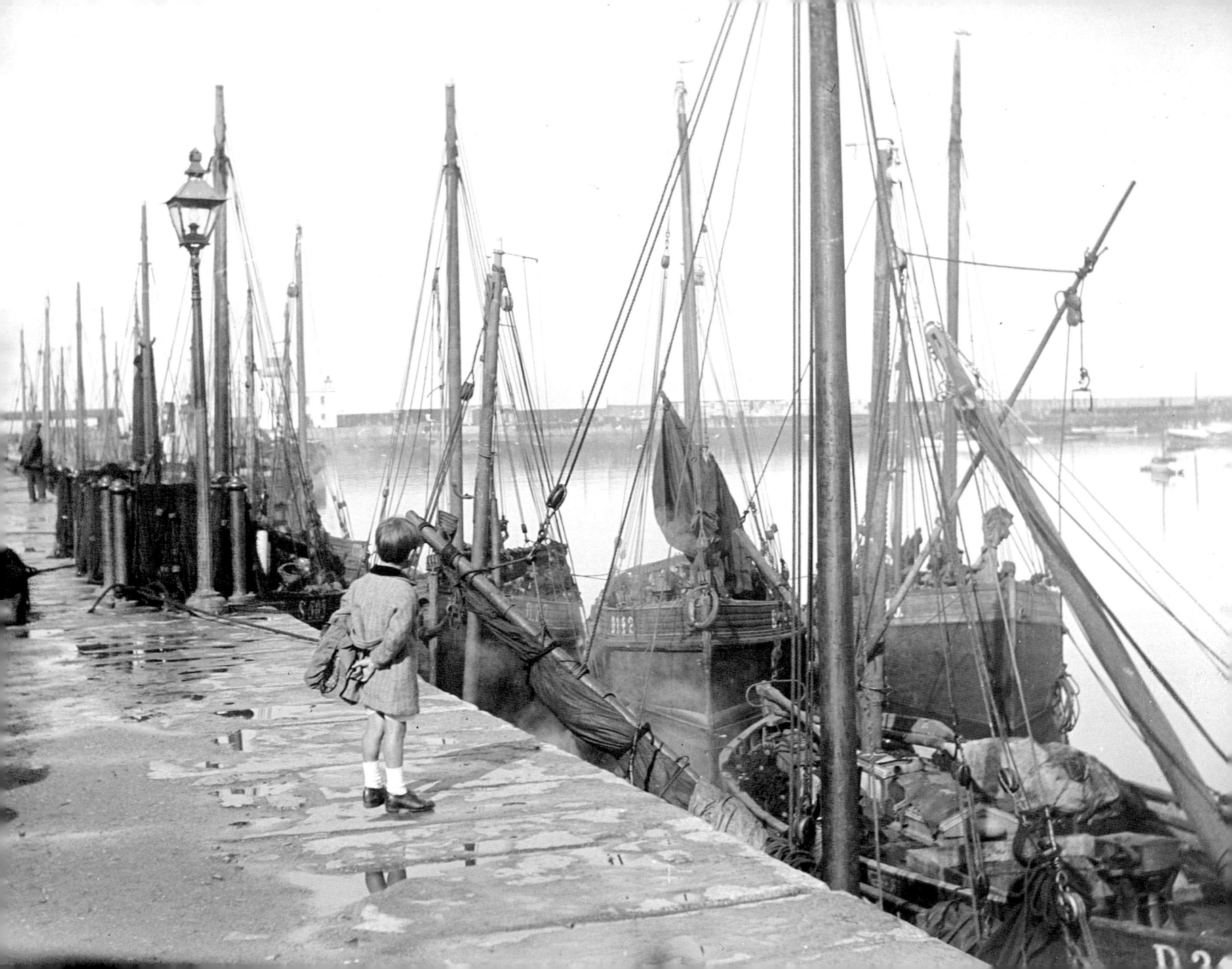

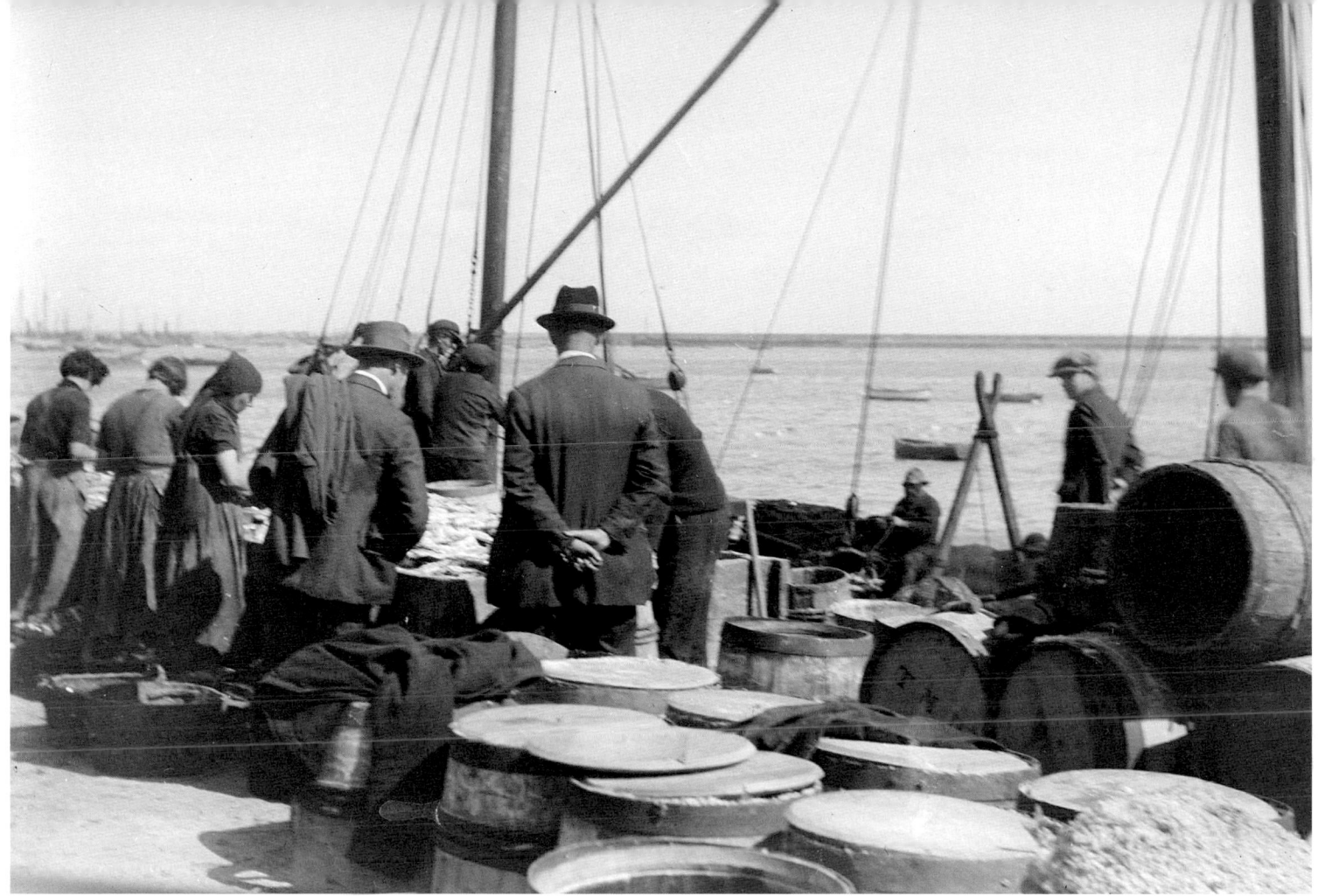

Above: Salting herring, Howth Harbour (E 1154)
2 p.m., 4 September 1925

Wellington Anti Screen, f11, 1/50 sec

Facing page: Ronnie Chapman watching the herringboats at Howth Harbour (E 1153)

5 p.m., 1 August 1925

Wellington Anti Screen, f11, 1/50 sec

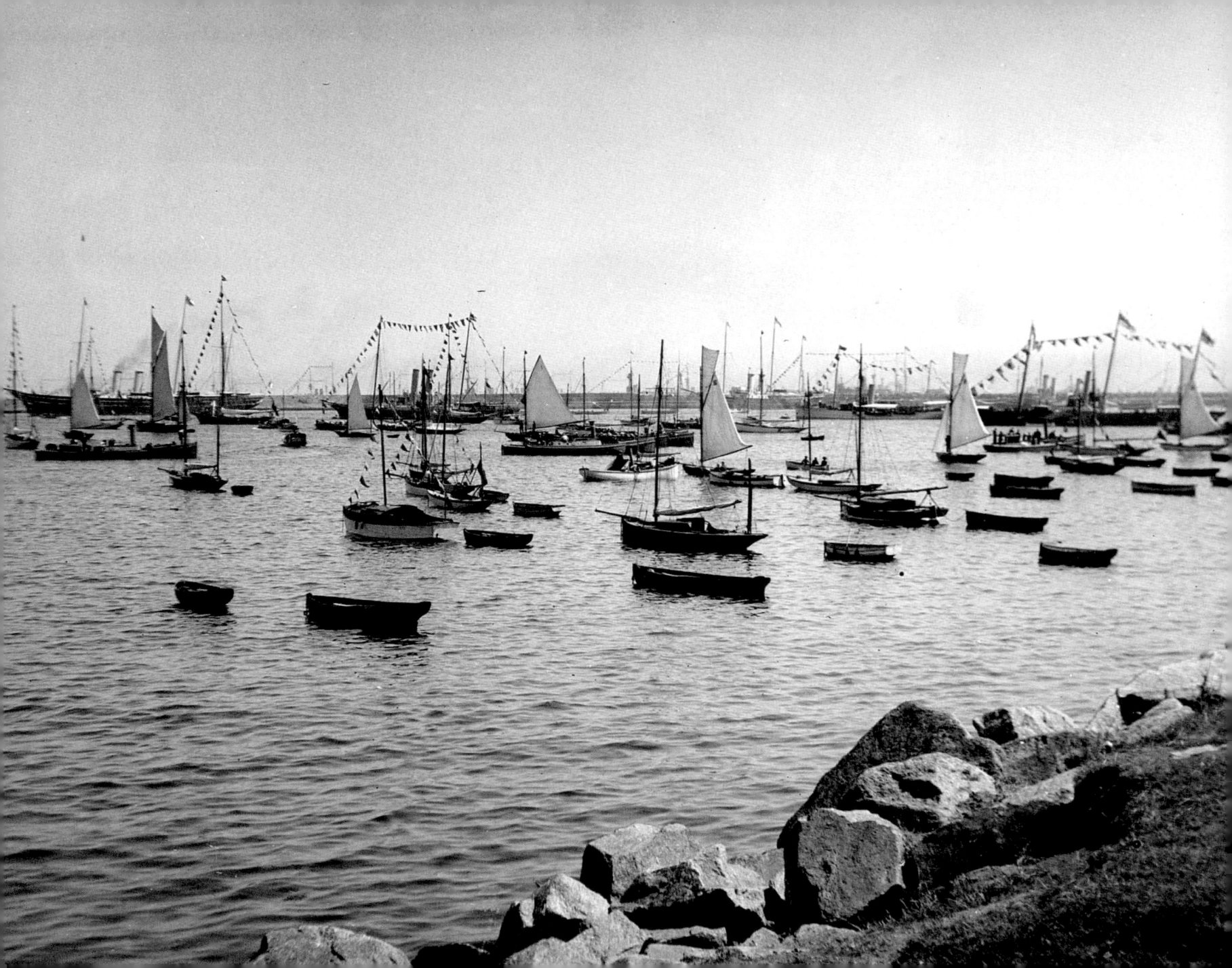

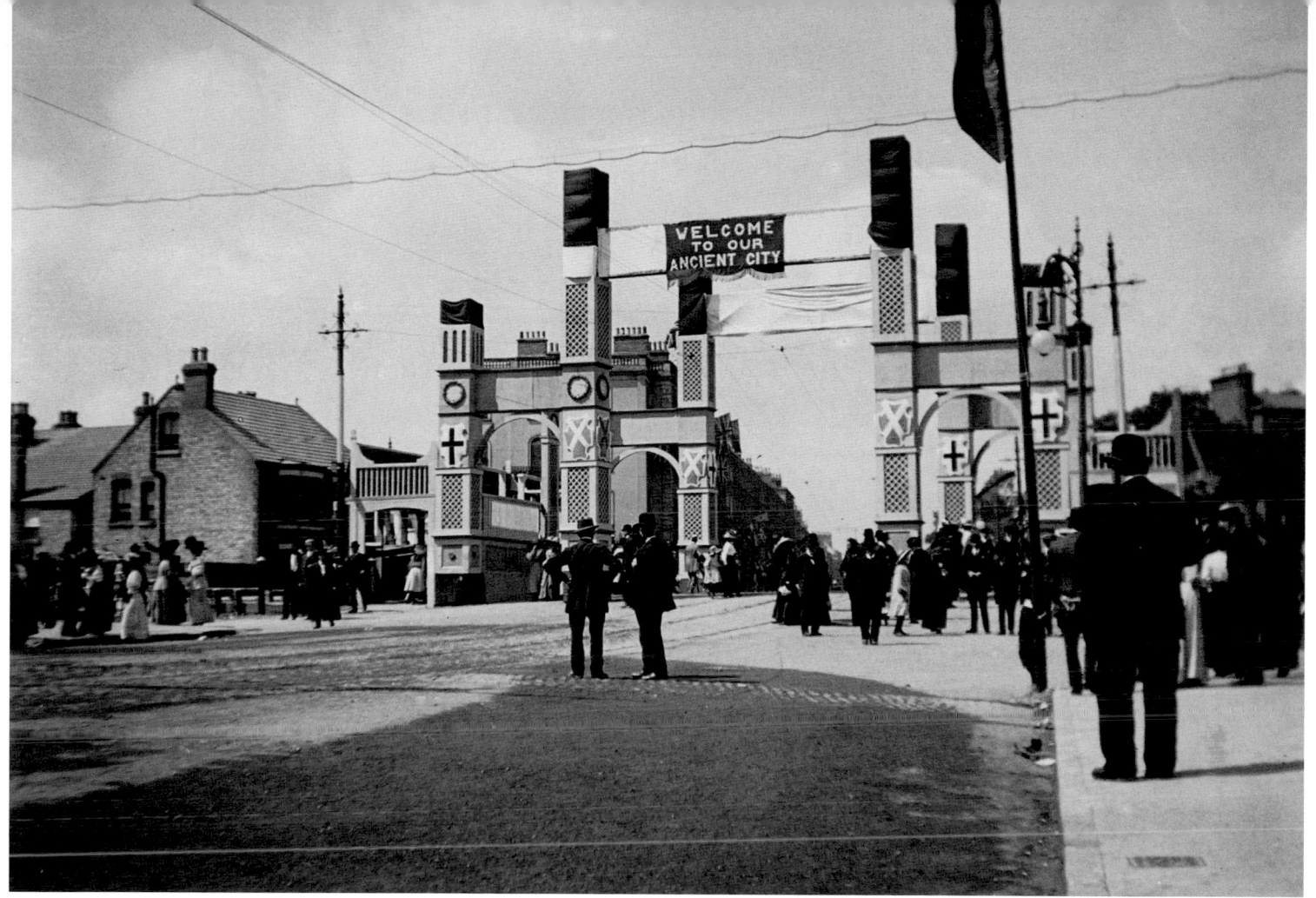

Above: Arch on Leeson Street Bridge, Dublin, decorated for the 1911 Royal Visit [of King George V] (E 160)

1.30 p.m., 8 July 1911

Edwards Isochromatic Auto Screen, f8, 1/50 sec

Facing page: Dun Laoghaire Harbour from Coastguard Station during 1911 Royal Visit (E 159)

11.30 a.m., 8 July 1911

Edwards Isochromatic Auto Screen, f16, 1/50 sec

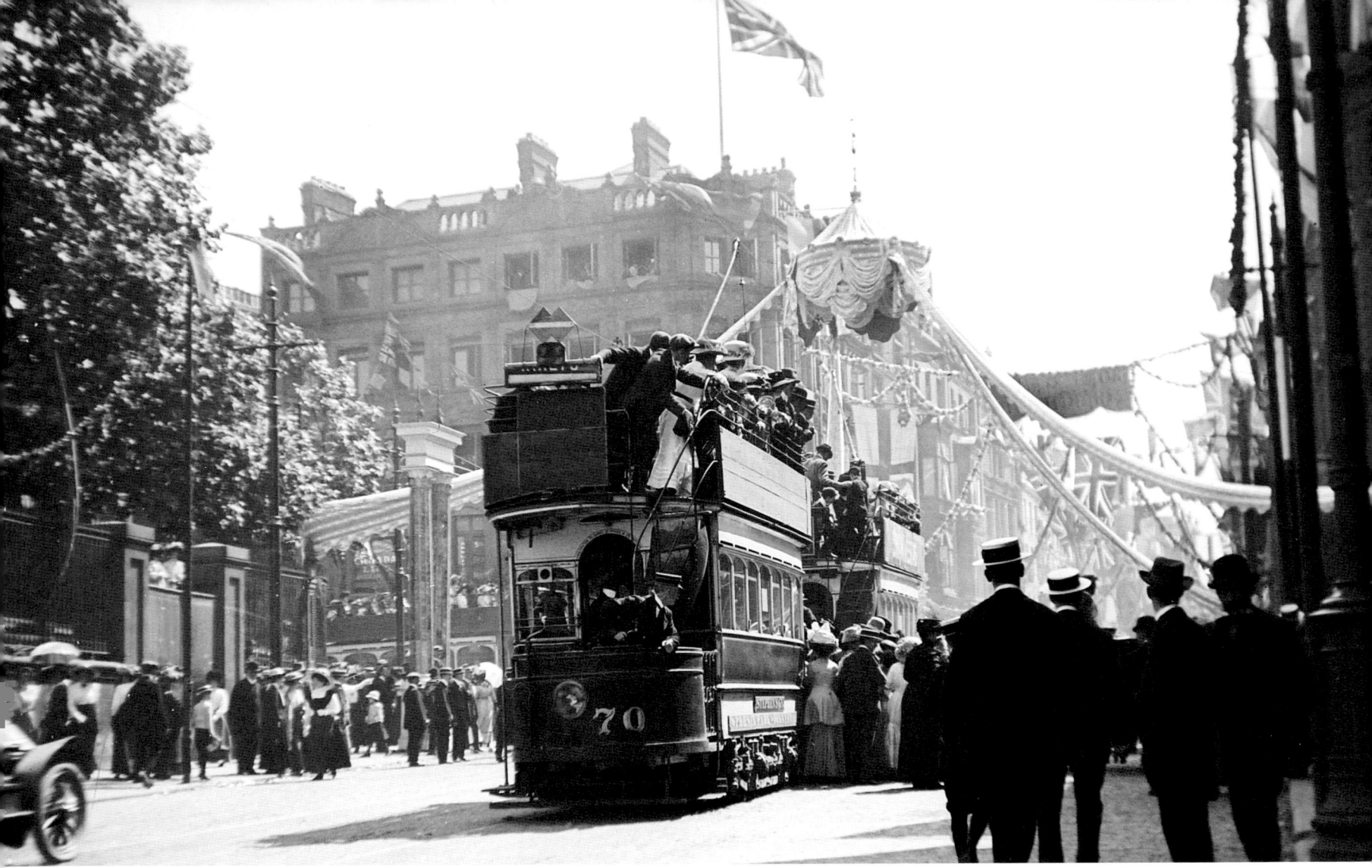

Corner of Grafton Street, Dublin, decorated for 1911 Royal Visit (E 161)

1.45 p.m., 8 July 1911

Edwards Isochromatic Auto Screen, f8, 1/50 sec

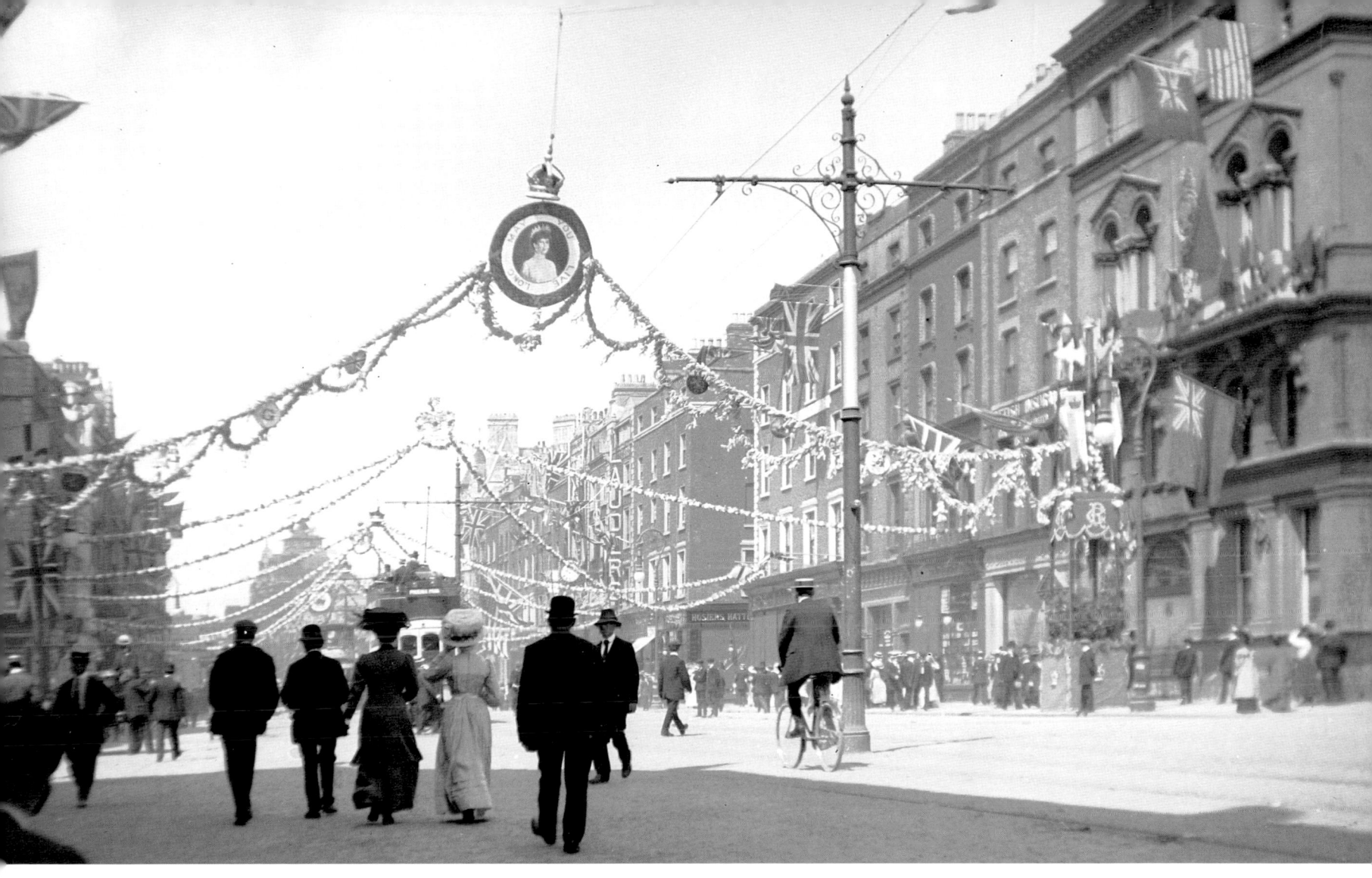

Westmoreland Street, Dublin, decorated for 1911 Royal Visit (E 162)

1.45 p.m., 8 July 1911

Edwards Isochromatic Auto Screen, f8, 1/50 sec

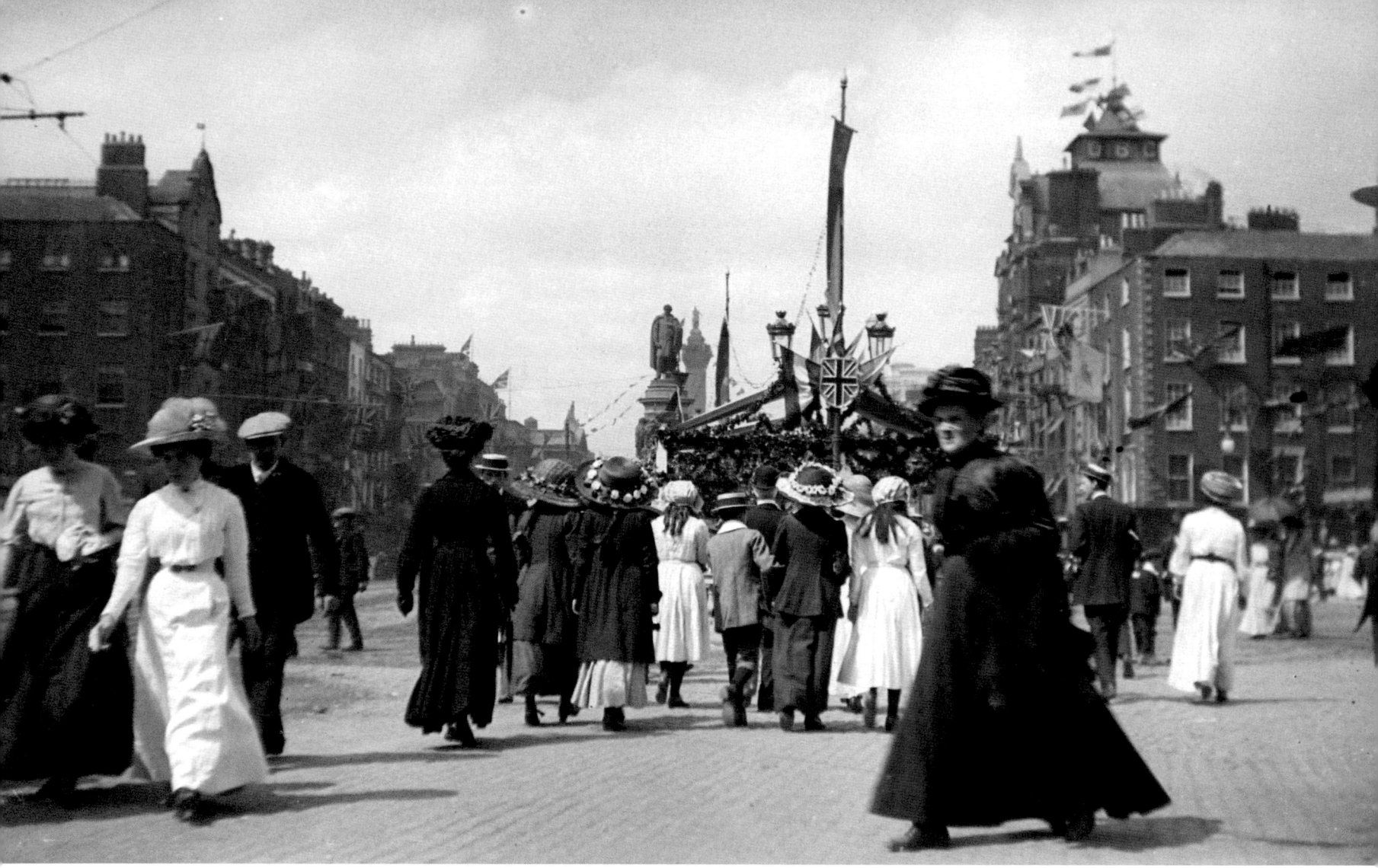

Carlisle Bridge, Dublin, decorated for 1911 Royal Visit (E 163)

1.45 p.m., 8 July 1911

Edwards Isochromatic Auto Screen, f8, 1/50 sec

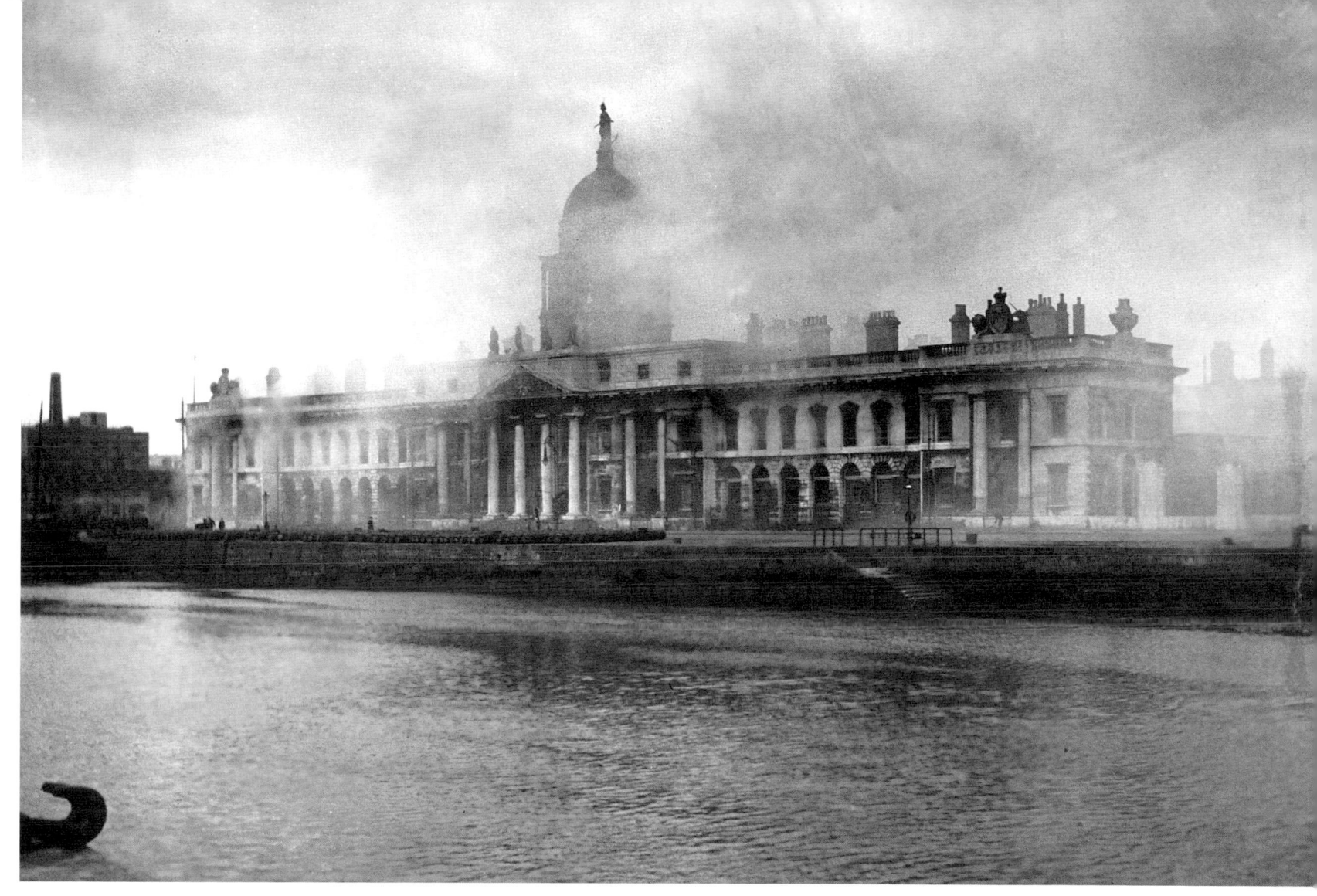

Burning of the Custom House, Dublin (E 757)

9.00 a.m., 26 May 1921

Primo Film, f6.3, 1/50 sec

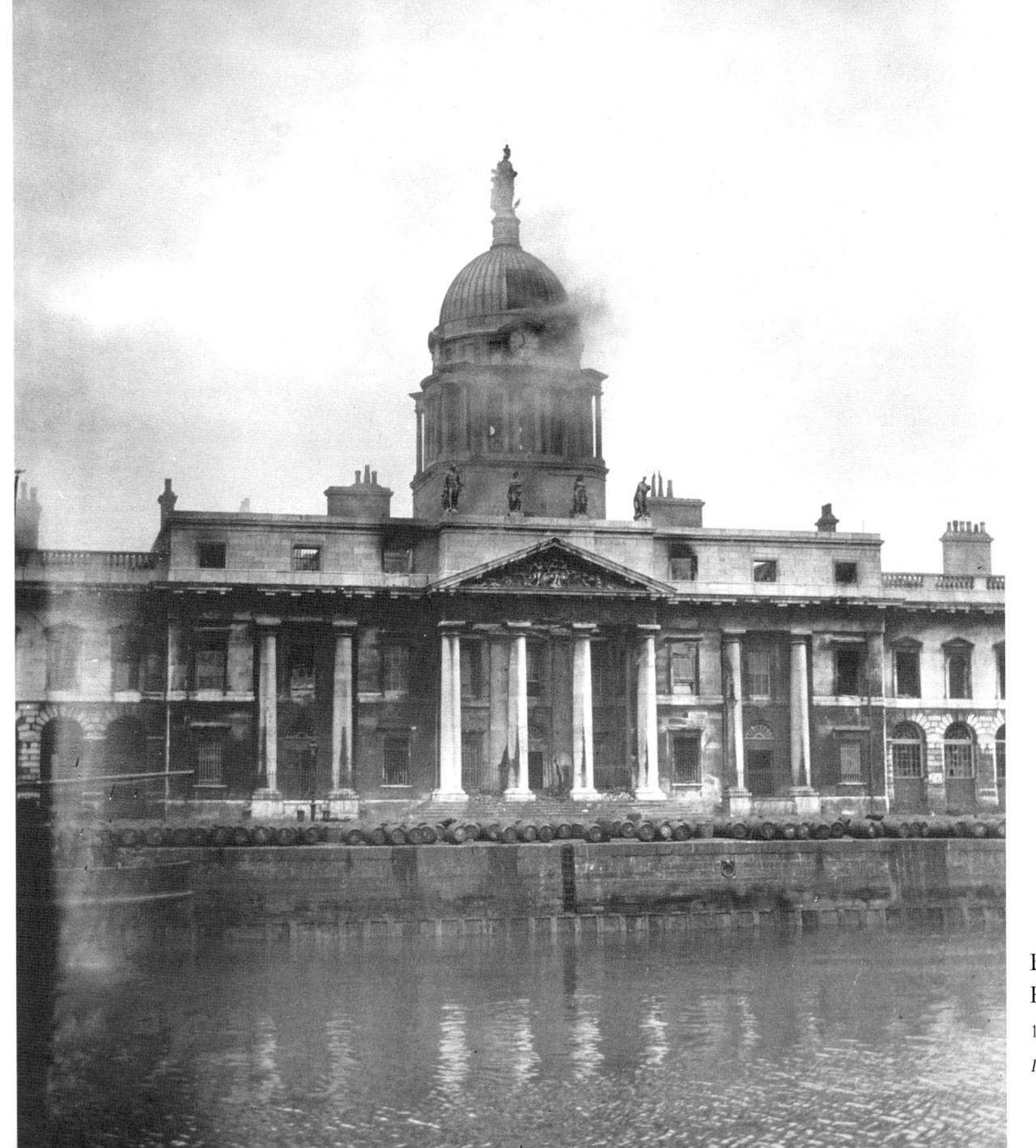

Burning of the Custom
House, Dublin (E 760)

12.15 p.m., 26 May 1921

Primo Film, f8, 1/50 sec

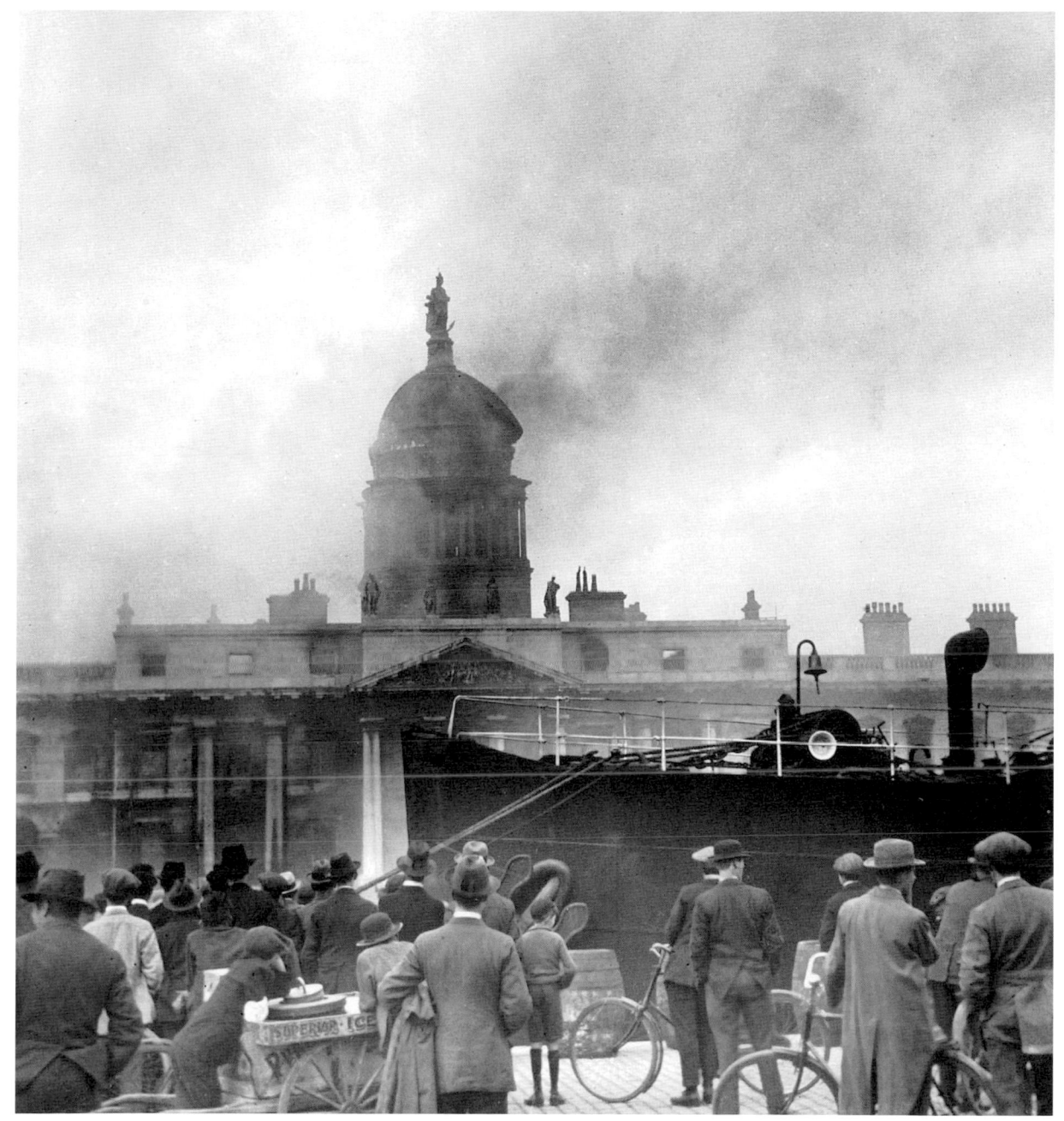

Burning of the Custom
House, Dublin (E 762)

2.30 p.m., 26 May 1921

Primo Film, f8, 1/50 sec

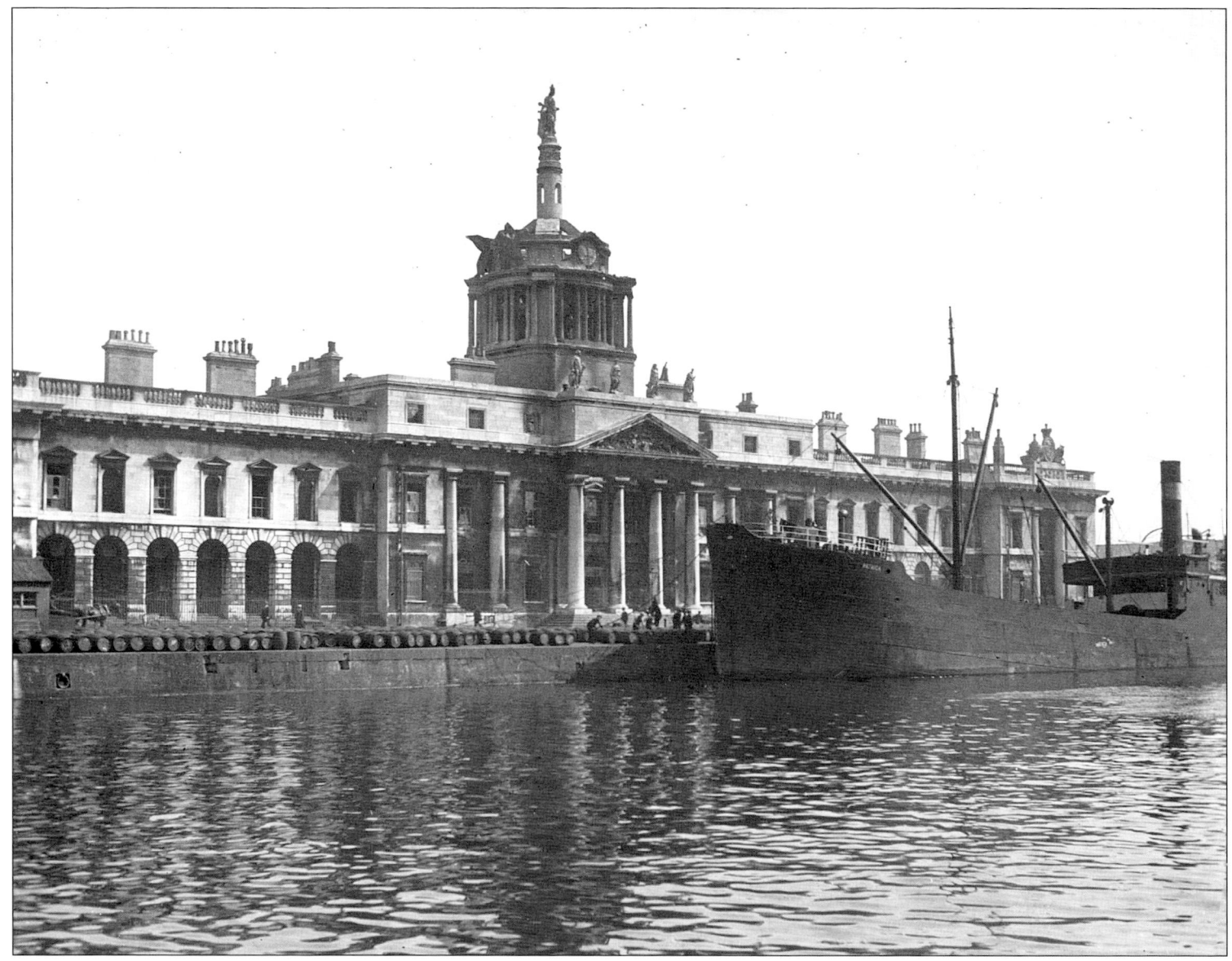

Facing page: Burnt out ruins of Custom House, Dublin (E 764)

11.00 a.m., 4 June 1921

Primo Film, f11, 1/50 sec

On Wednesday 25 May 1921, the Dublin Brigade of the IRA set fire to the Custom House. This was one of the most symbolic attacks on the British administration in Ireland during the War of Independence. The building burned for five days, by which time little was left of the original interior of the building. On the day of the fire RLC recorded in his diary:

Returning back to office from lunch. Saw Custom House in flames. Saw it several times during the day, burning furiously. It was set on fire by the IRA shortly after which the military surrounded it & kept guard as usual after the damage had been done. Tried to get down to the Quays after tea but too much shooting going on. Building still burning.

The following day RLC returned with his camera and took several photographs of the progress of the fire during the day. By this time a large crowd had gathered to witness the scene. It would appear that such was the crowd that one industrious boy can be seen in one of RLC's photographs standing over an ice-cream cart, keen for business. Later that day he wrote in his diary:

Passed Custom House on way into office. Still ablaze but tower untouched. Towards midday latter took fire & spurted out flame. The copper dome held out till the afternoon, when the flames burst out underneath it & caused it to belly out like the sails of a ship. Finally the sheeting gave way disclosing the pedestal of the statue of Hope. Huge crowds watching the fire.

Facing page: Rathfarnham Police Barracks blown up by the IRA (E 914)

9 a.m., 12 January 1923

Imperial Non-filter Orthochromatic, f11, 1 sec

RLC deliberately came early on the morning of 12 January 1924 to photograph the remains of Rathfarnham Police Barracks, blown up the previous night by the IRA. In his diaries he recorded that the previous night he was cycling through Rathfarnham shortly before the explosion:

All quiet in village. Had hardly passed through 10 minutes, when was startled by loud explosion which shook the ground & echoed back & forth from the mountains. It was followed by what sounded like a burst of machine gun fire far away, so took it to be more liveliness in city. Returning home … noticed an unusual glitter & crackle underwheel in Rathfarnham. Dismounted to investigate & found whole place littered with broken glass & a heap of ruins to mark the place where the police barracks was. Yet hardly any damage was done to adjoining houses & street lamps though only a few yards away were untouched. Heard afterwards that it was a mine. No one injured as inhabitants warned first & police removed from building.

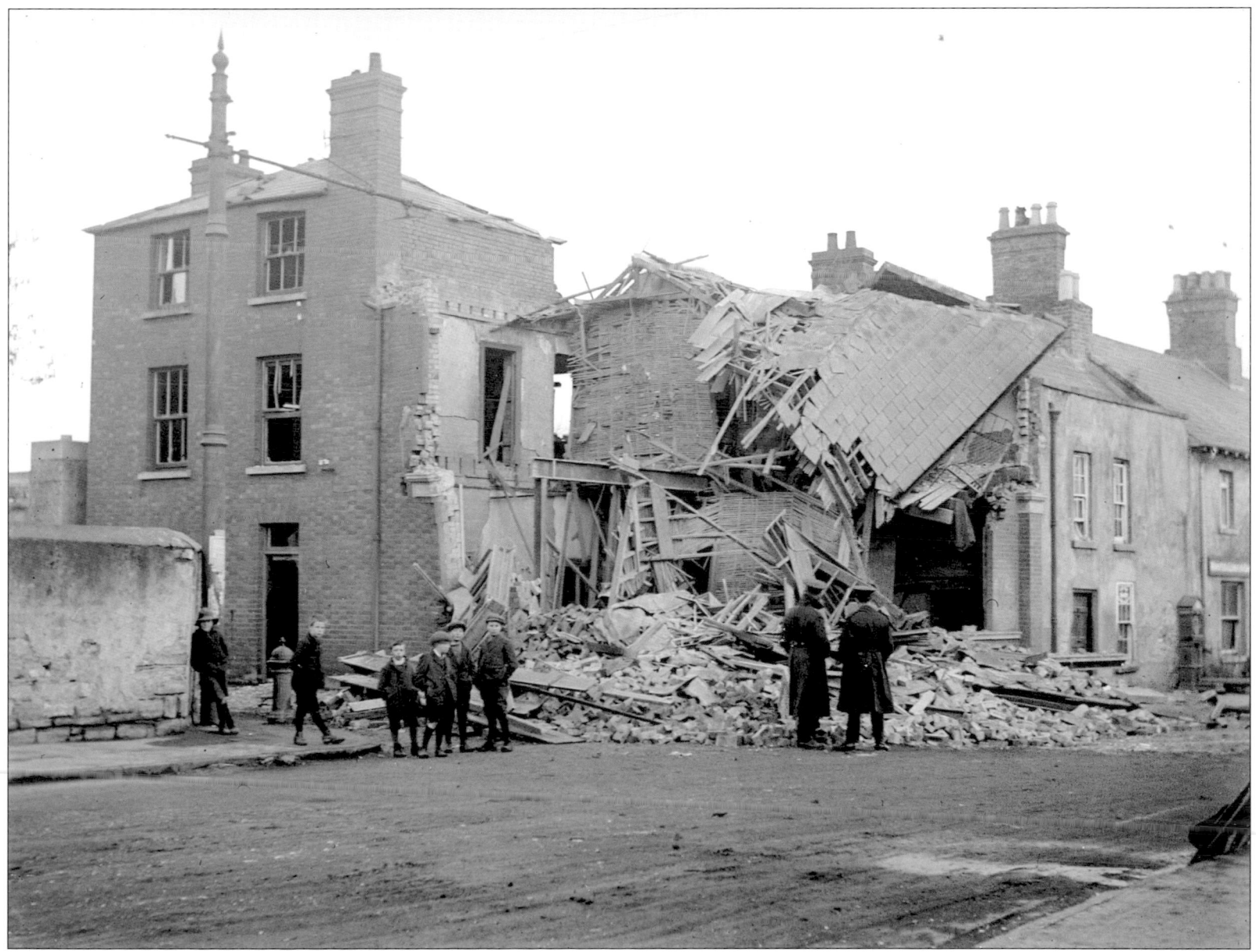

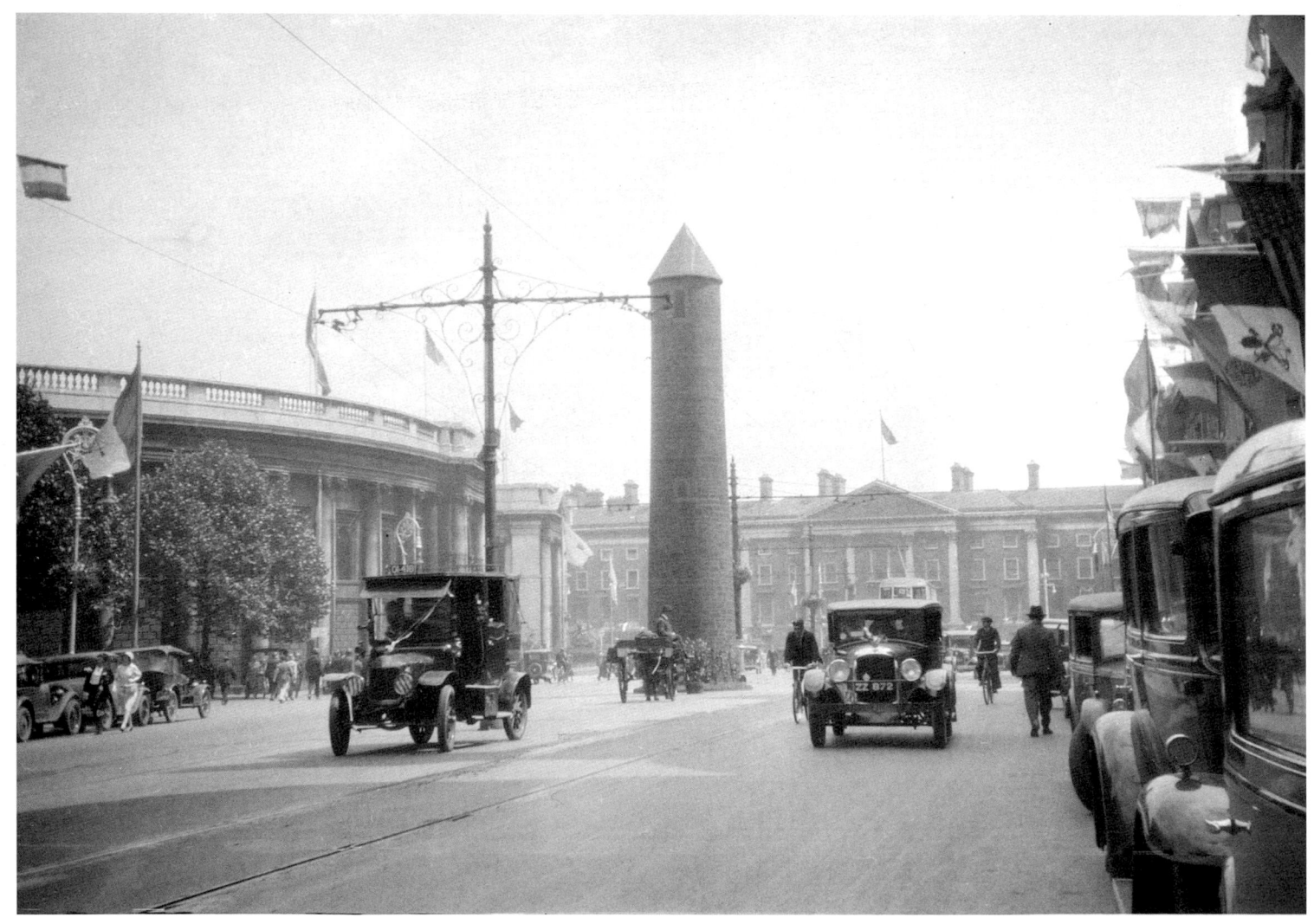

Round Tower during Eucharistic Congress at College Green, Dublin (G 452)

12.30 p.m., 25 June 1932

KF [possibly Kodak Film], f11, 1/25 sec

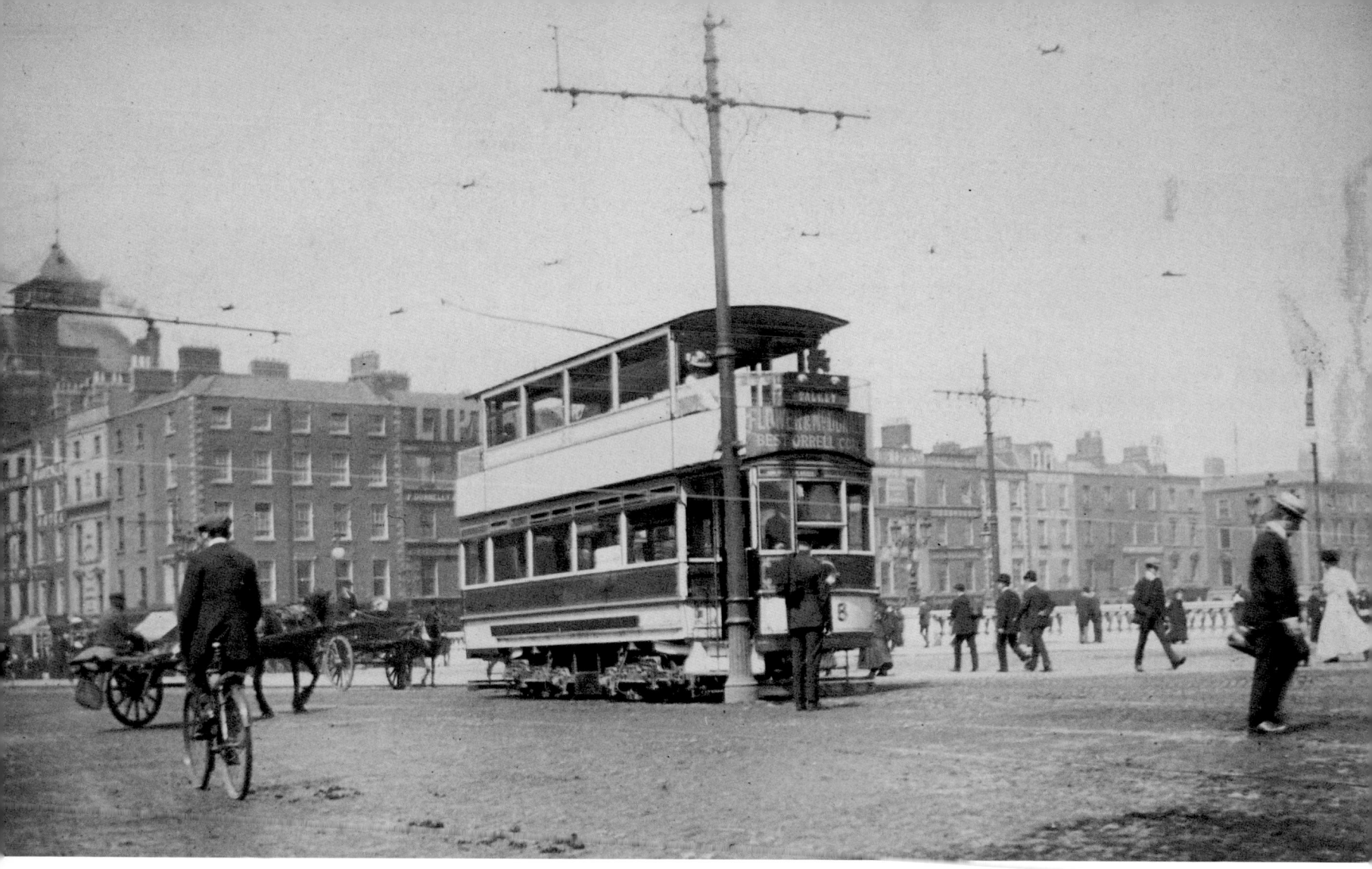

Tram on O'Connell Bridge, Dublin (E 5)

June 1908

Edwards Snapshot Isochromatic, f9, 1/100 sec

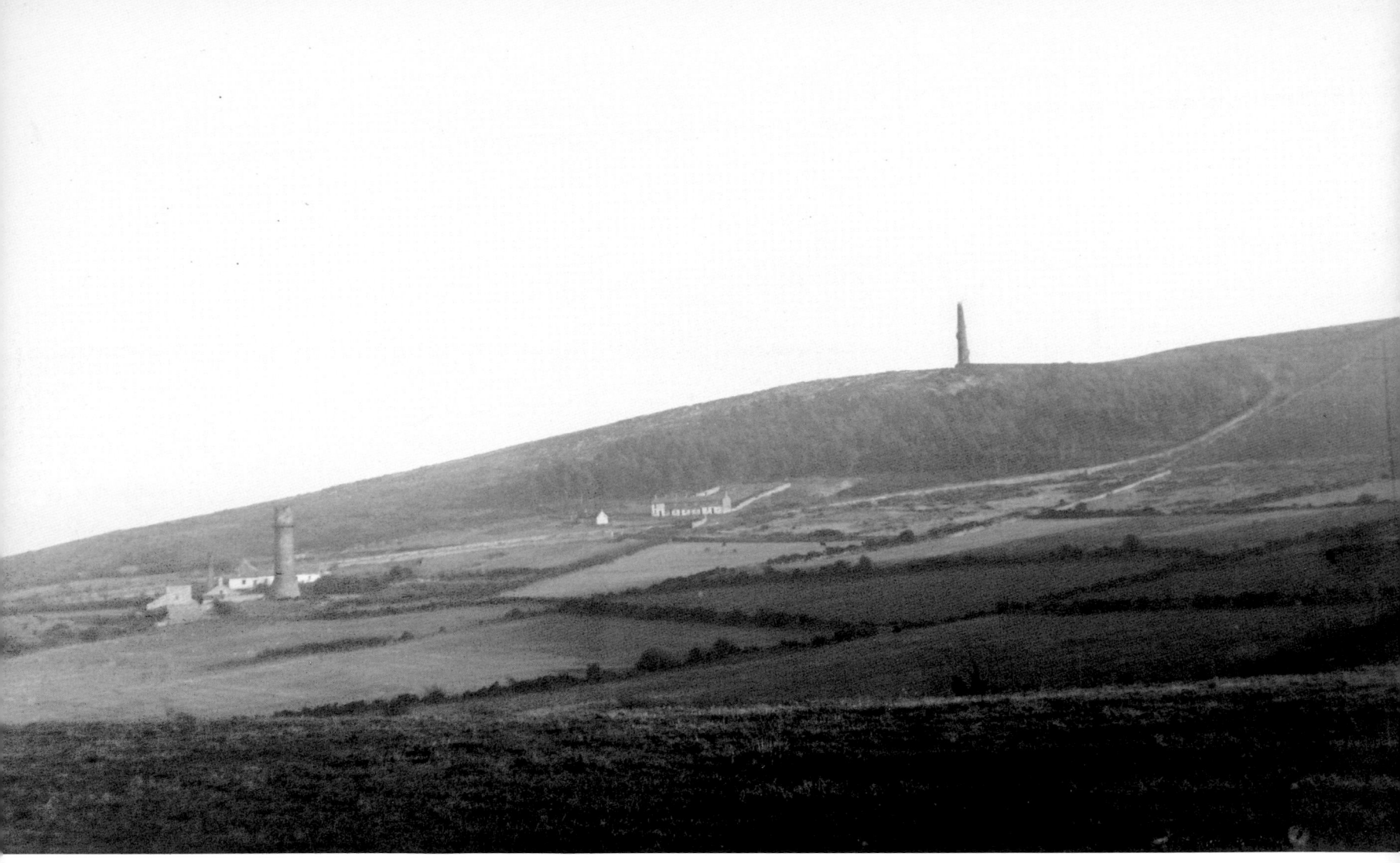

Above: Ballycorus Mountain from the Scalp,
County Dublin (E 147)

2.15 p.m., 1 January 1911

Ilford Special Rapid, f32, 1 sec

Facing page: River Liffey, Lucan Demesne,
County Dublin (E 176)

4.30 p.m., 13 August 1911

Edwards Isochromatic Auto Screen, f22, 1/5 sec

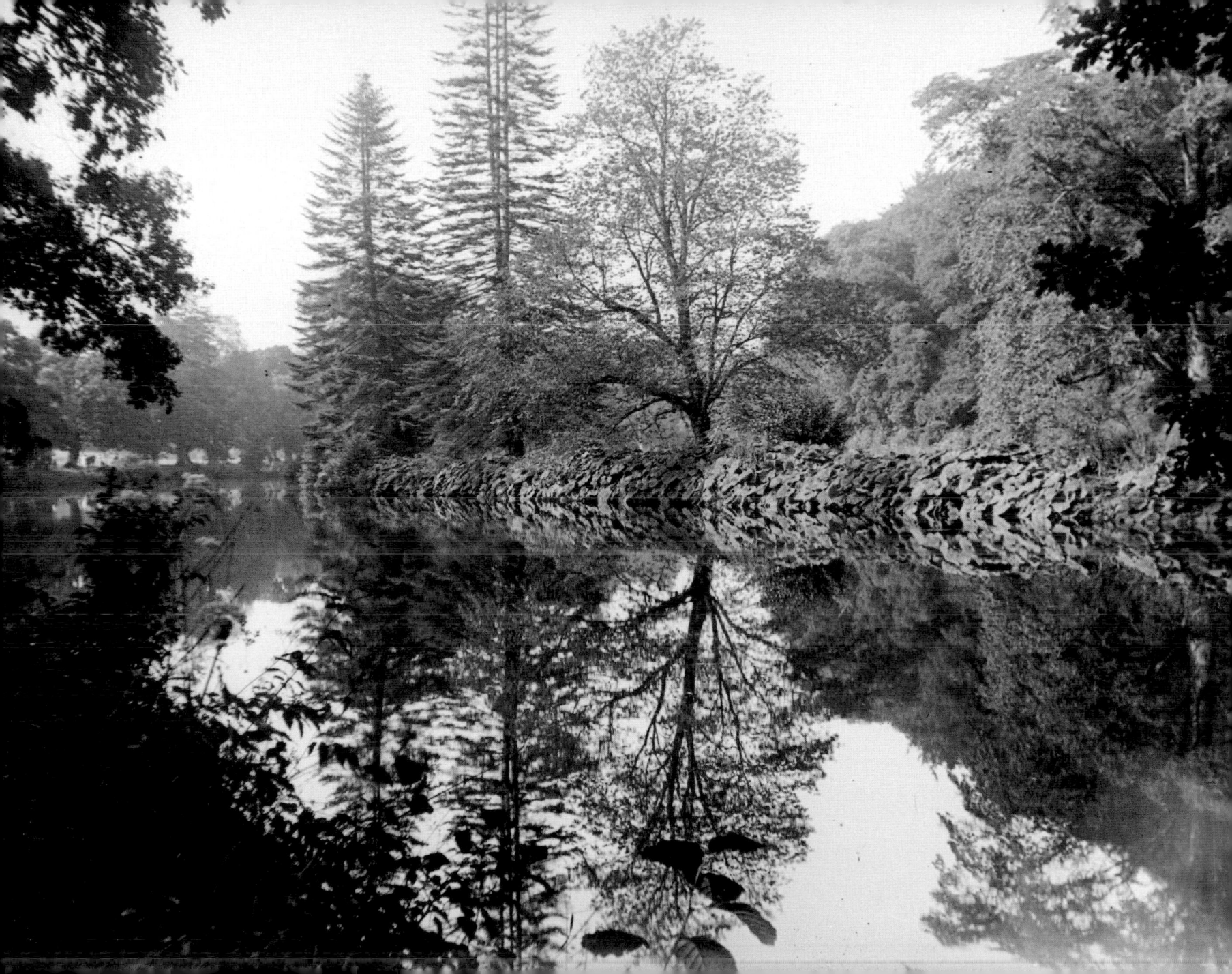

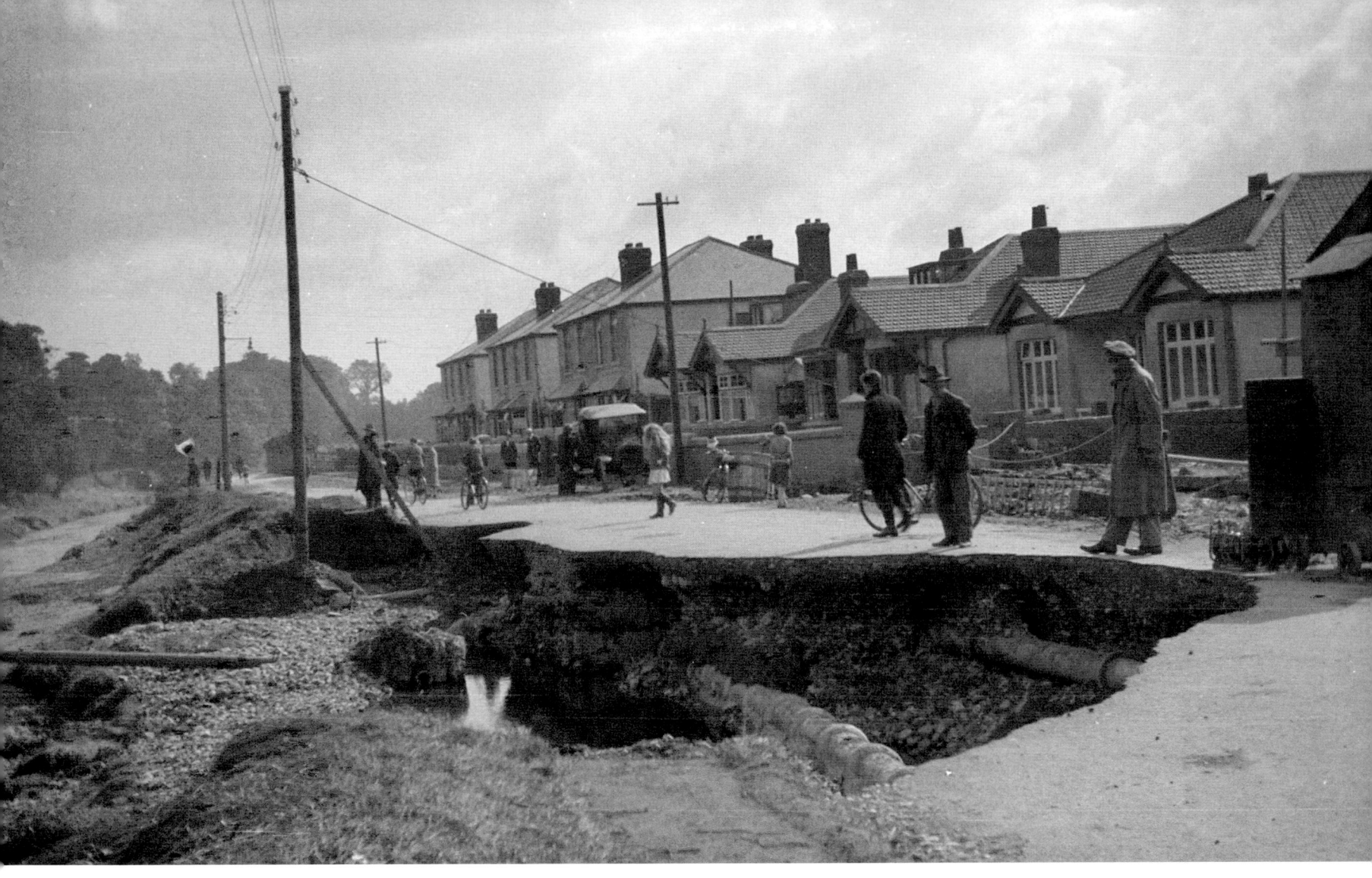

Road washed away by floods, River Dodder, near Rathfarnham, County Dublin (G 400)

11.30 a.m., 5 July 1931

VF [possibly Verachrome Film], f11, 1/25 sec

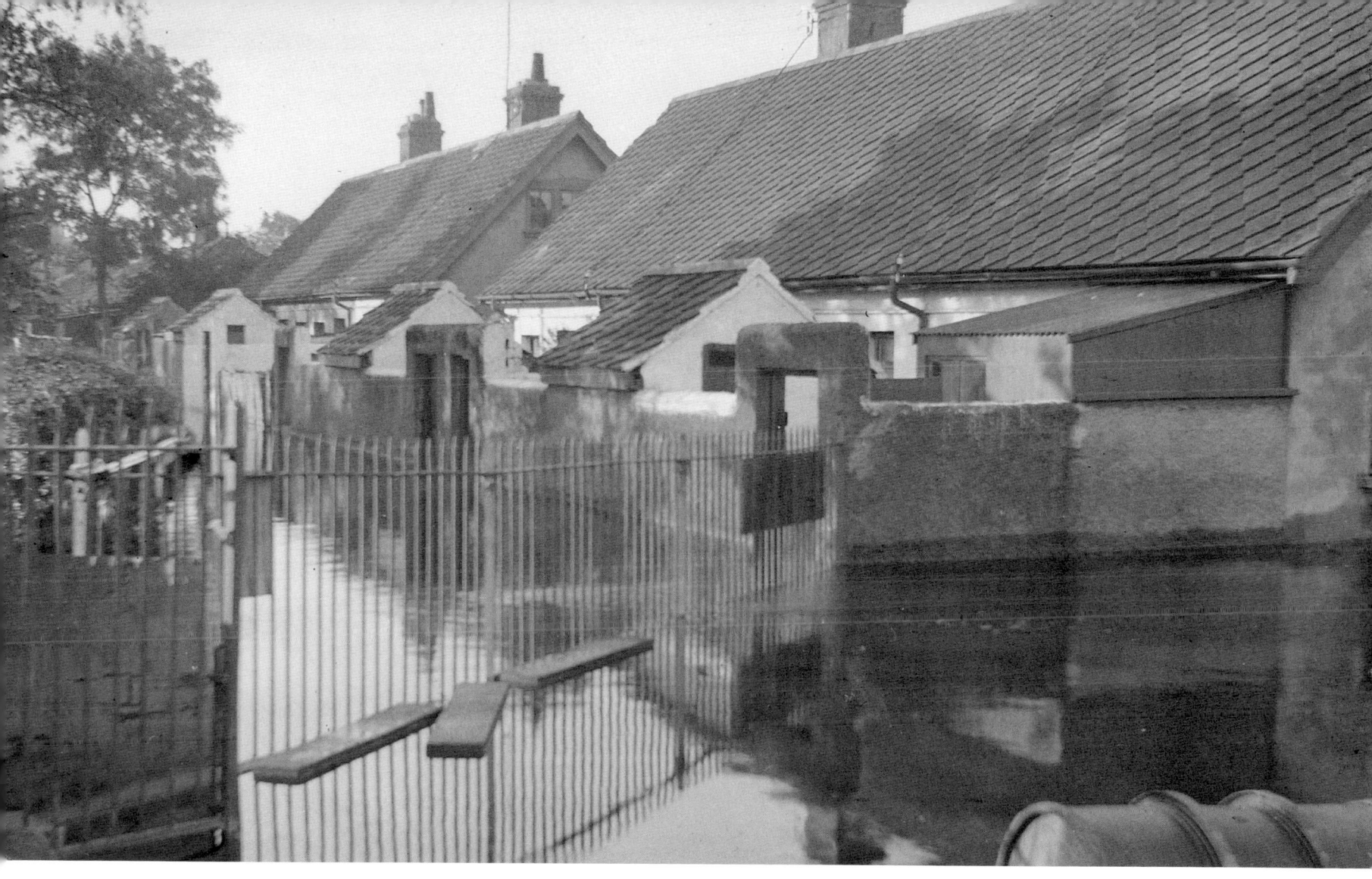

Floods at cottages, Foxrock, County Dublin (E 1293)

8.30 a.m., 5 September 1931

Ilford Iso Zenith, f11, 1/10 sec

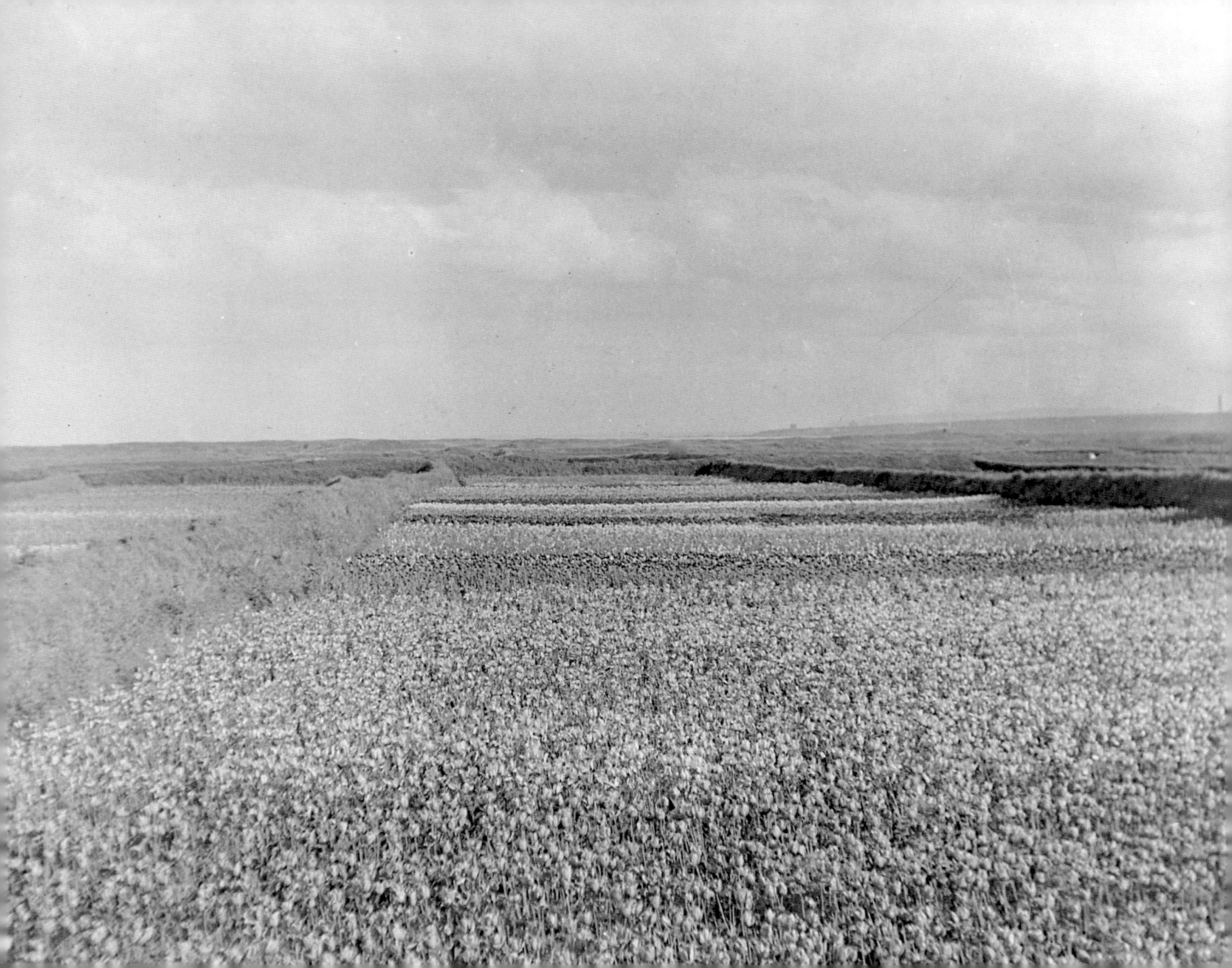

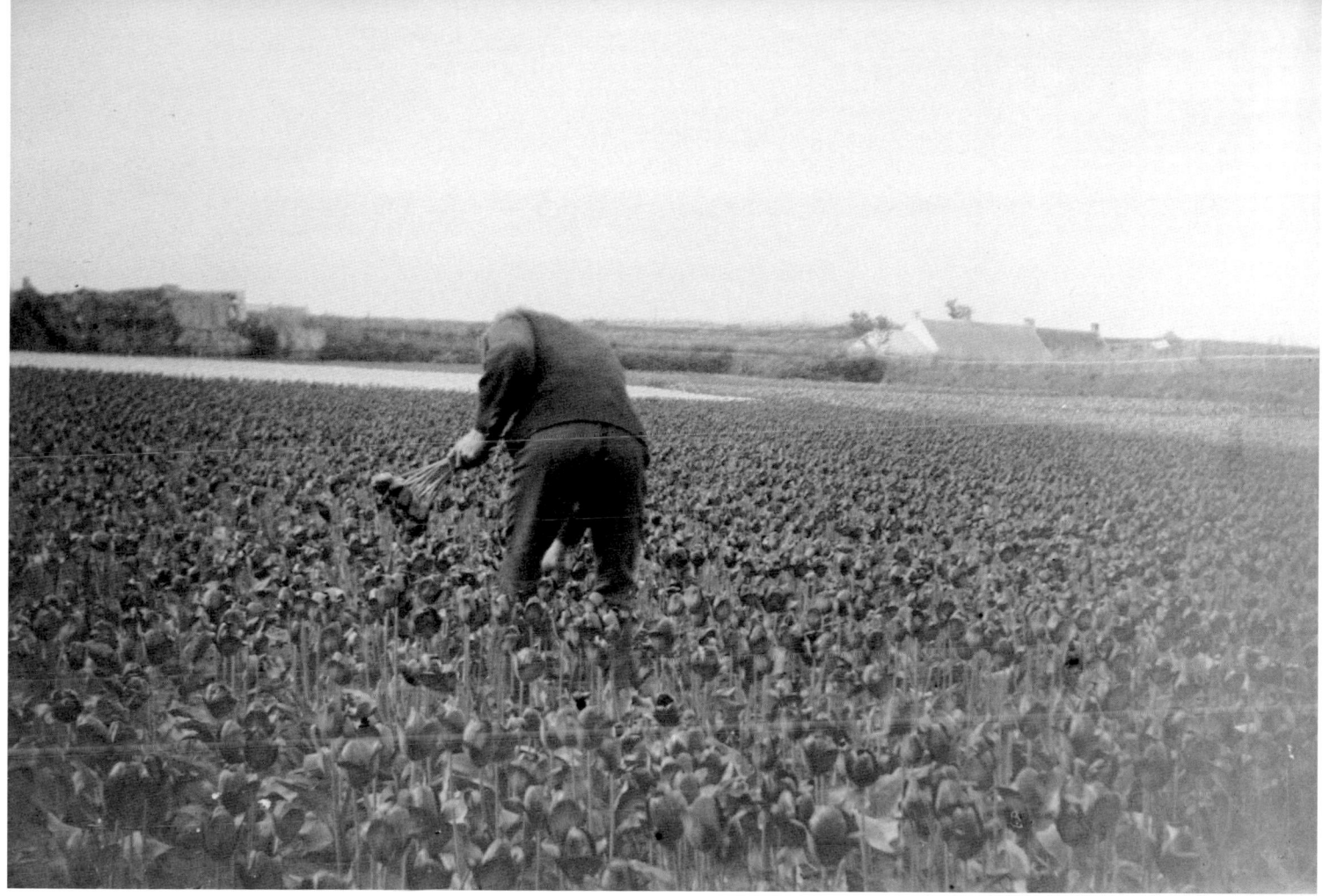

Above: Field at bulb farm, Rush, County Dublin (E 4)

May 1908

Edwards Snapshot Isochromatic, f9, 1/20 sec

Facing page: Field of tulips, Rush, County Dublin (E 642)

6.15 p.m., 22 May 1920

Imperial Non-filter Orthochromatic, f11, 1/25 sec

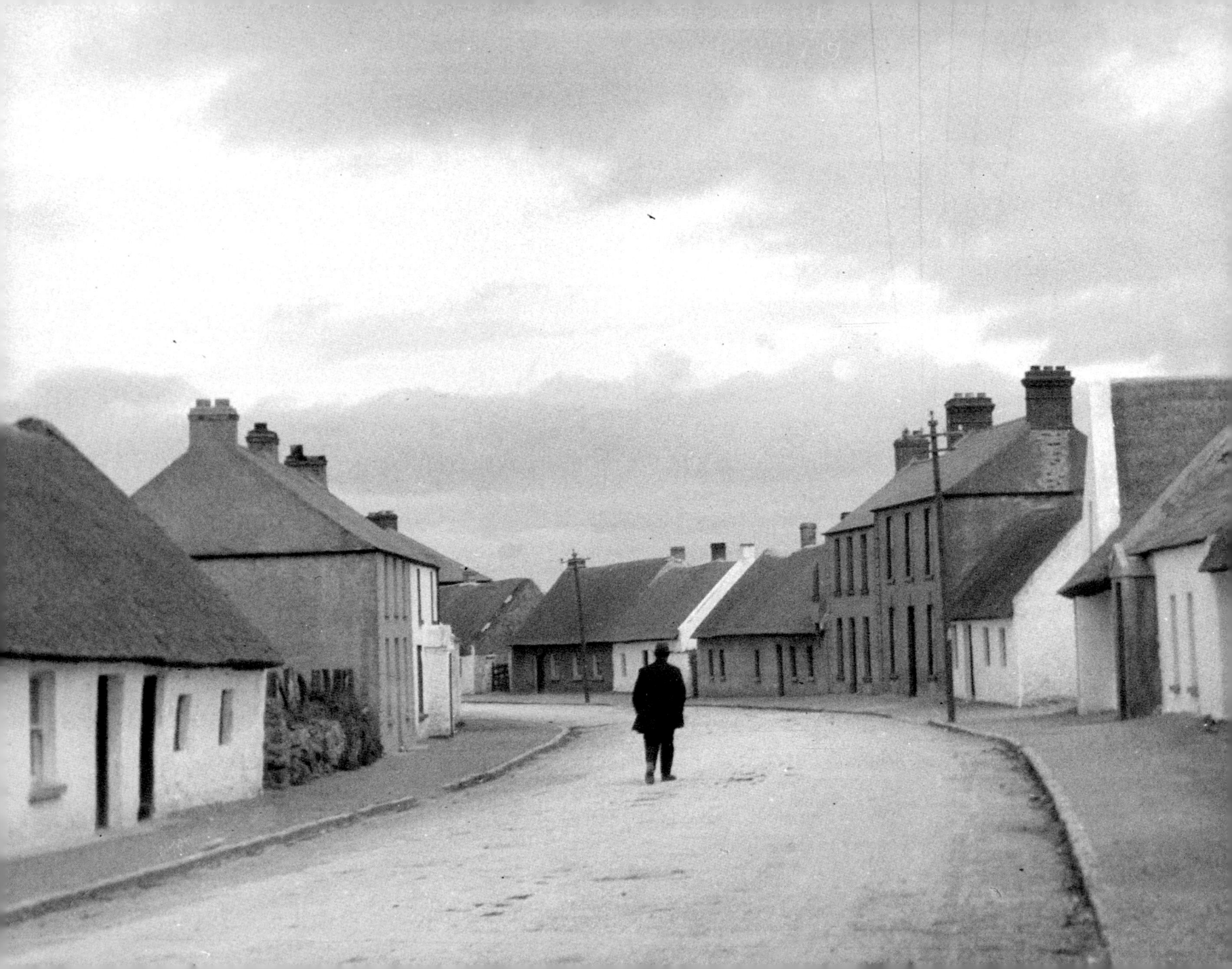

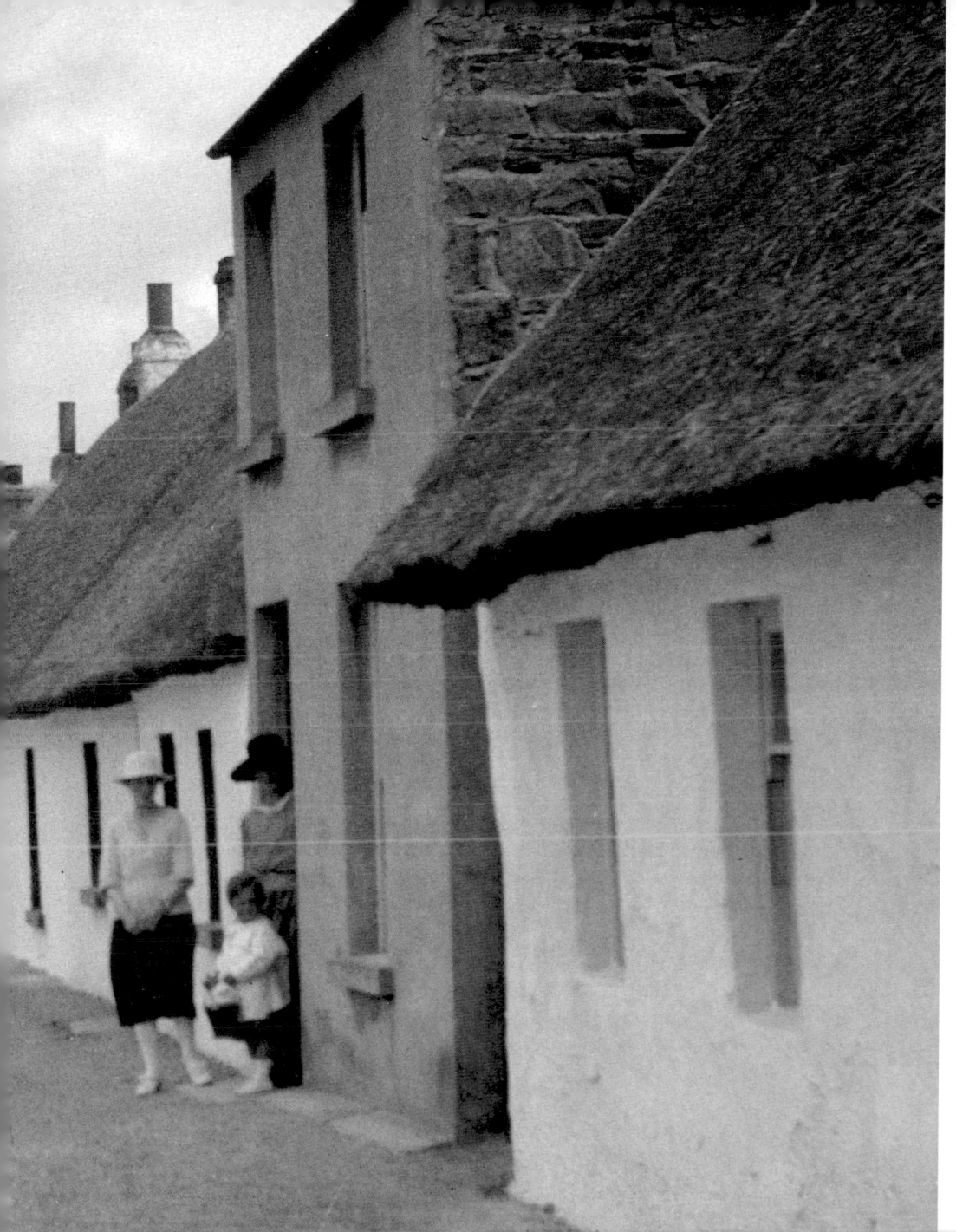

Lower Main Street, Rush, County Dublin (E 864)

4 p.m., 18 June 1922

Primo Film, f11, 1/50 sec

ON 1 JUNE 1922, RLC RECORDED IN HIS DIARY:

Set off for Rush from office having arranged to spend the month there with Ethel & Ronnie. Had small 2 storey house. Rooms small & a staircase never intended for the corpulent. Water supply of village very bad. In spite of sandy soil, every spare bit of ground cultivated, mostly potatoes with a fair amount of peas, scallions, carrots etc. Donkeys, carts & goats seem to outnumber the inhabitants who spend most of their time drawing water. Majority of houses are thatched. Rents low, same being let for £1 to £5 per annum.

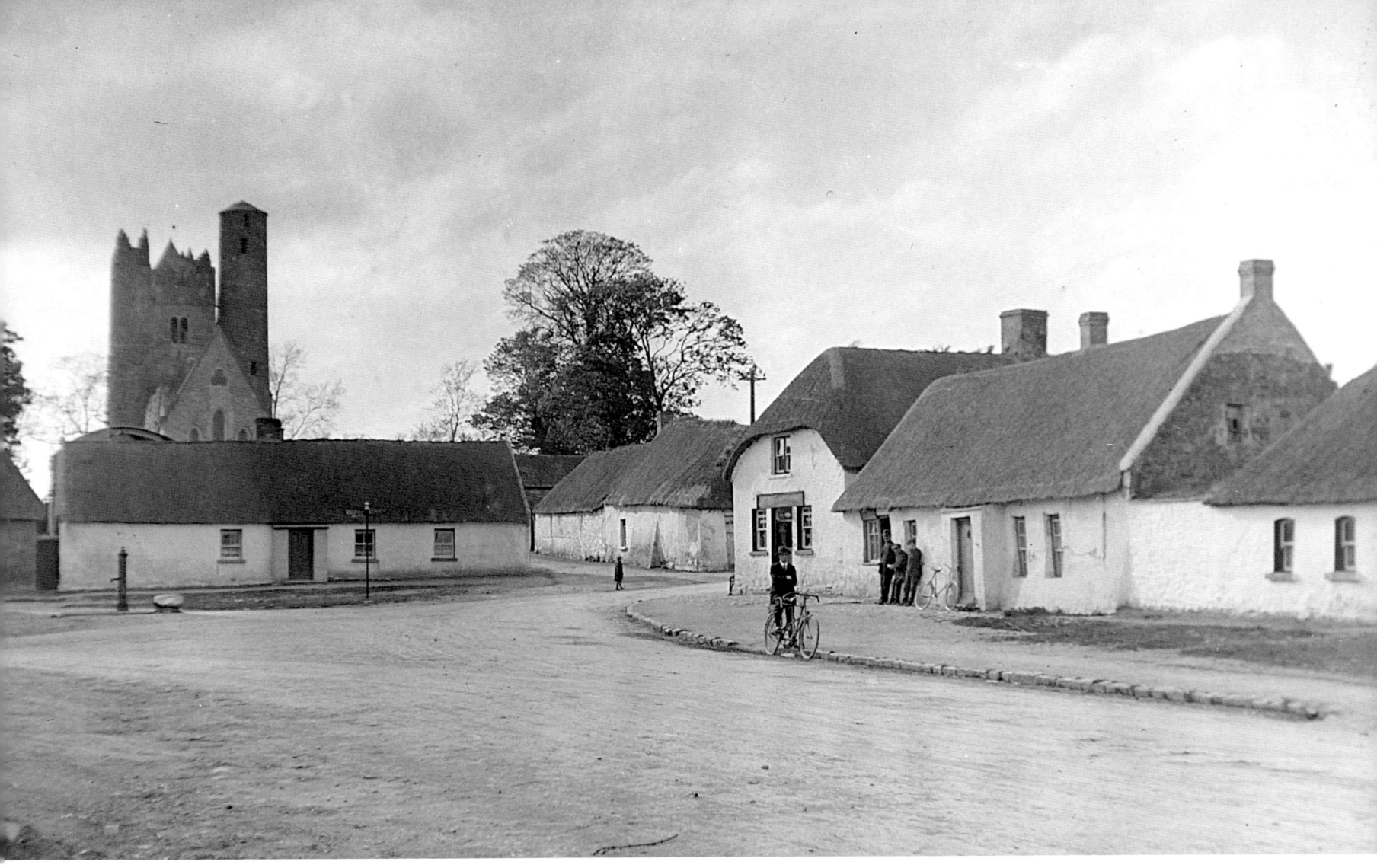

Above: Thatched houses, Lusk, County Dublin (E 640)

6 p.m., 22 May 1920

Imperial Non-filter Orthochromatic, f11, 1/25 sec (old camera)

Facing page: Portmarnock beach, County Dublin (E 948)

5.30 p.m., 5 August 1923

Imperial Non-filter Orthochromatic, f10, 1/50 sec

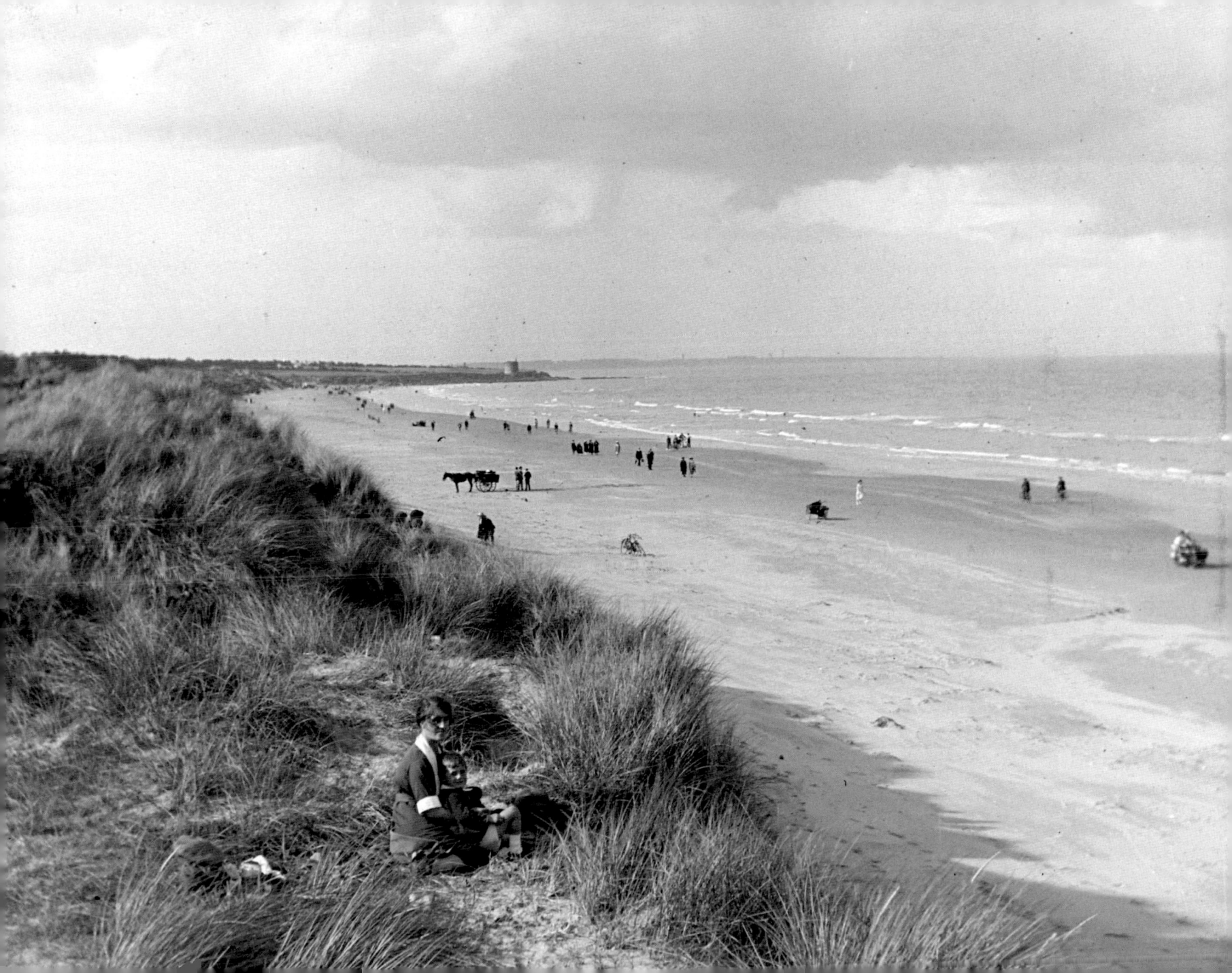

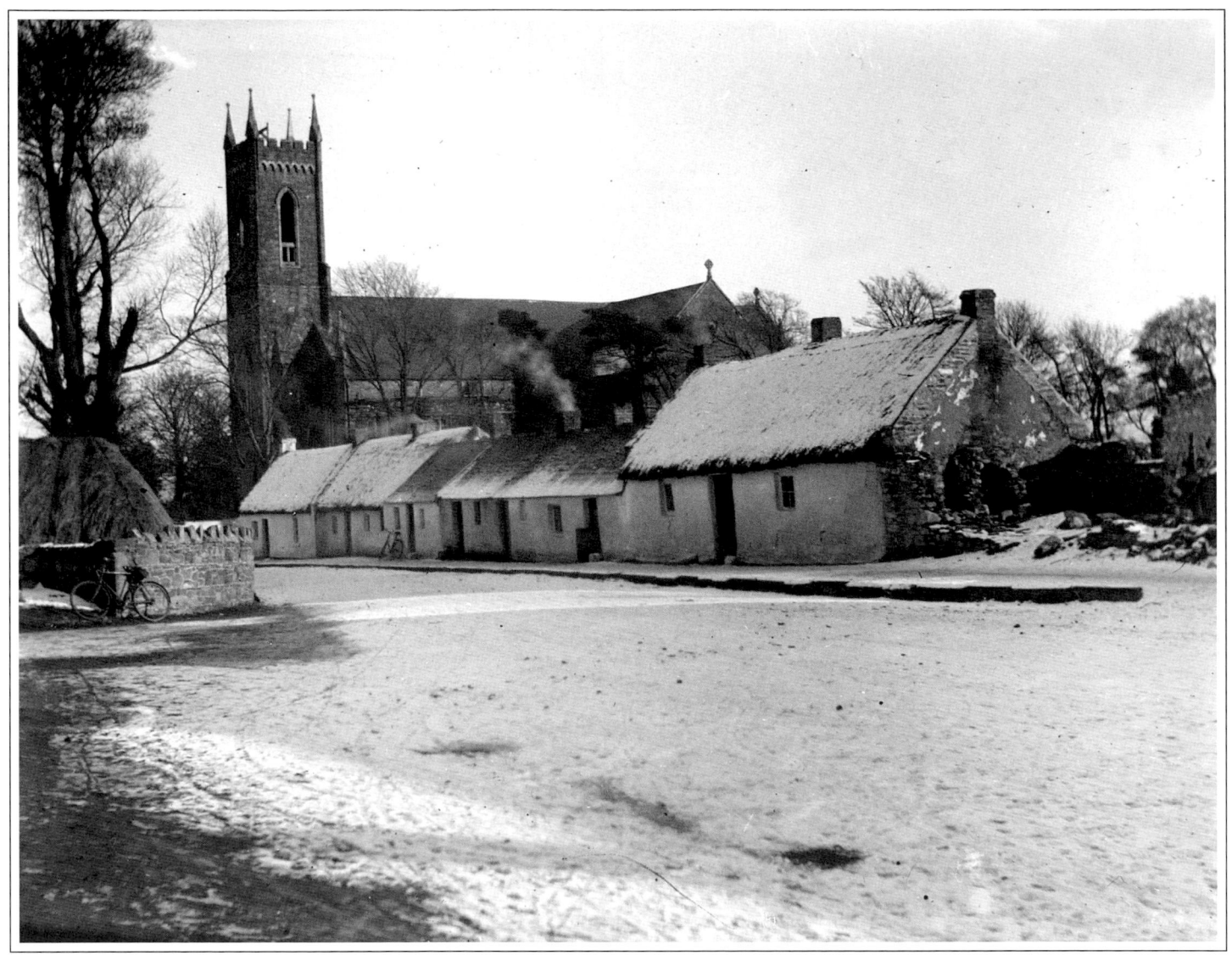

Saggart, County Dublin (E 1018)

1 p.m., 25 November 1923

Barnet Matt Screen, f6.8, 1/50 sec

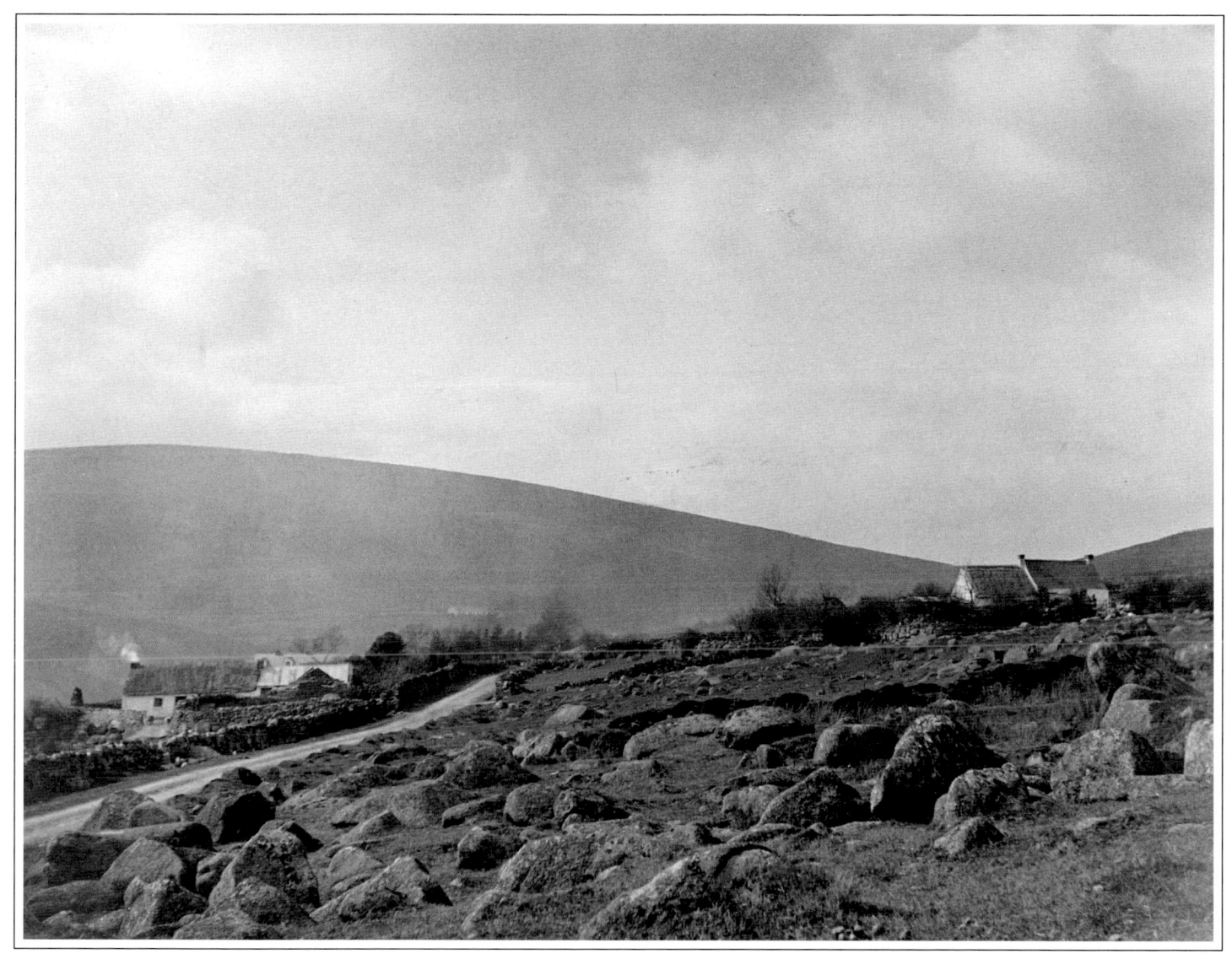

Glencullen, County Dublin (E 1041)

2 p.m., 30 March 1924

Agfa Film, f18, 1/5 sec

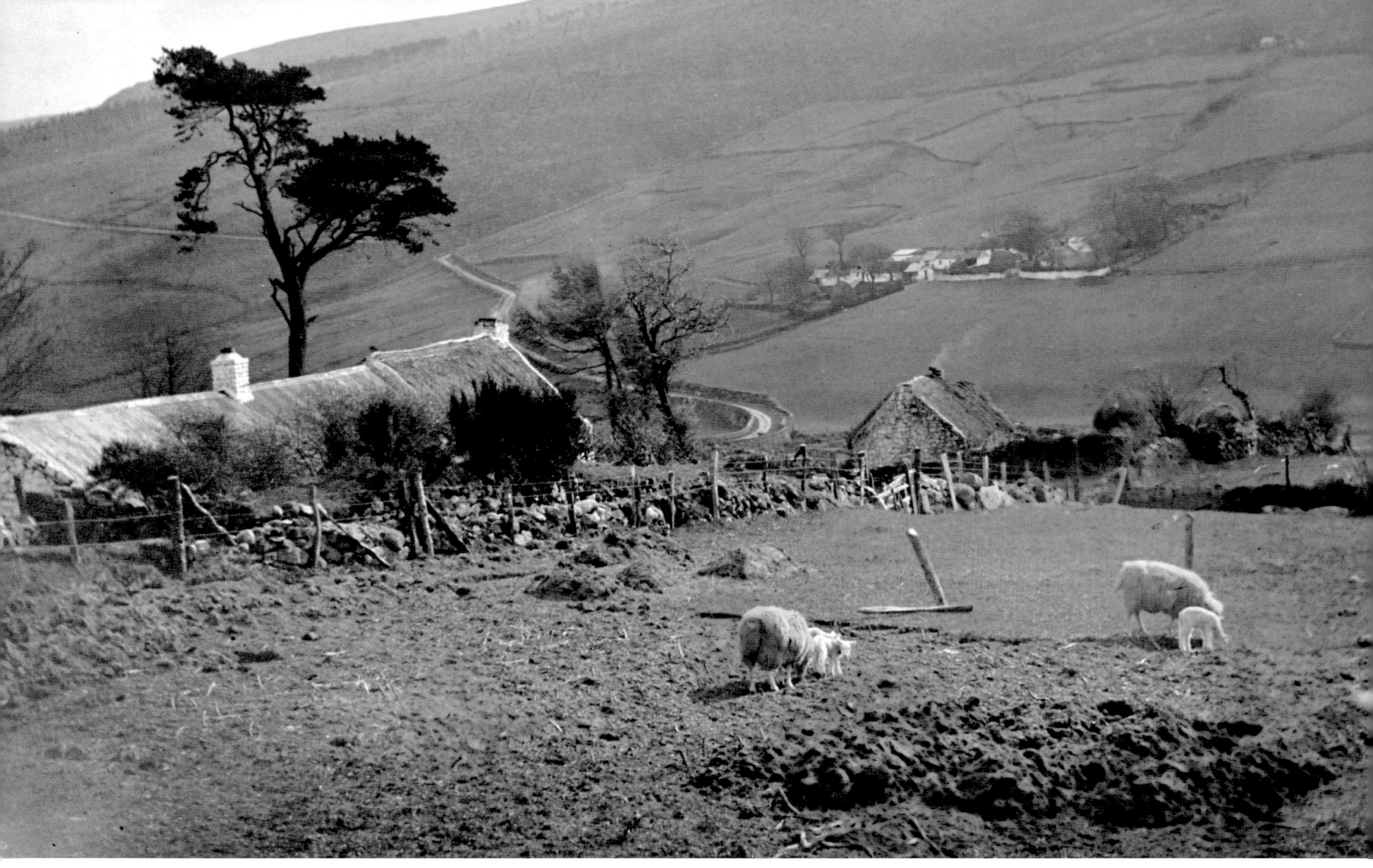

Glencullen, County Dublin (E 1042)

2 p.m., 30 March 1924

Agfa Film, f8, 1/50 sec

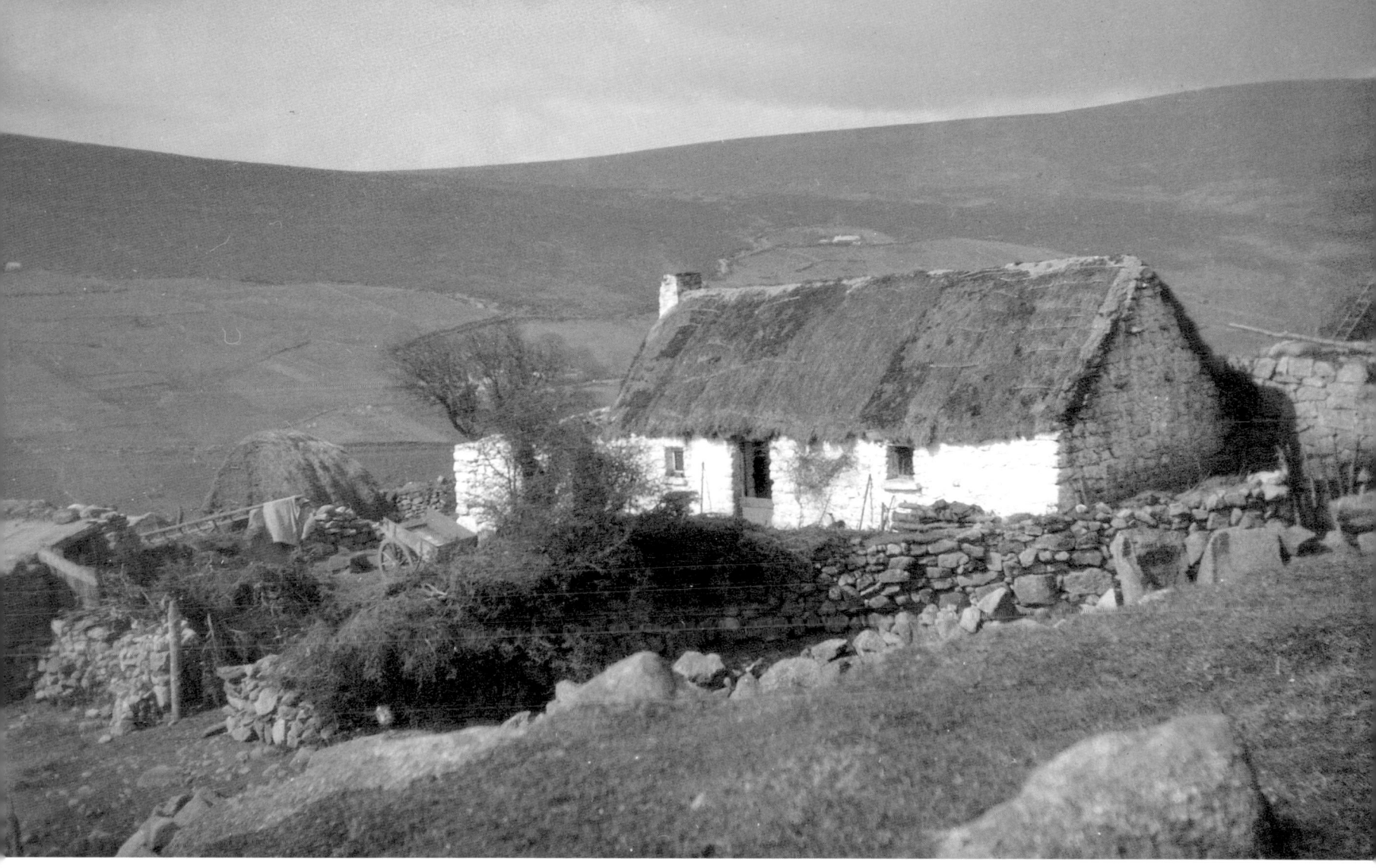

Cottage near Ballybrew, [Enniskerry] County Wicklow (G 84)

11 a.m., 15 April 1927

KF [Kodak Film?], f11, 1/25 sec

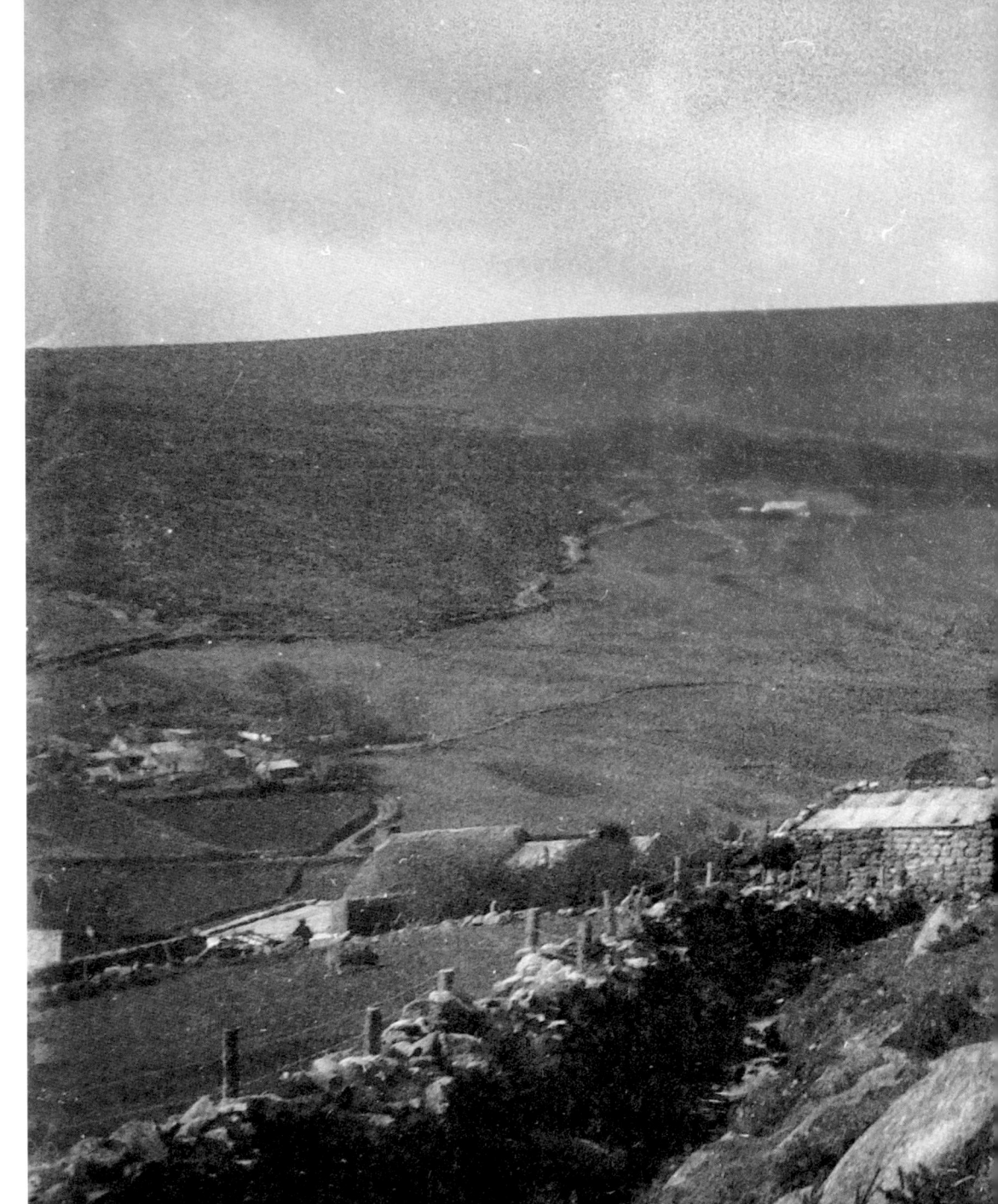

Near Ballybrew, County Wicklow
(G 83)

11 a.m., 15 April 1927

KF [Kodak Film?], f16, 1/25 sec

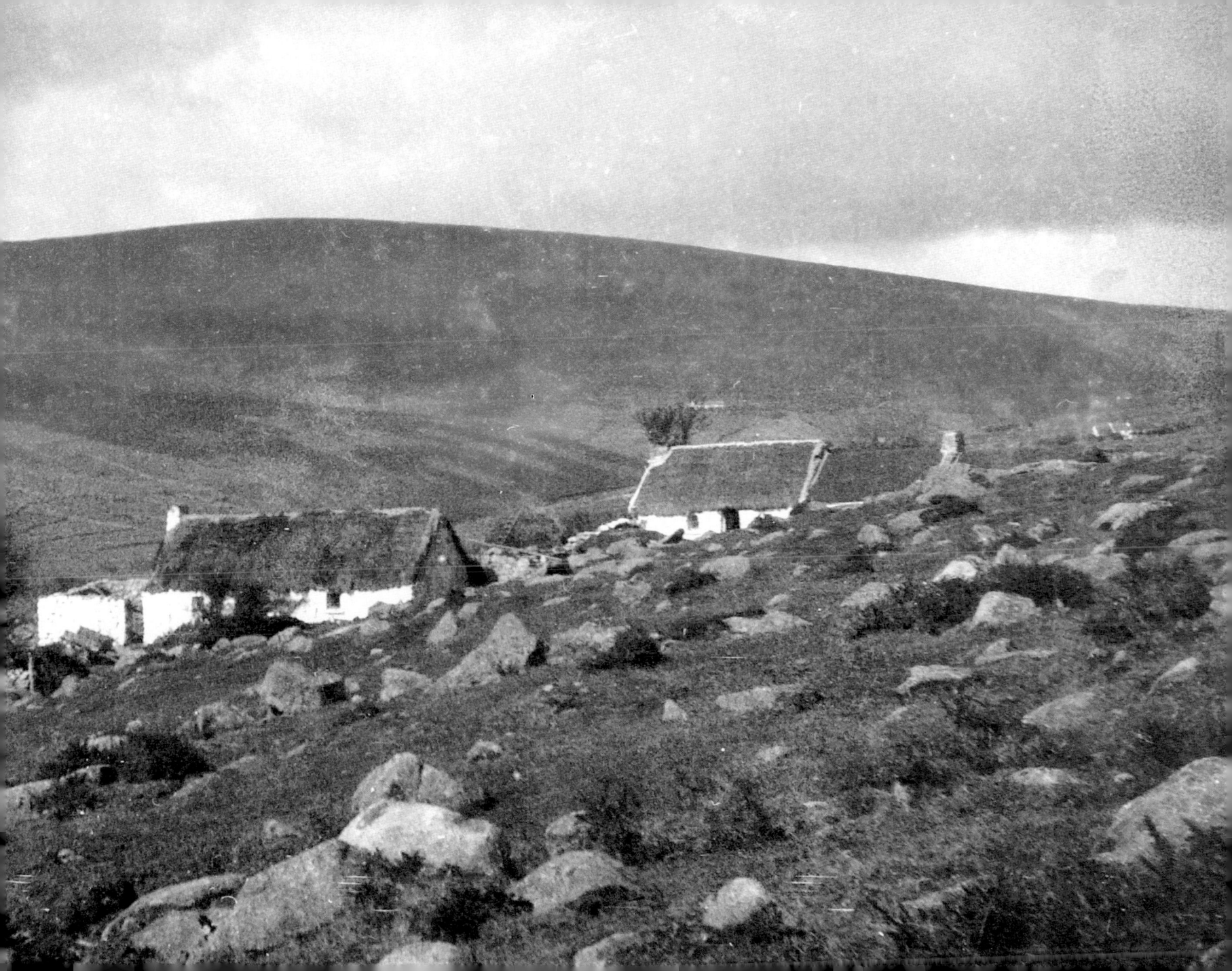

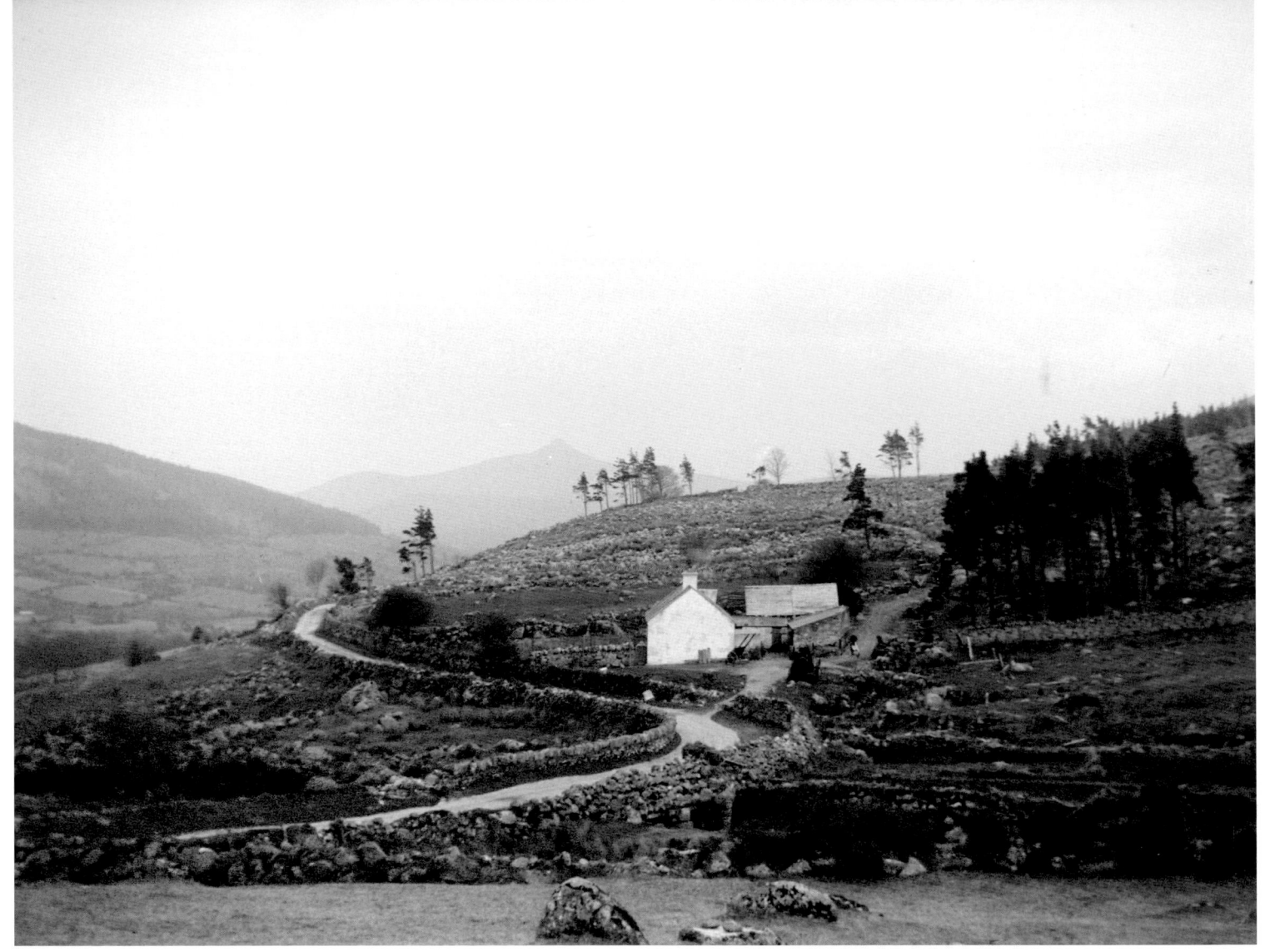

Glencree Valley, County Wicklow (E 1229)

5.30 p.m., 9 April 1927

Wellington Anti Screen, f11, 1/5 sec

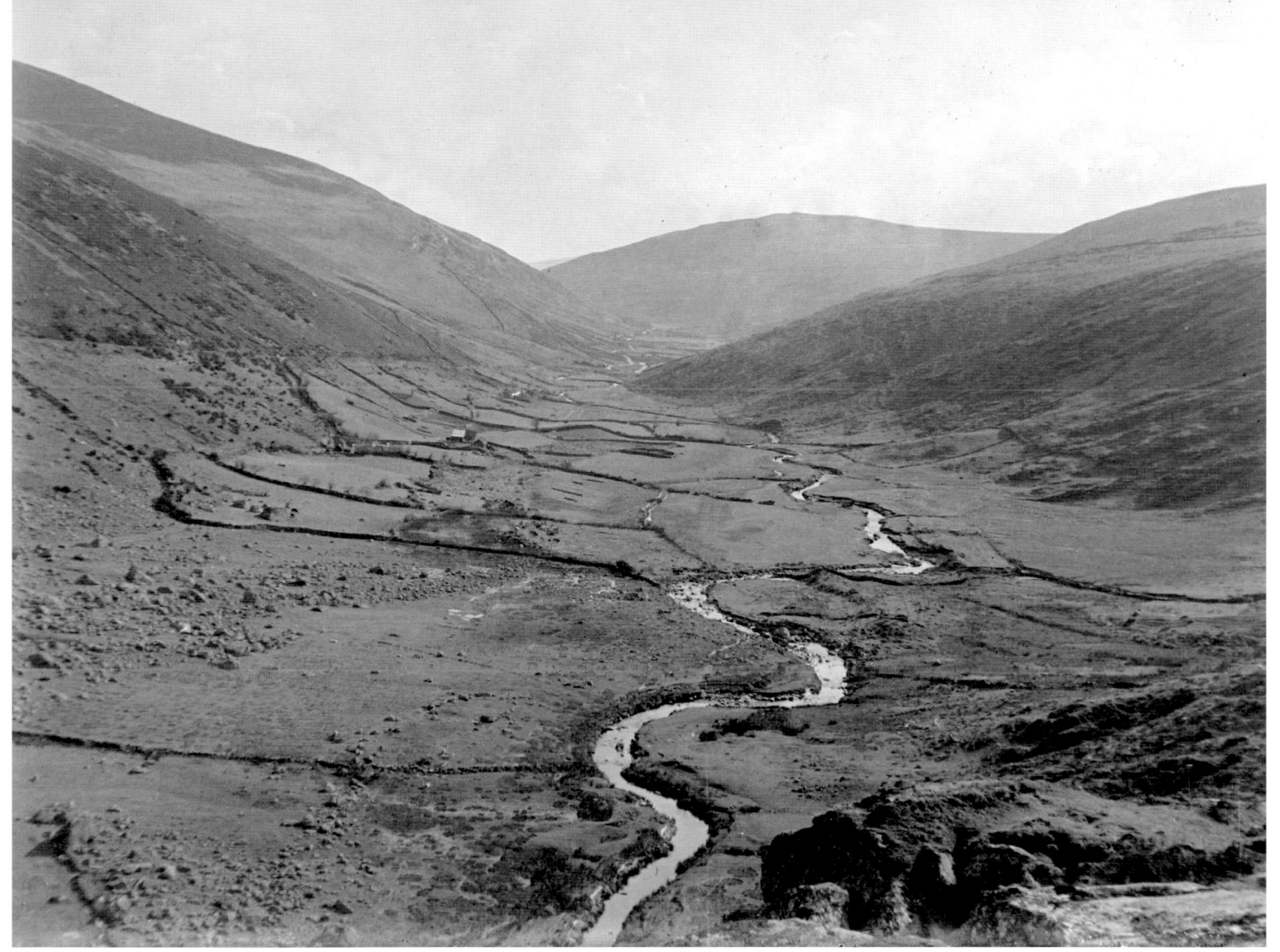

Looking down Glenmacnass, County Wicklow (E 425)

2 p.m., 22 March 1914

Edwards Isochromatic Auto Screen, f22, 1/5 sec

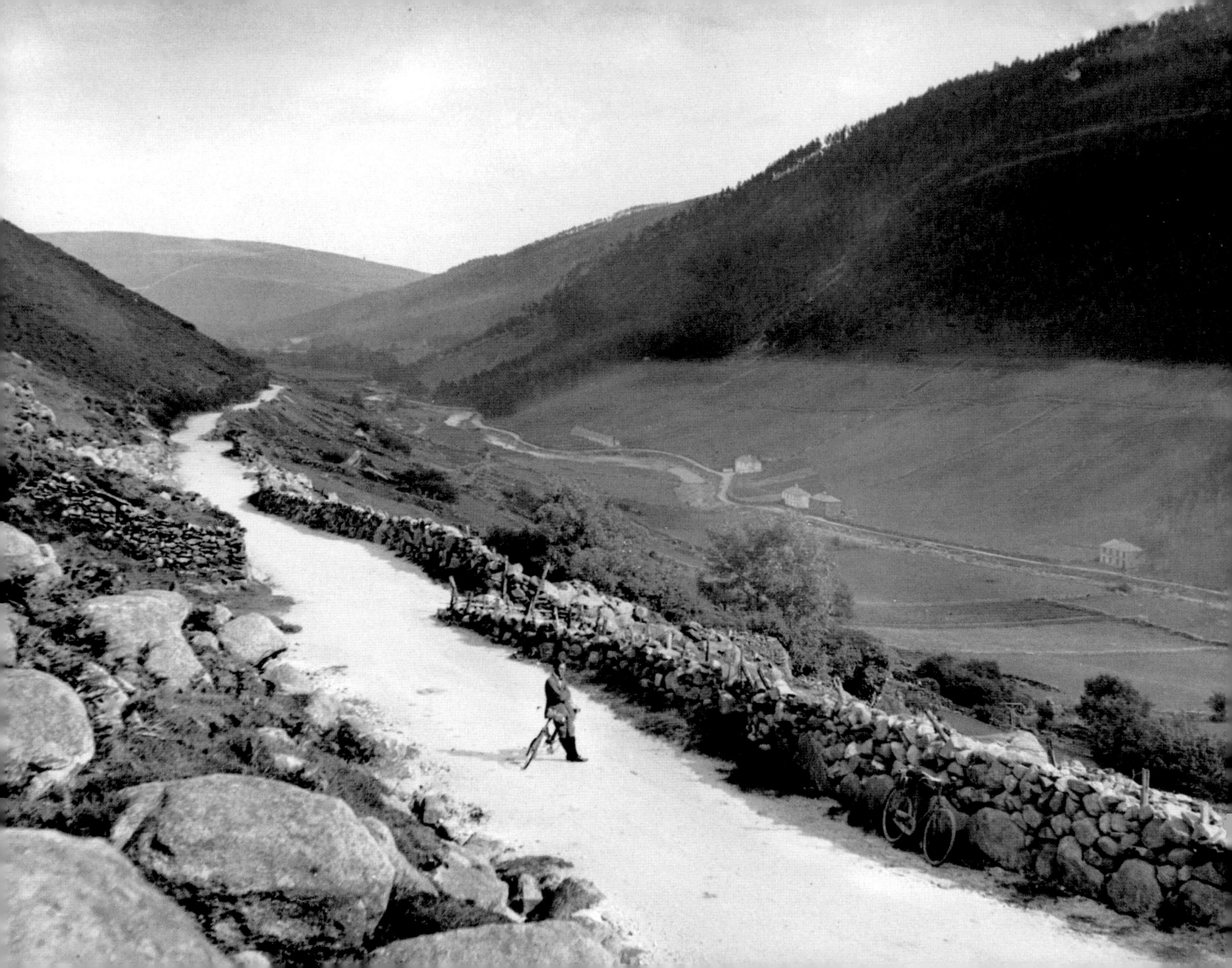

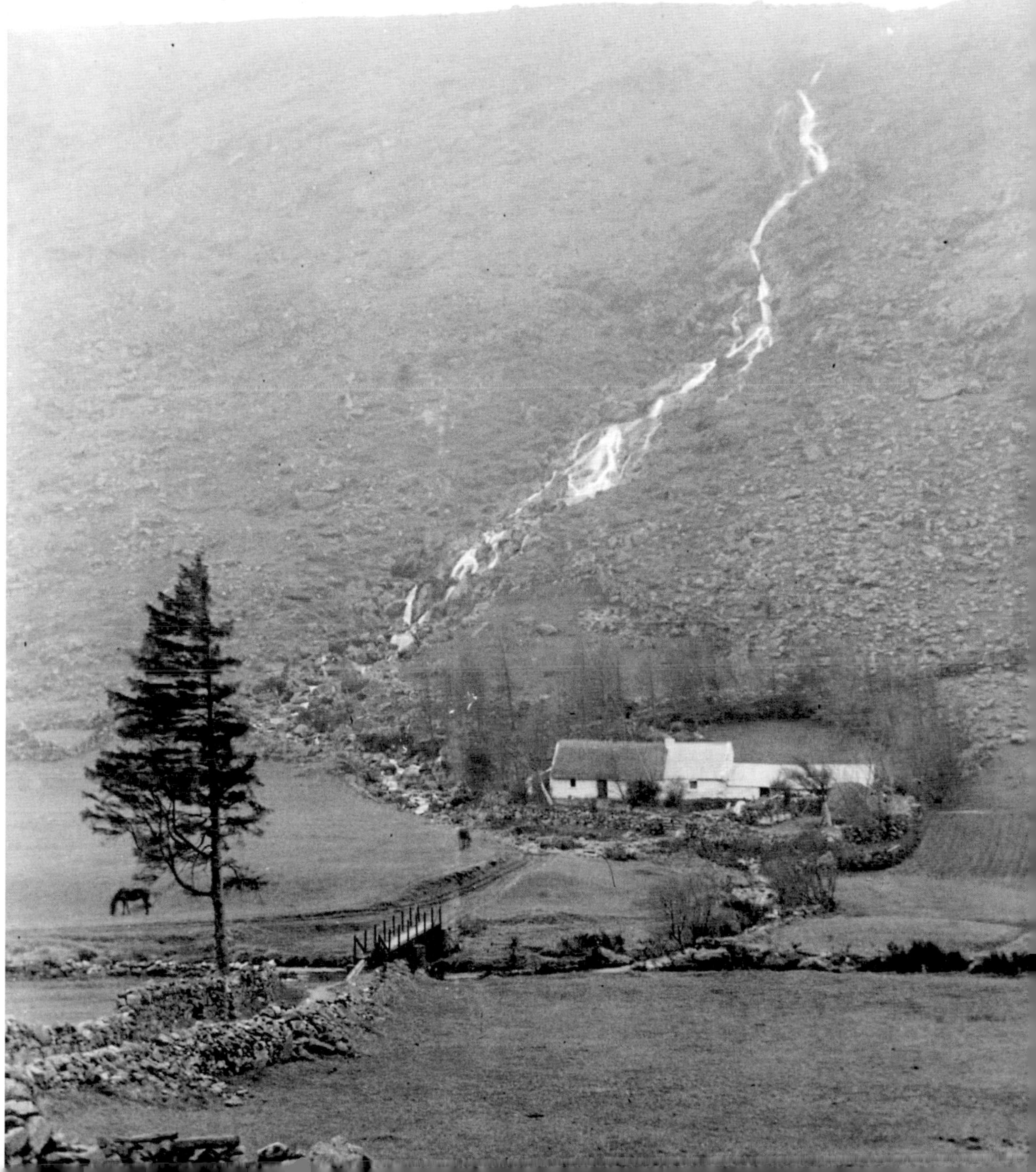

Right: Carrawaystick Waterfall,
Glenmalure, County Wicklow
(E 826)

6 p.m., 26 March 1922

Primo Film, f8, 4 sec

Facing page: Wicklow Gap,
County Wicklow (E 879)

5 p.m., 30 July 1922

*Imperial Non-filter Orthochromatic,
f18, 1/5 sec*

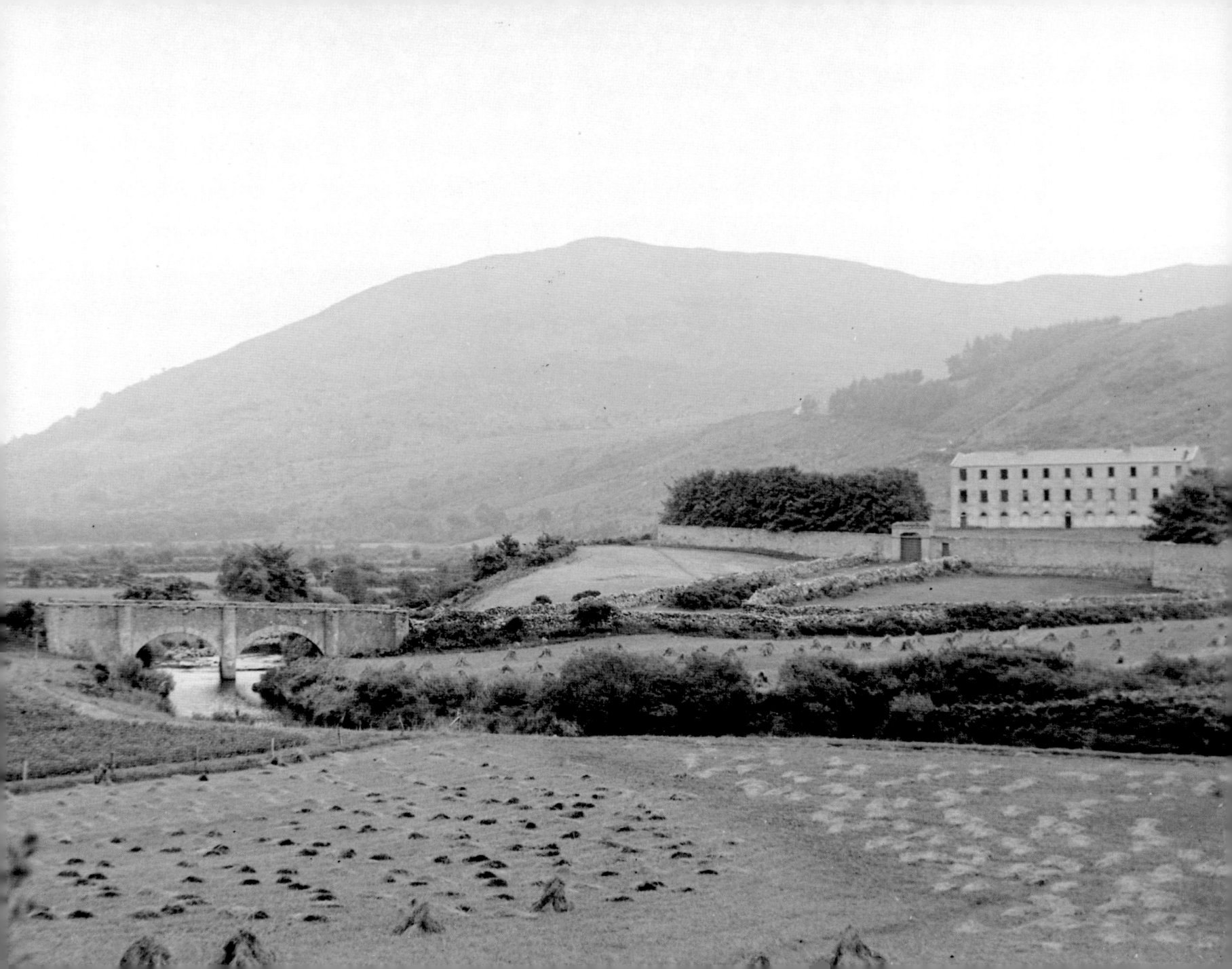

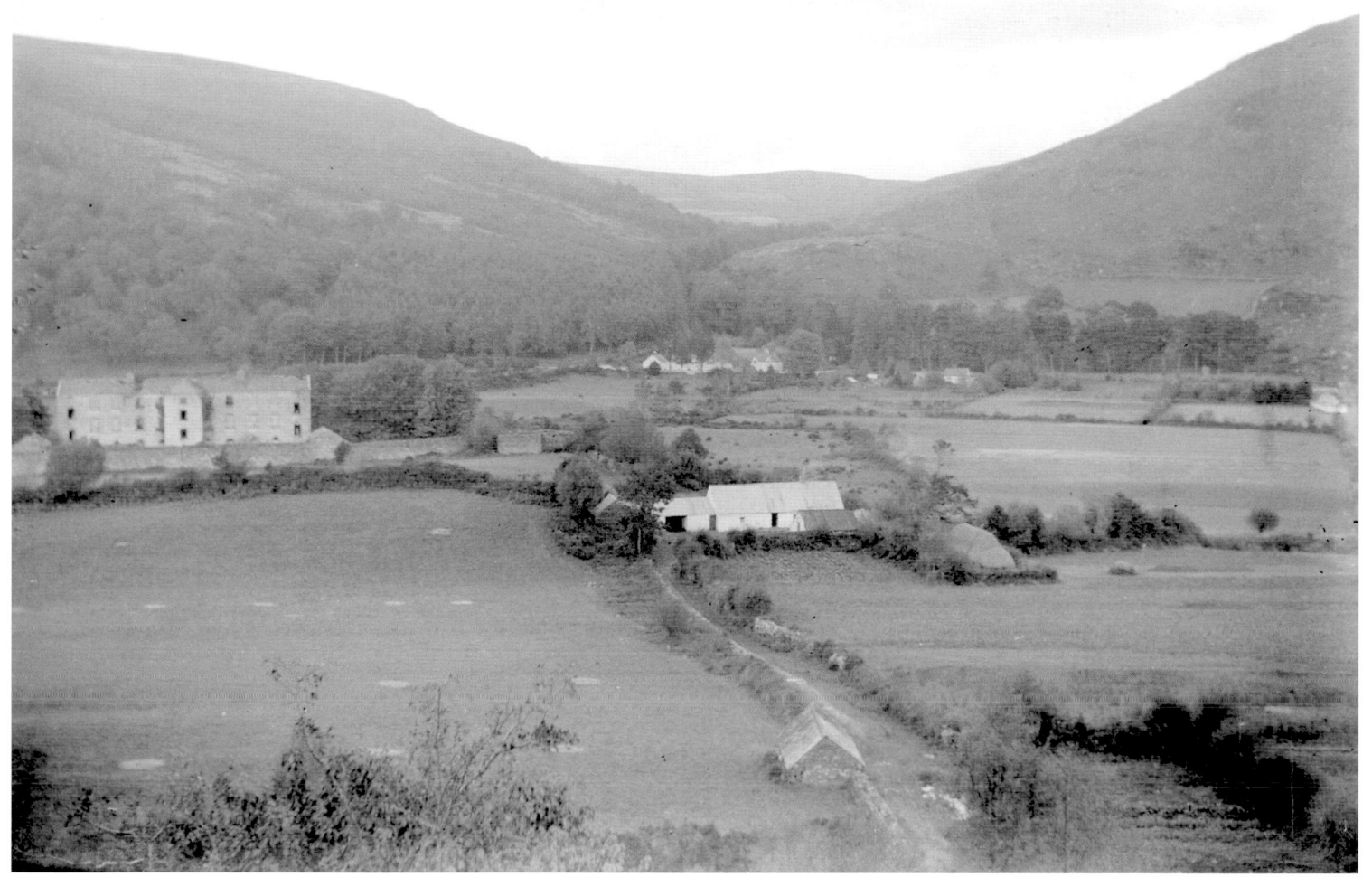

Above: Drumgoff, Glenmalure, County Wicklow (E 1307)

4 p.m., 23 October 1932

Ilford Auto-Filter, f11, 10 sec

Facing page: Drumgoff Bridge & Barrack, Glenmalure, County Wicklow (E 180)

3.45 p.m., 20 August 1911

Edwards Isochromatic Auto Screen, f22, 1/5 sec

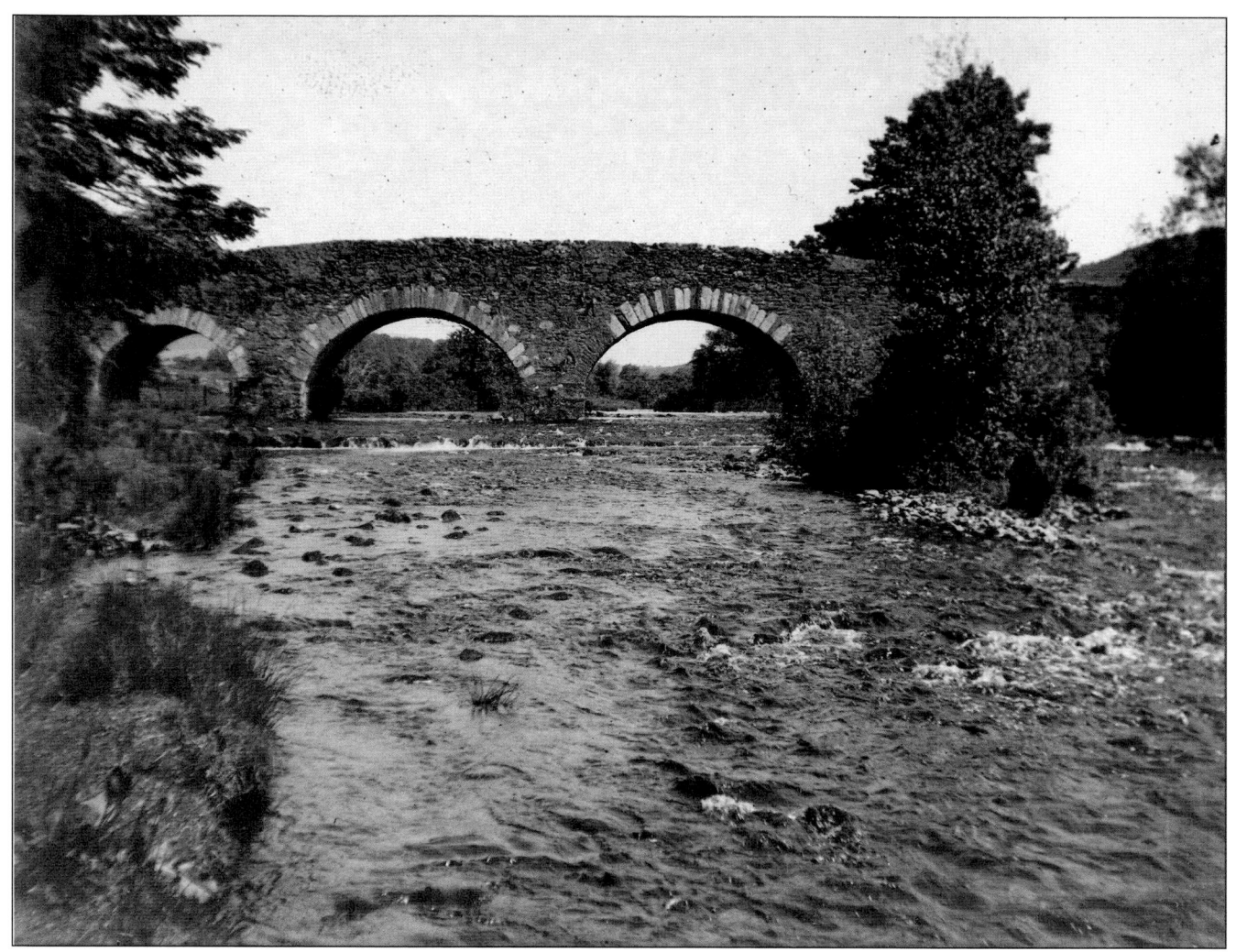

Above: Annamoe Bridge and River Avonmore,
County Wicklow (E 75)

9.30 a.m., 12 June 1910

Imperial Non-filter Orthochromatic, f11, 1/50 sec

Facing page: Evening on the River,
Wicklow (E 842)

8 p.m., 30 April 1922

Wellington Anti Screen, f8, 1/5 sec

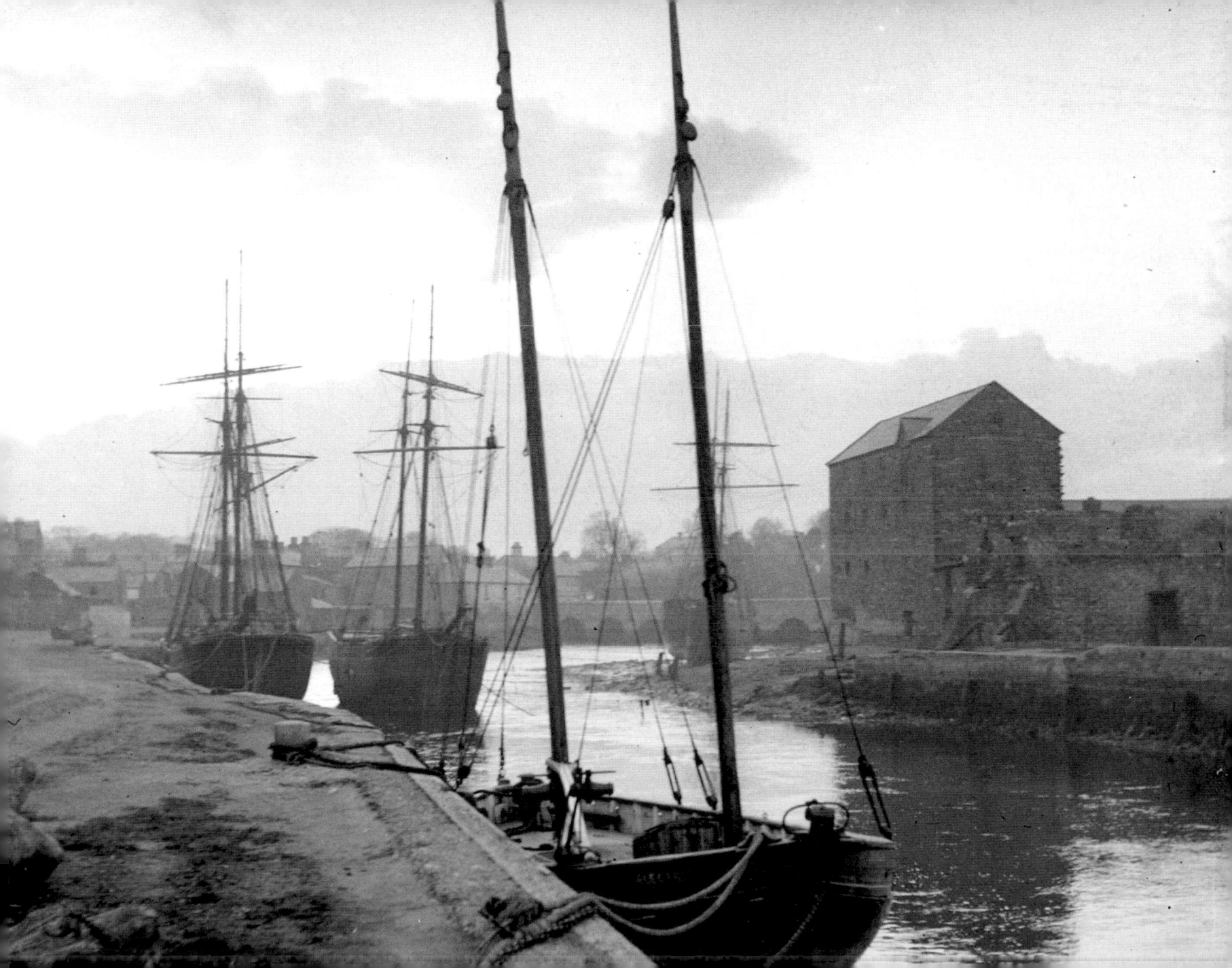

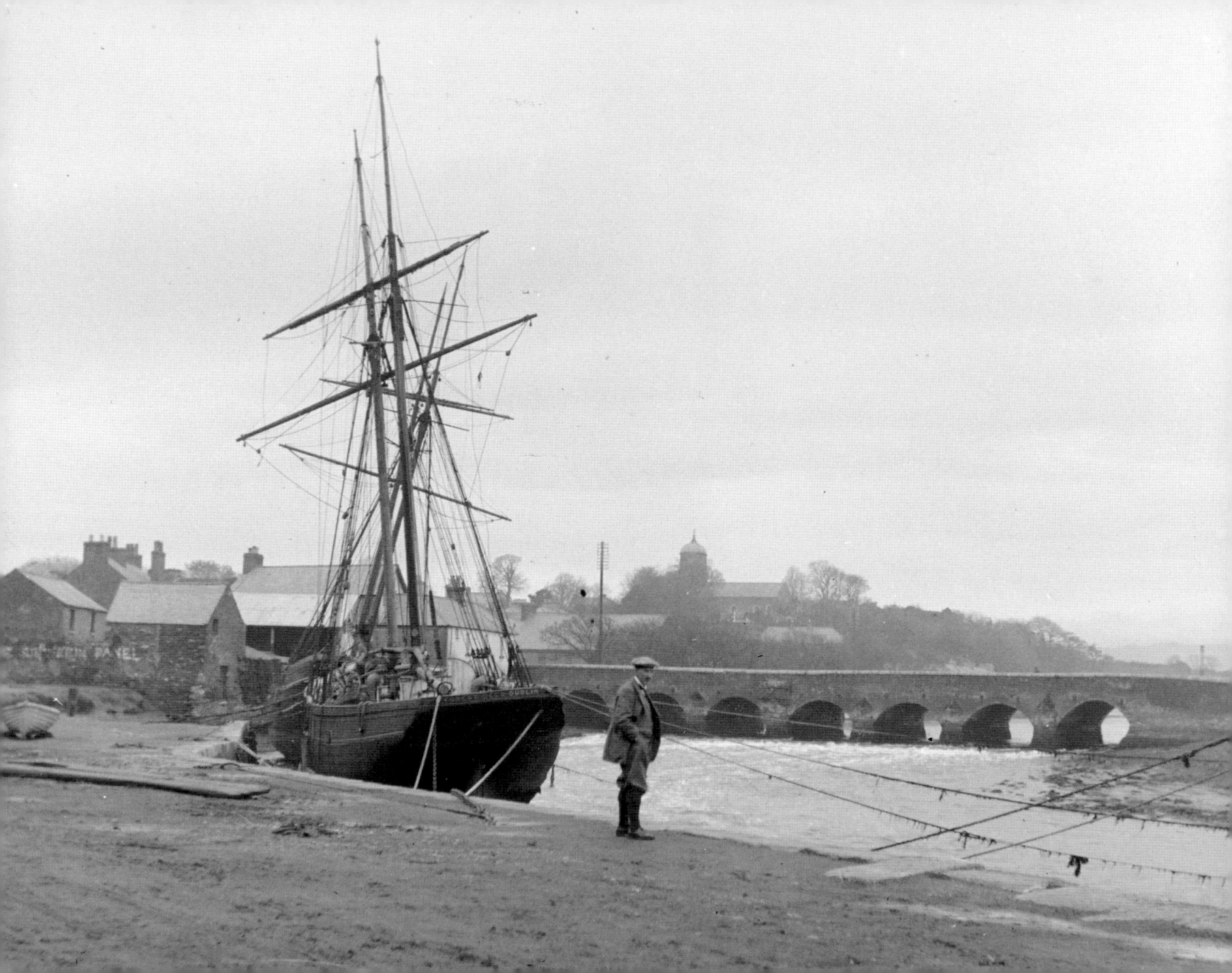

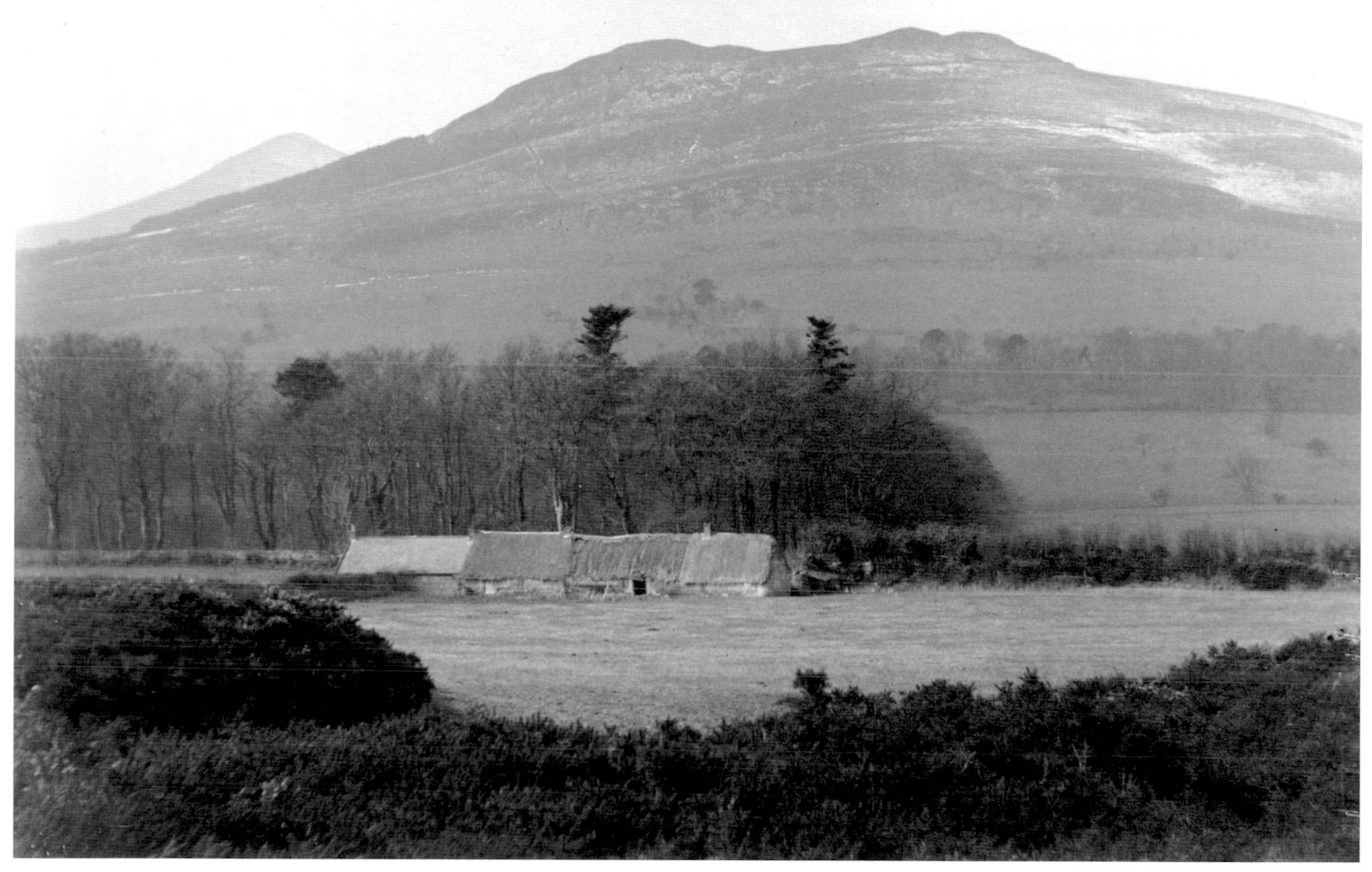

Above: Little Sugar Loaf from Windgates, County Wicklow (E 830)

11 a.m., 2 April 1922

Imperial Non-filter Orthochromatic, f10, 1/50 sec

Facing page: Old bridge and quays, Wicklow Town (E 926)

4 p.m., 15 April 1923

Ilford Screened Chromatic, f11, 1/5 sec

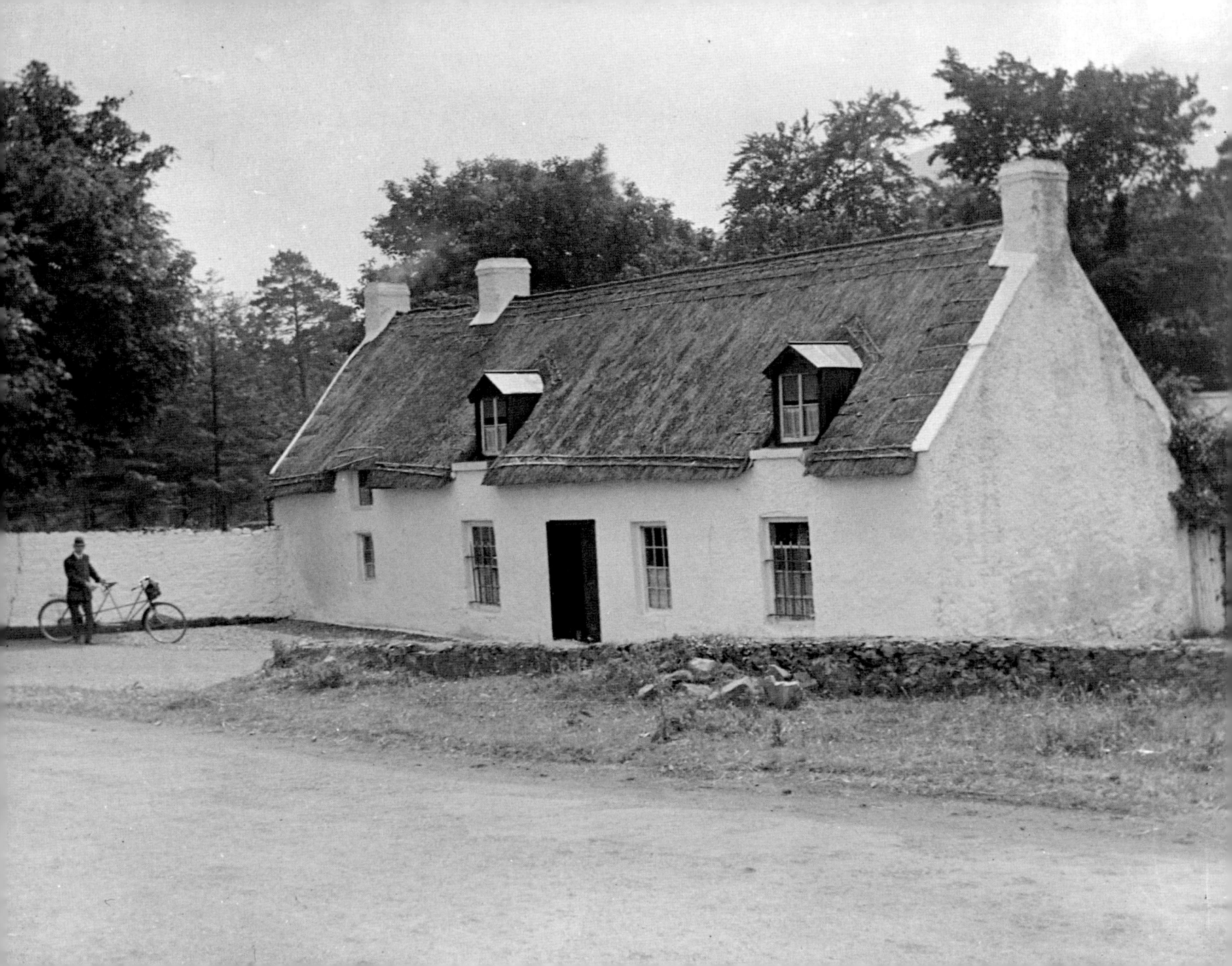

Right:
Cottage at Kilmacanogue,
County Wicklow (E 769)

2 p.m., 26 June 1921

Imperial Non-filter Orthochromatic,
f11, 1/50 sec

Facing page:
Thatched cottage near
Ballinalea, Ashford,
County Wicklow (E 1012)

3 p.m., 22 November 1923

Agfa Film, f12, 1 sec

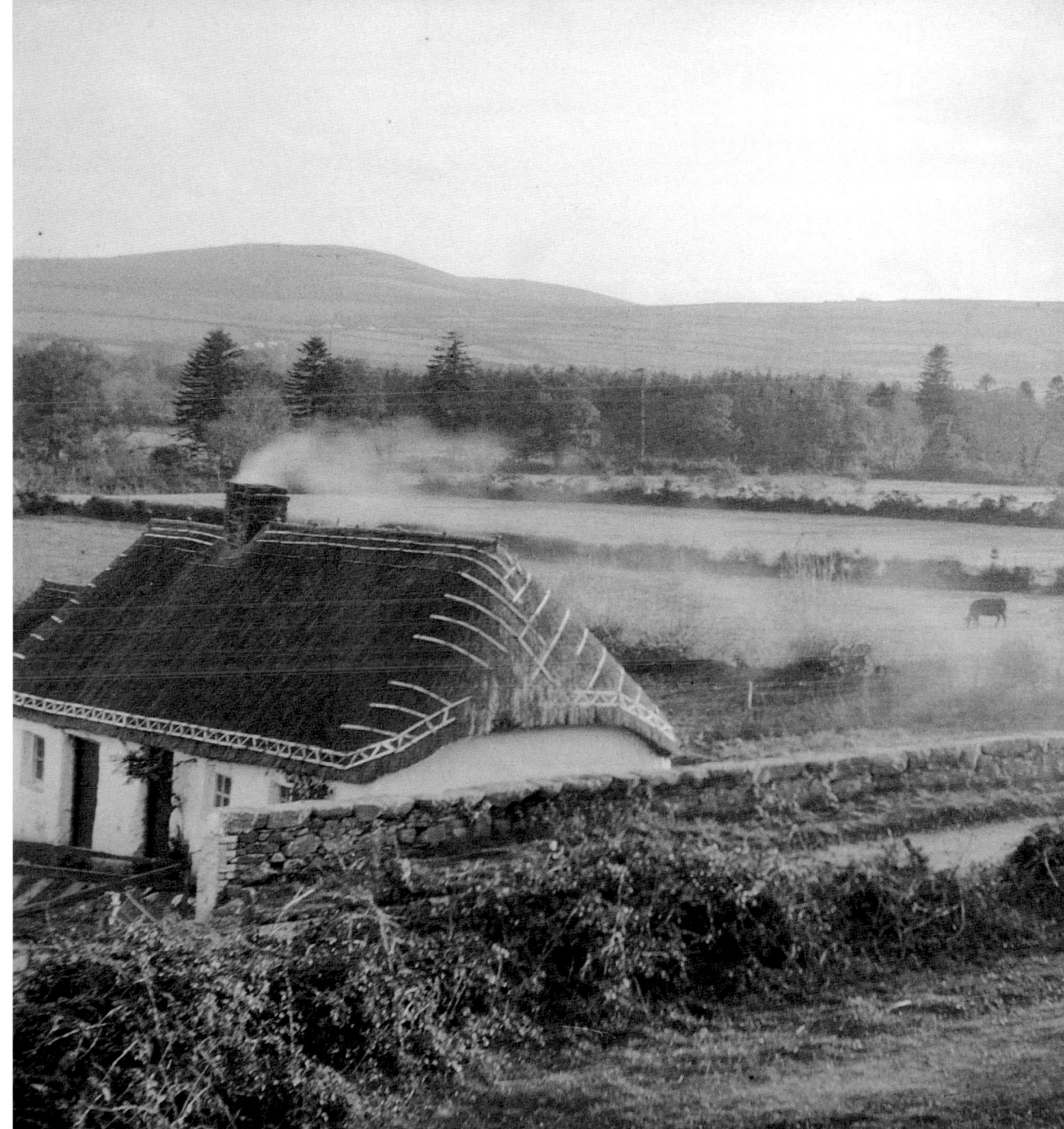

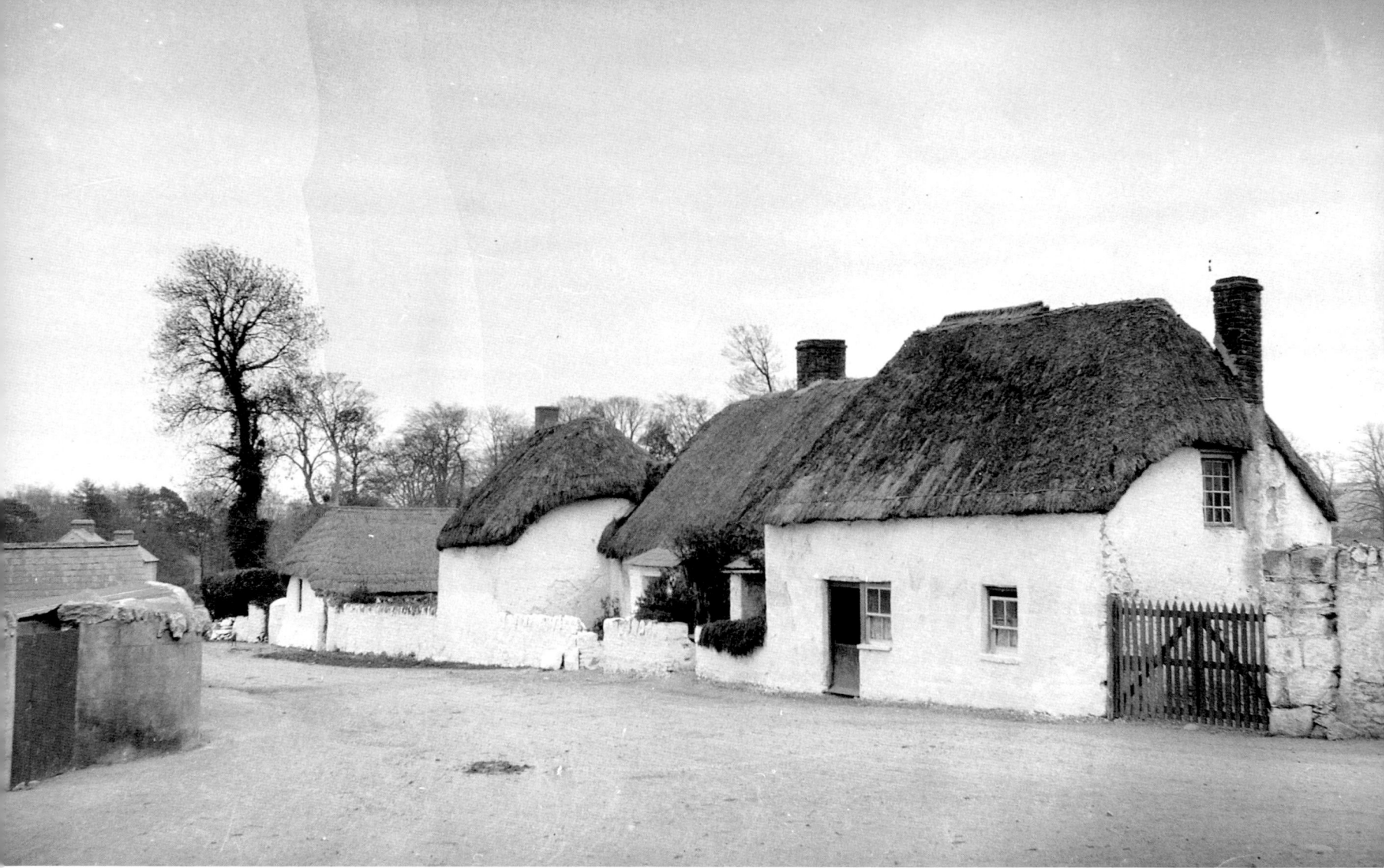

Thatched Cottage, Ballinalea, Ashford, County Wicklow (G 95)

2.30 p.m., 18 April 1927

KF [Kodak Film?], f22, ½ sec

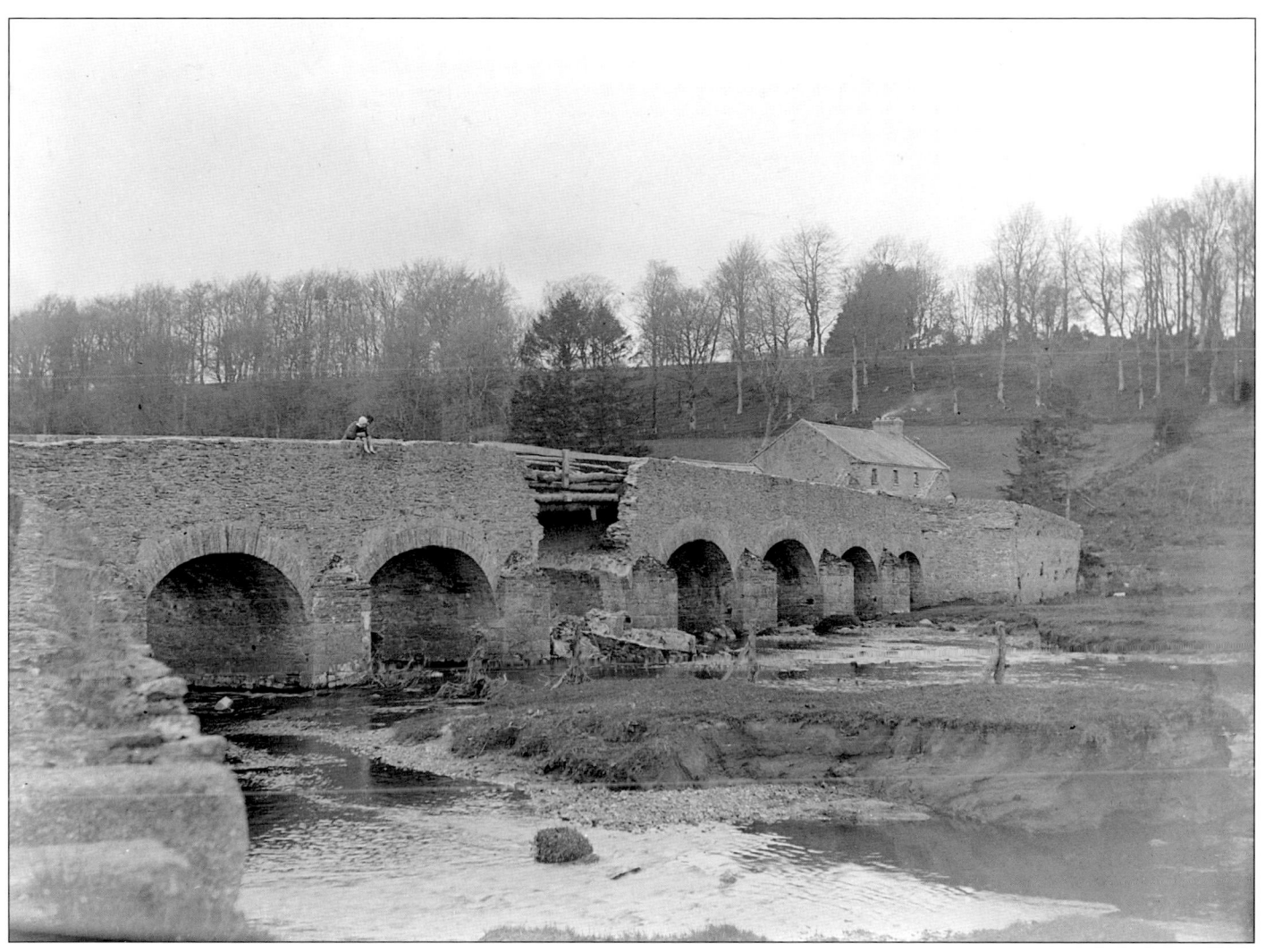

Blessington Bridge, County Wicklow, blown up by the IRA in 1923 (E 1043)

4 p.m., 4 May 1924

Barnet Matt Screen, f14, ½ sec

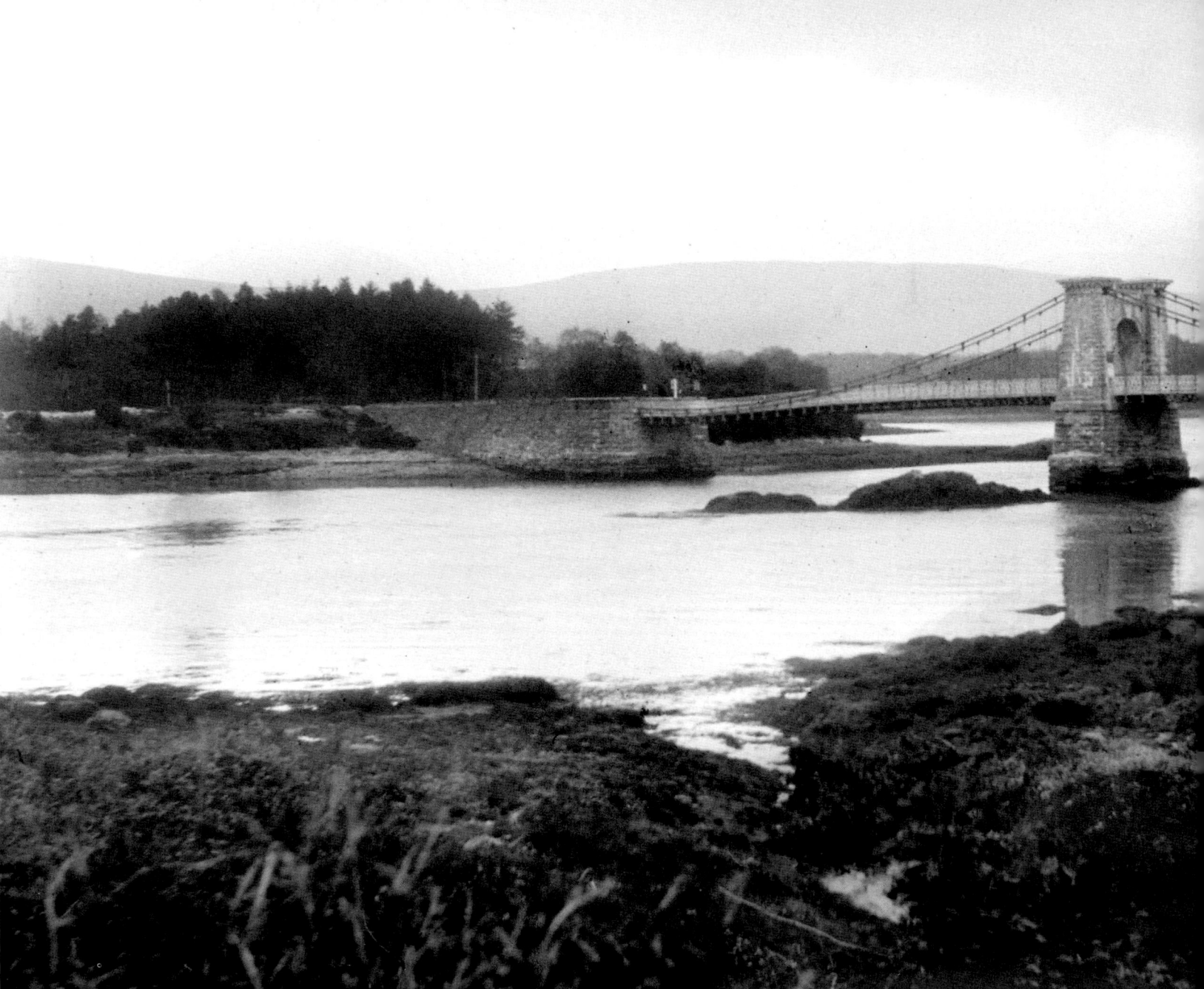

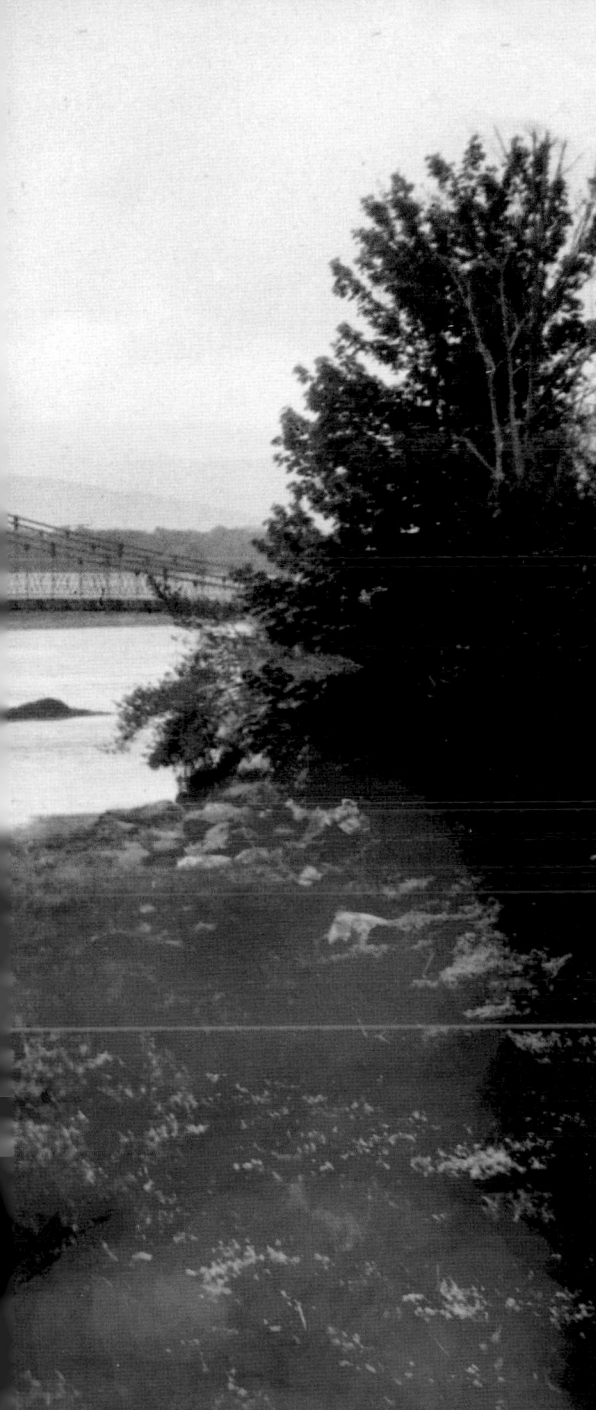

Suspension Bridge, Kenmare, County Kerry (E 514)

12 noon, 12 May 1915

Primo Film, f16, 1/50 sec

During the First World War many photographers found themselves curtailed, and indeed prohibited from taking photographs of coastal scenes. While taking this photograph of the suspension bridge at Kenmare in Kerry RLC found himself being challenged by a local magistrate, but was able to point out that it was possible to purchase postcards of the bridge in the town:

> *Was taking photograph of this bridge, when observed a portly gentleman hurrying down his garden in a great state of agitation 'What are you doing? he called out. 'Don't you know that taking photographs on the coast is forbidden.' Explained to him that this was not the coast & that picture-postcards of the bridge were on sale less than ½ mile away. After making a great fuss & saying he was a magistrate, an English one to judge by his accent, he retired & left me in peace.*

12 MAY 1915

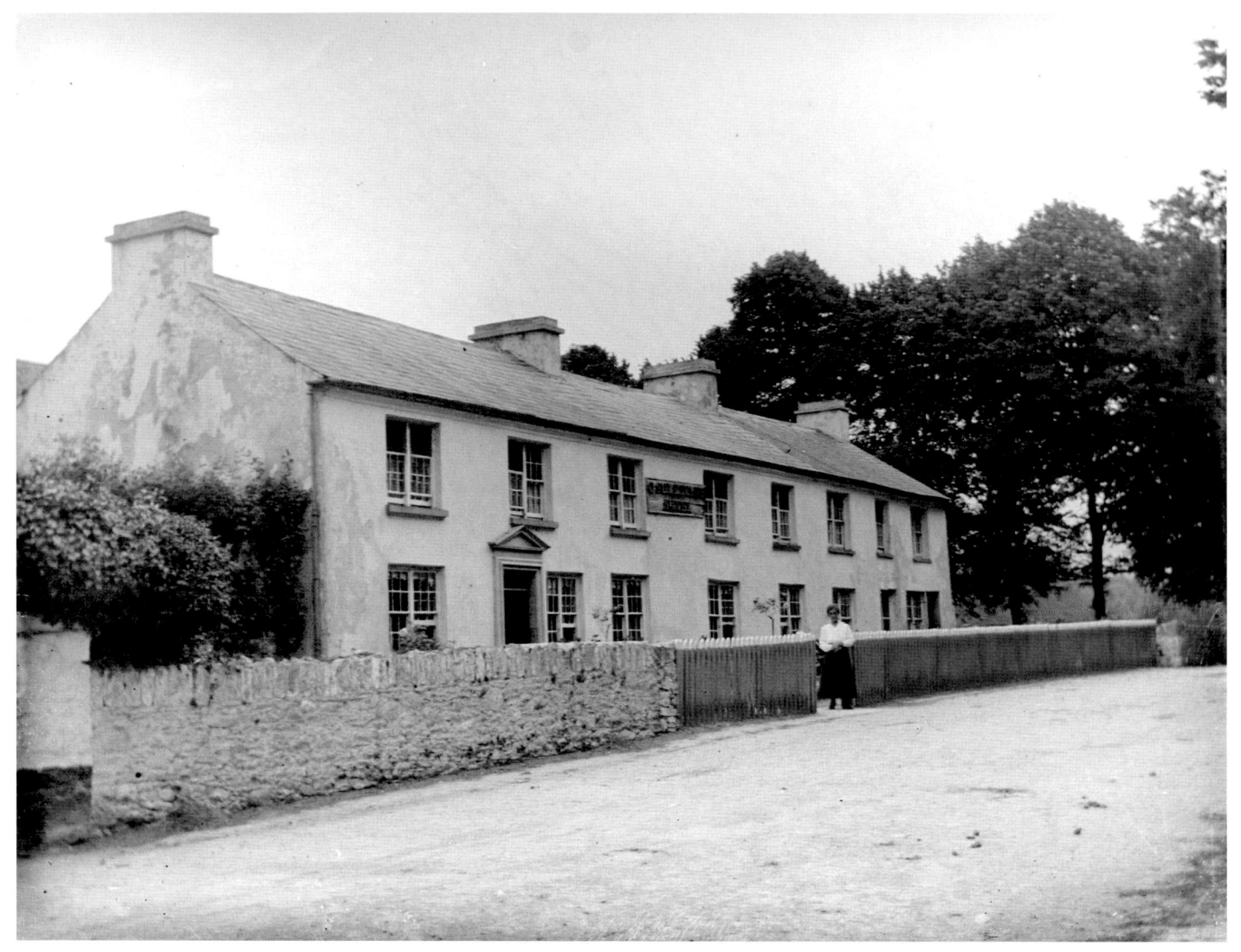

O'Sullivan's Hotel, Muckross, Killarney, County Kerry (E 603)

7 p.m., 6 June 1918

Edwards Isochromatic Auto Screen, f8, ½ sec

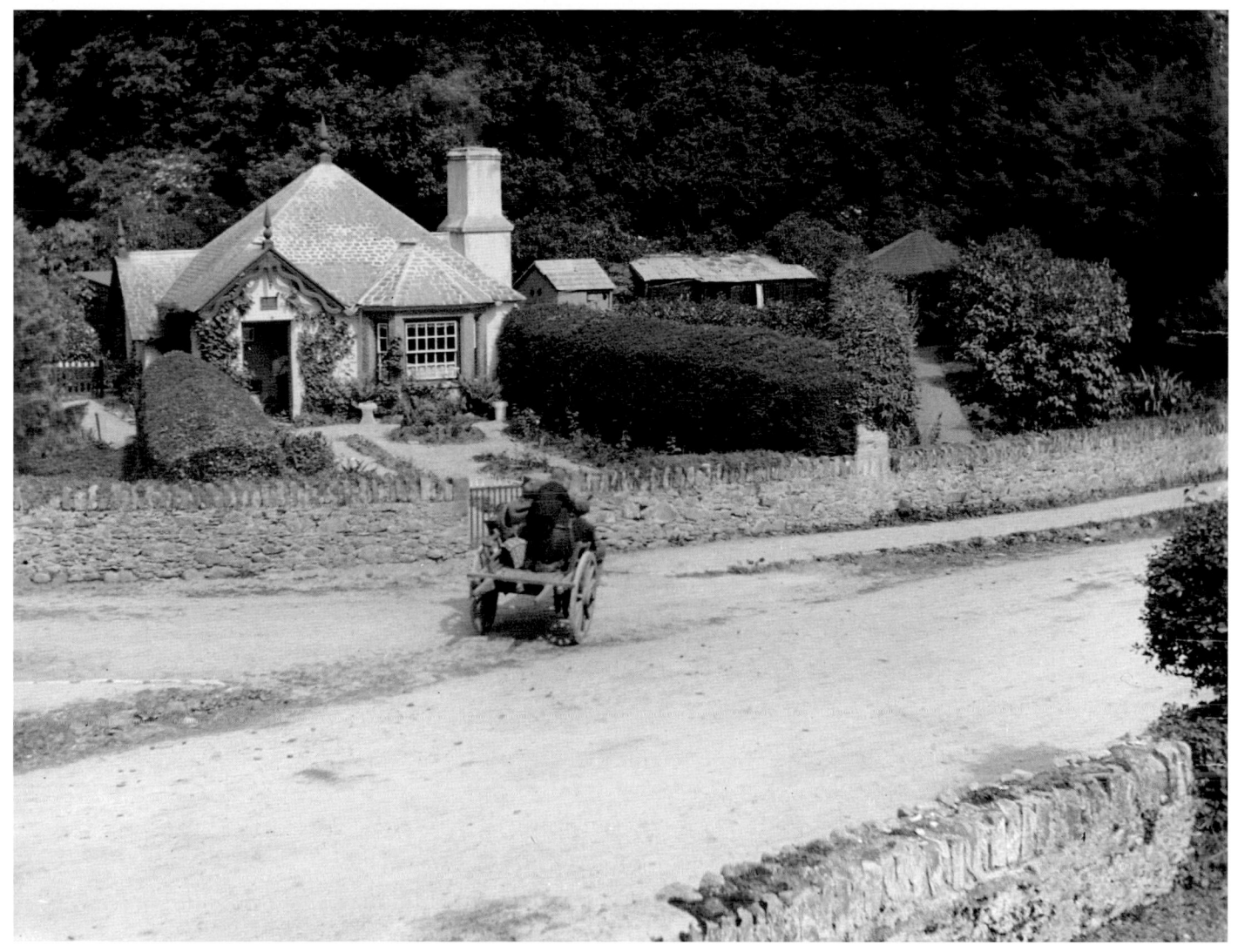

View from O'Sullivan's Hotel (E 606)

11 a.m., 8 June 1918

Edwards Isochromatic Auto Screen, f8, 1/50 sec

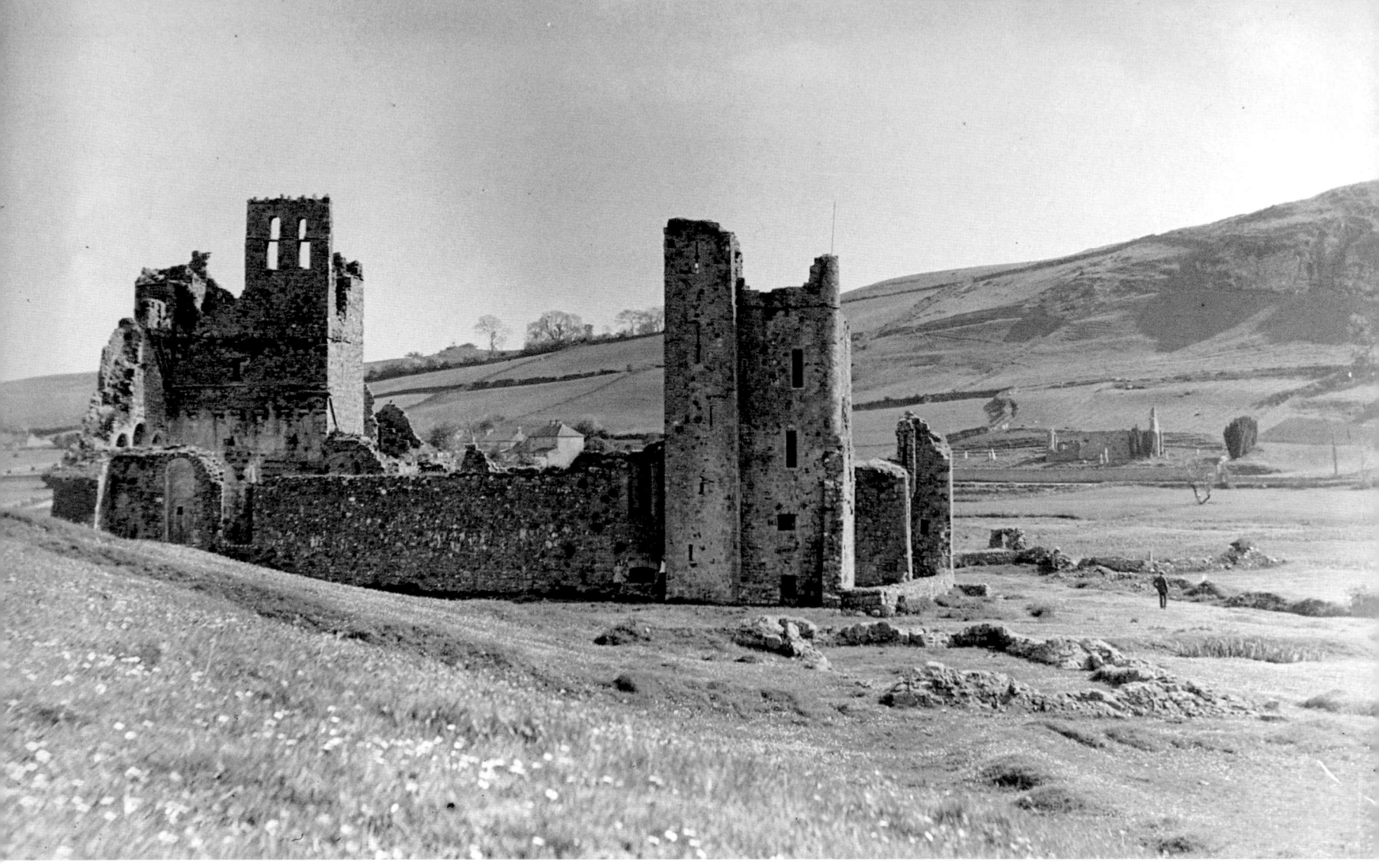

Fore Abbey, County Westmeath (E 859)

5.30 p.m., 28 May 1922

Imperial Non-filter Orthochromatic, f11, 1/5 sec

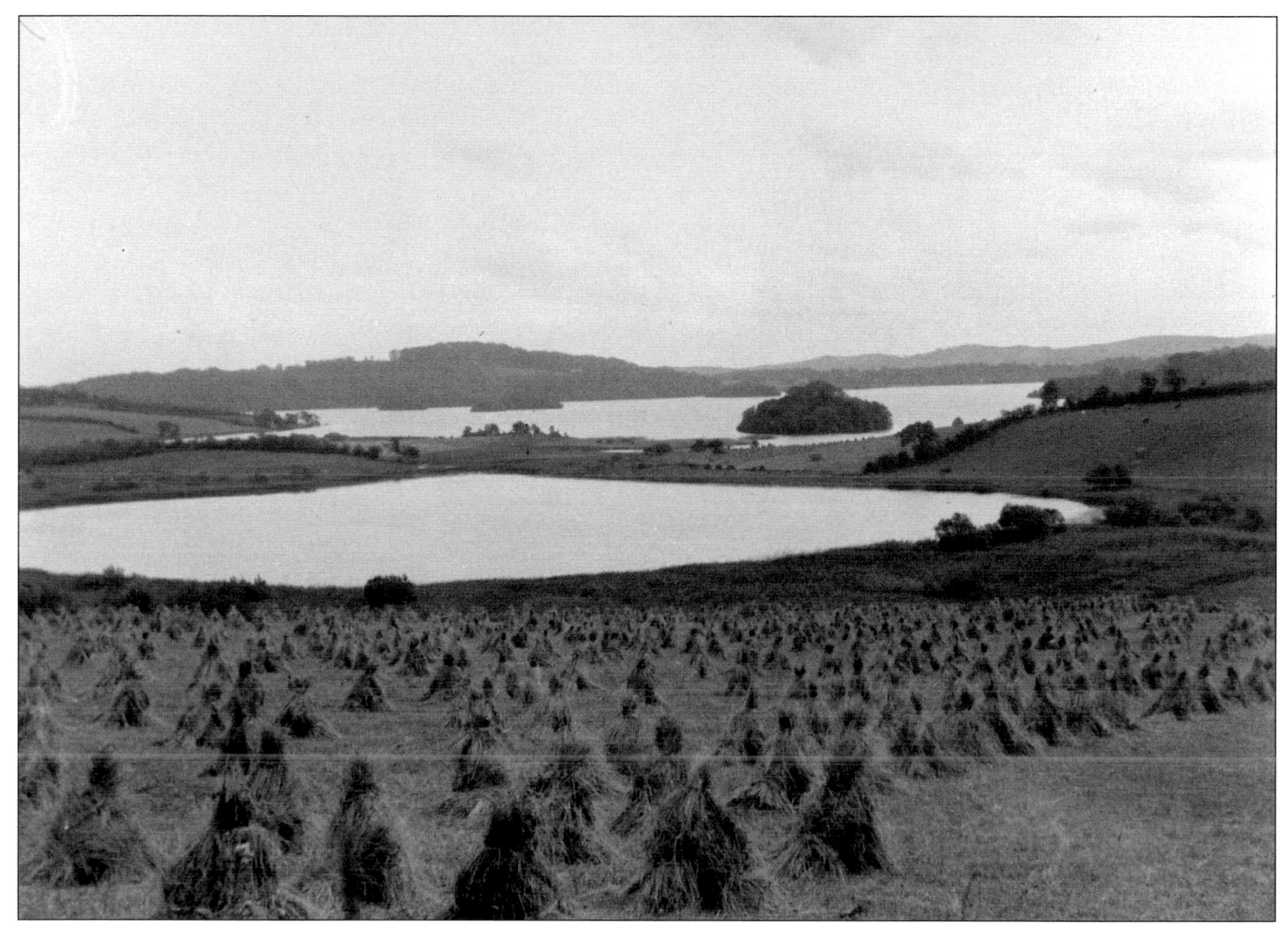

Lough Muckno near Church Hill, Castleblayney, County Monaghan (E 950)

5.30 p.m., 11 August 1923

Goerz Film, f15, 1/5 sec

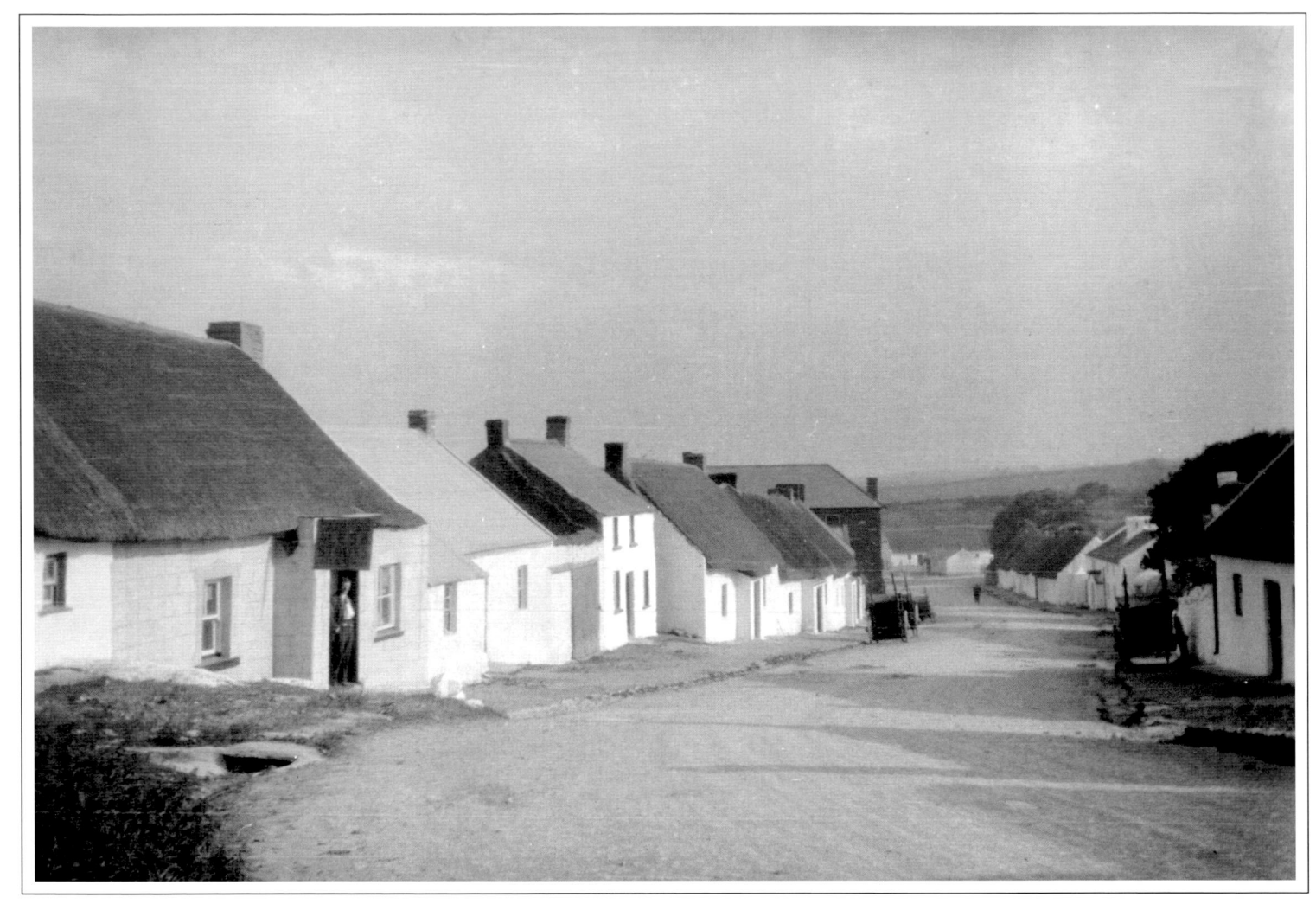

Clogher, [near Drogheda] County Louth (G 361)

7 p.m., 29 June 1930

Goerz Film, f11, 1/25 sec

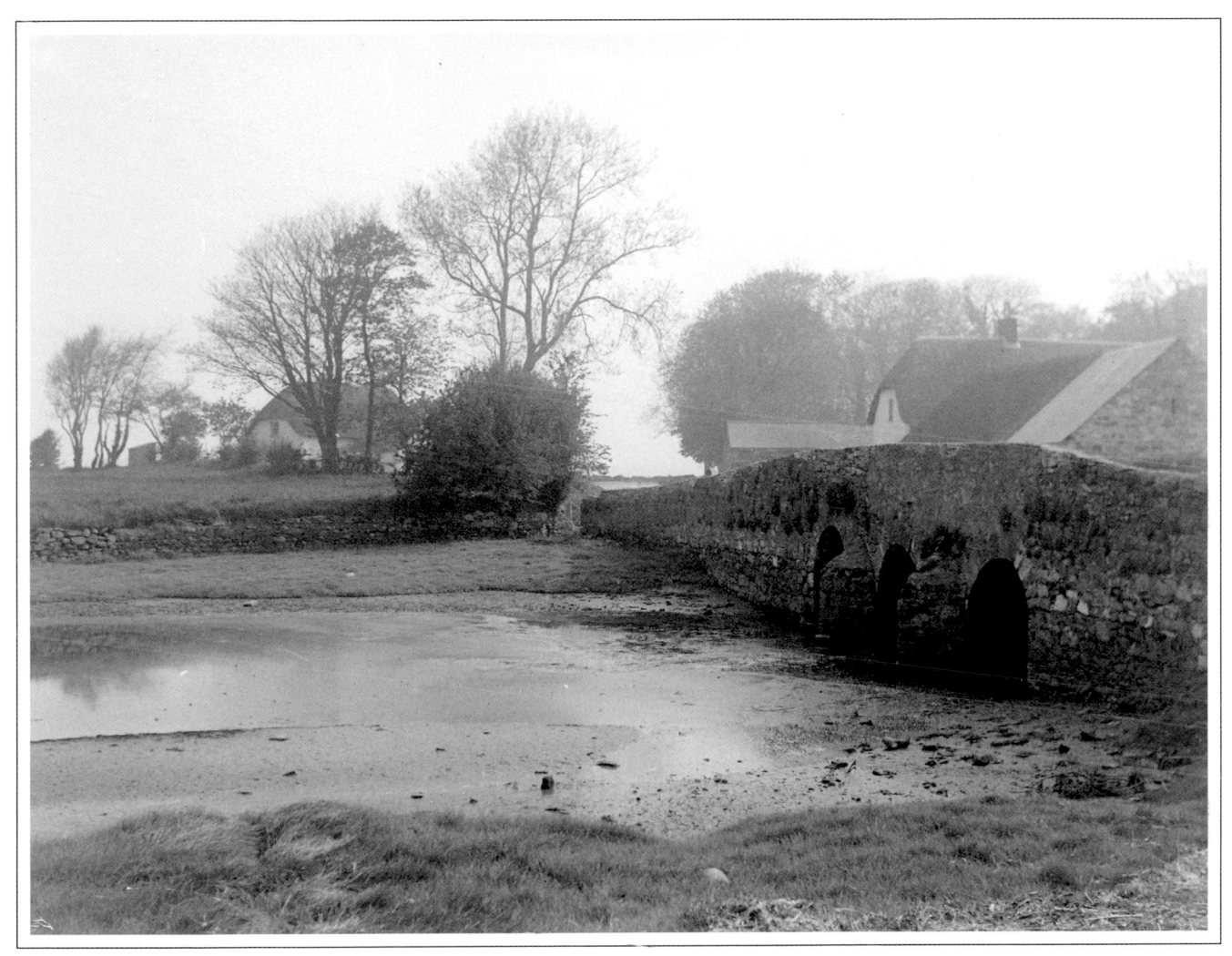

Baltray, [near Drogheda] County Louth (E 1242)

5 p.m., 7 May 1927

BMSC, f11, 1/25 sec

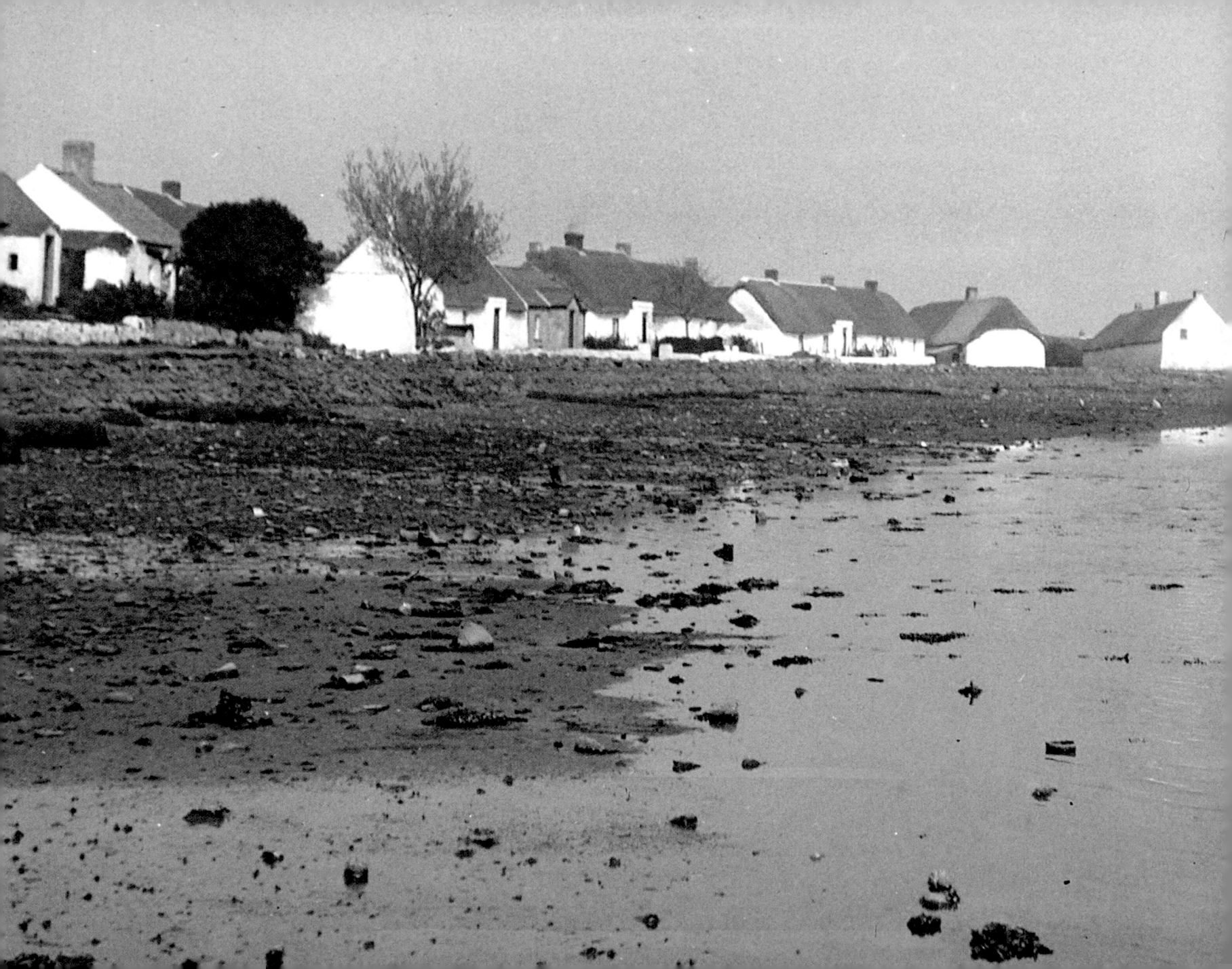

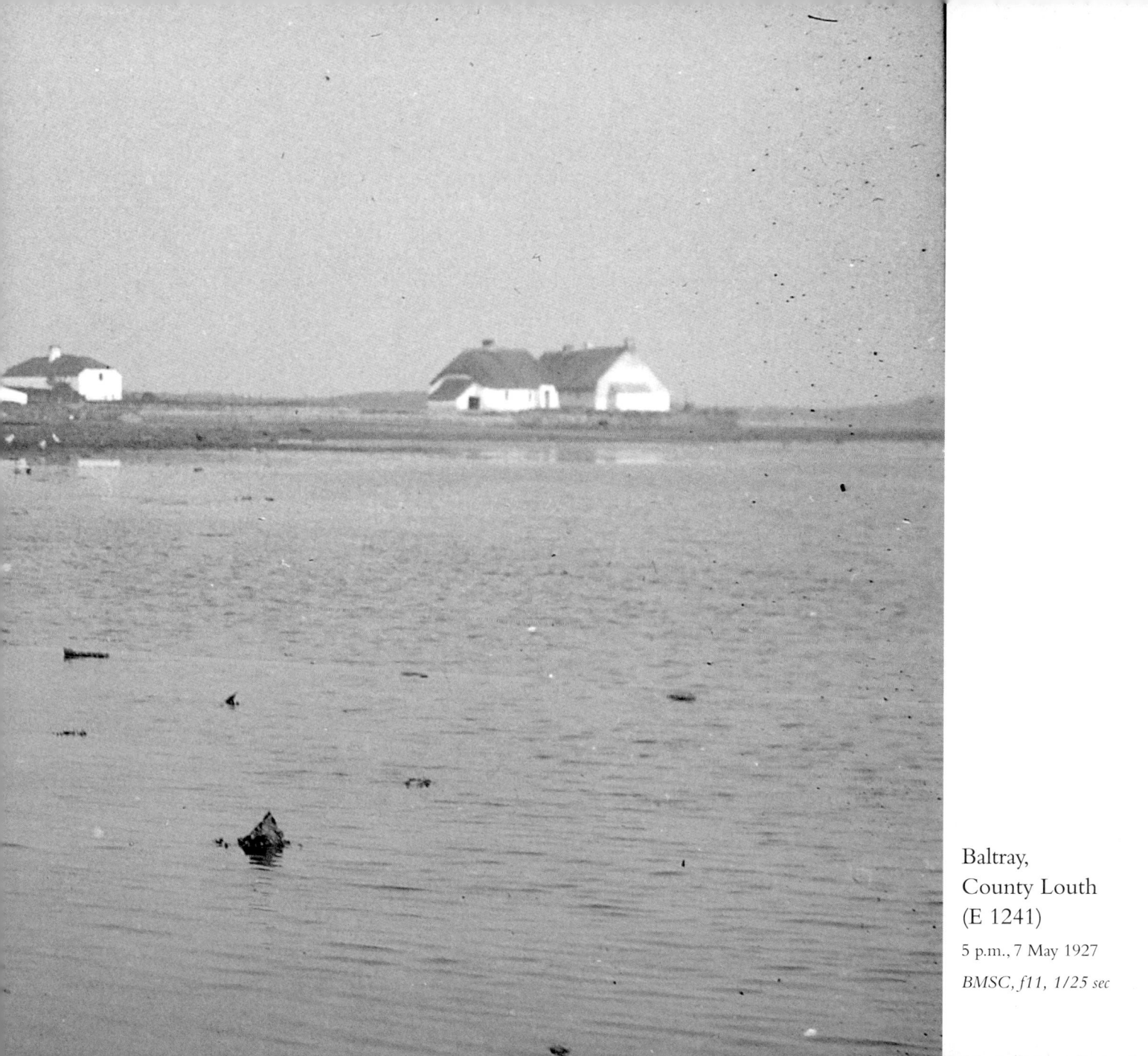

Baltray,
County Louth
(E 1241)

5 p.m., 7 May 1927

BMSC, f11, 1/25 sec

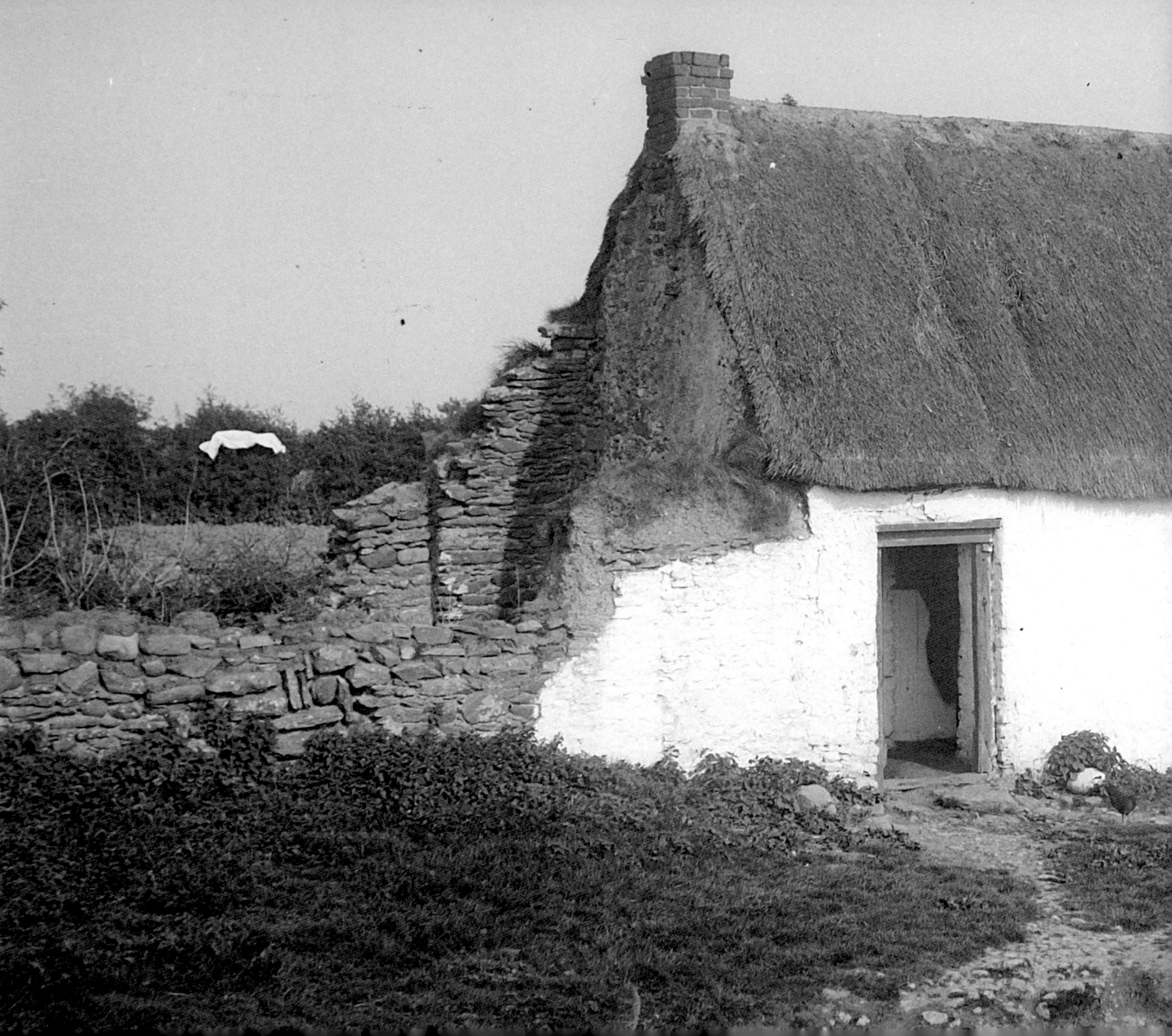

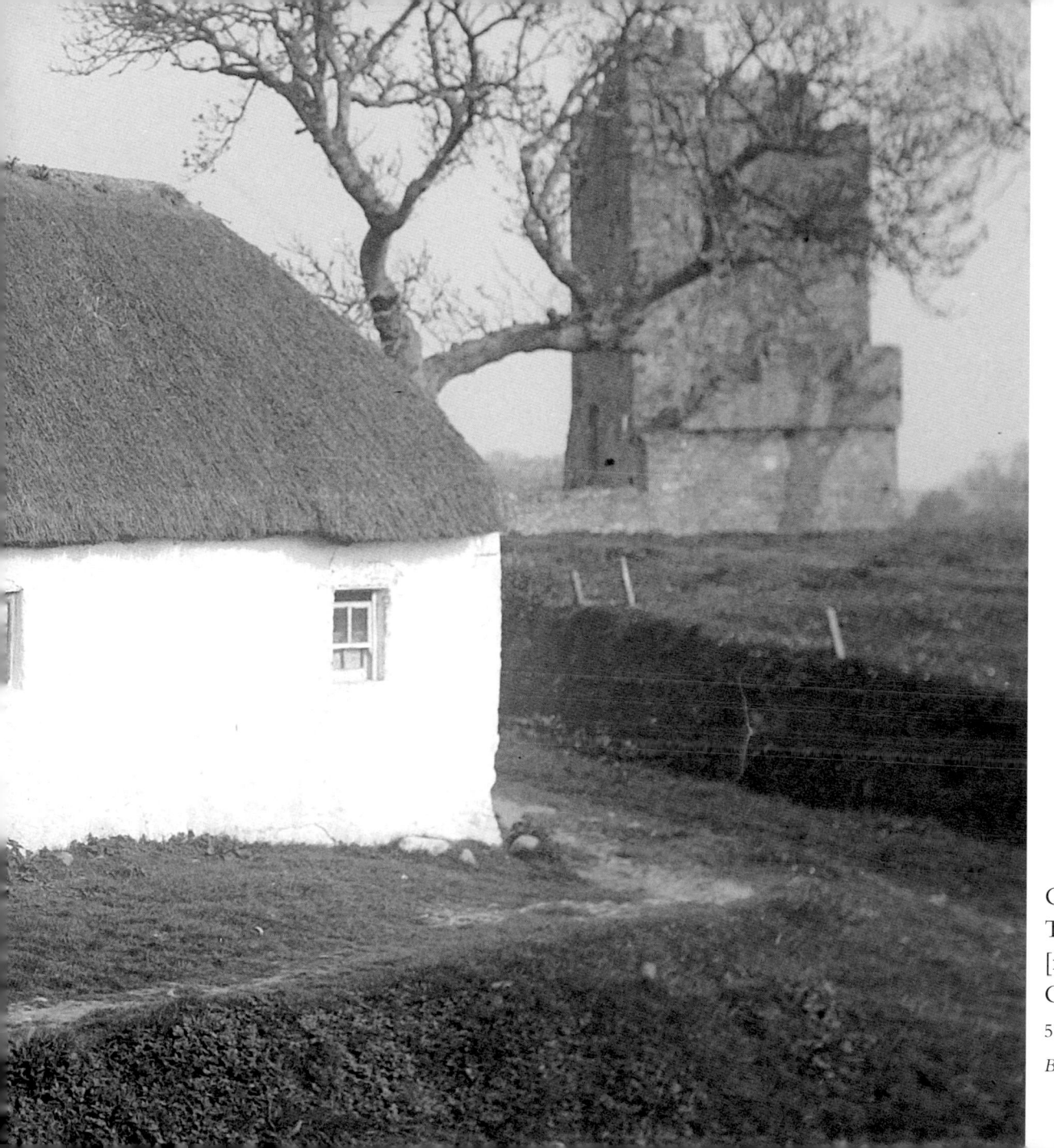

Cottage & Castle,
Termonfeckin,
[near Drogheda]
County Louth (E 1243)

5.30 p.m., 7 May 1927

BMSC, f8, 1/25 sec

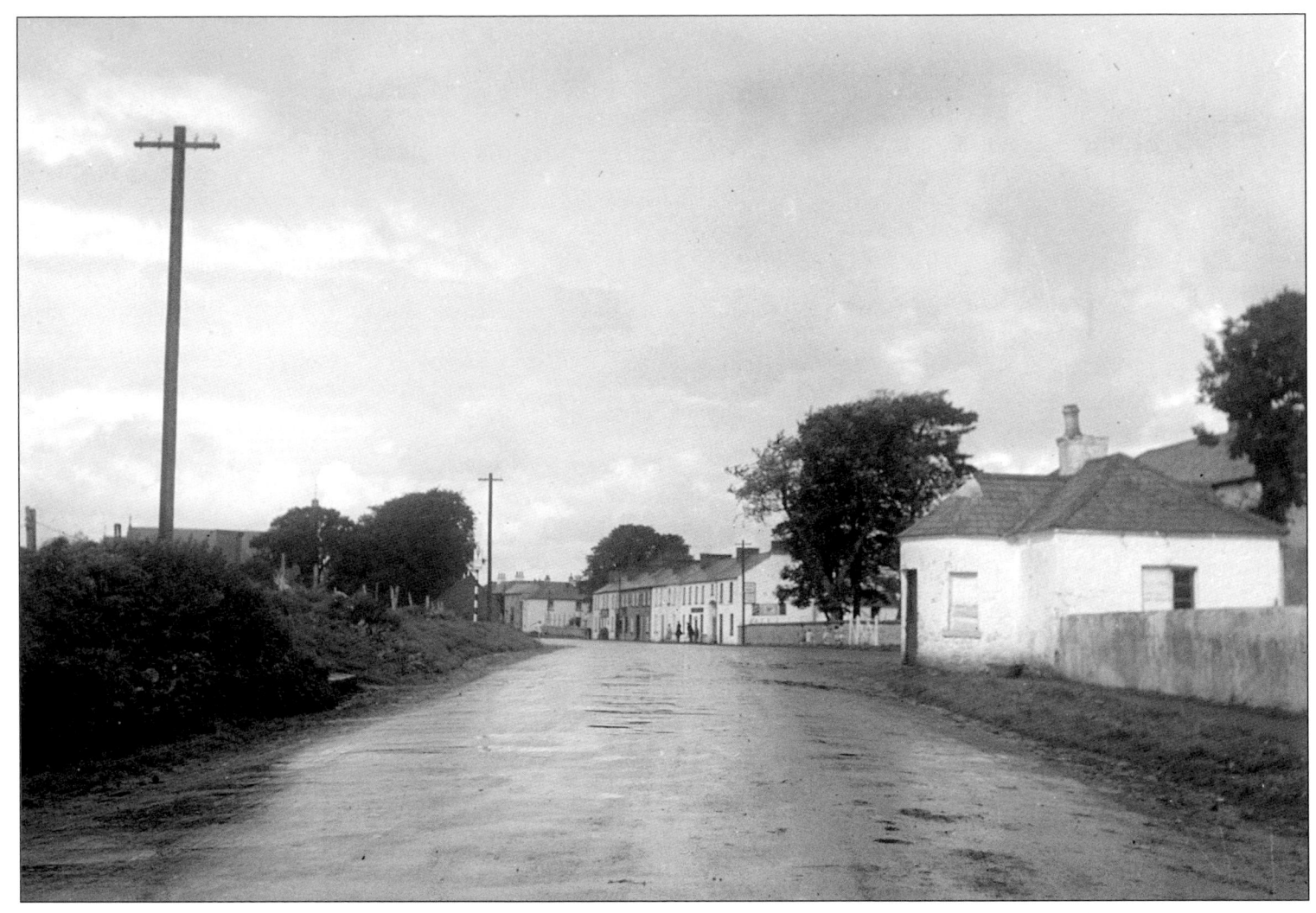

Above: Toll House, Ashbourne, County Meath (E 1301)

1.15 p.m., 25 September 1932

Wellington Anti Screen, f6.8, 1/25 sec

Facing page: Medieval cross and cottage at Duleek, [near Newgrange] County Meath (E 1240)

4 p.m., 7 May 1927

BMSC, f10, 1/25 sec

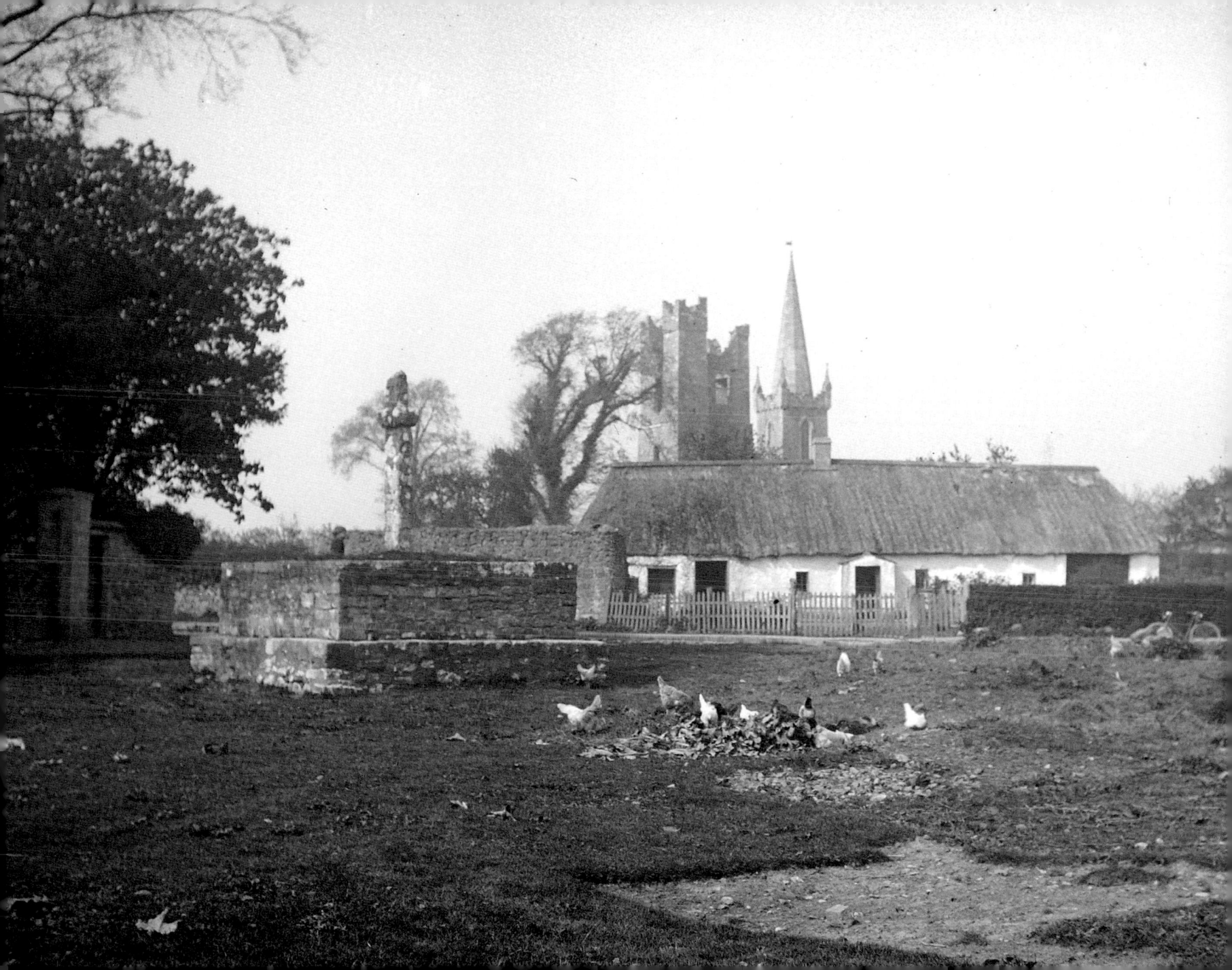

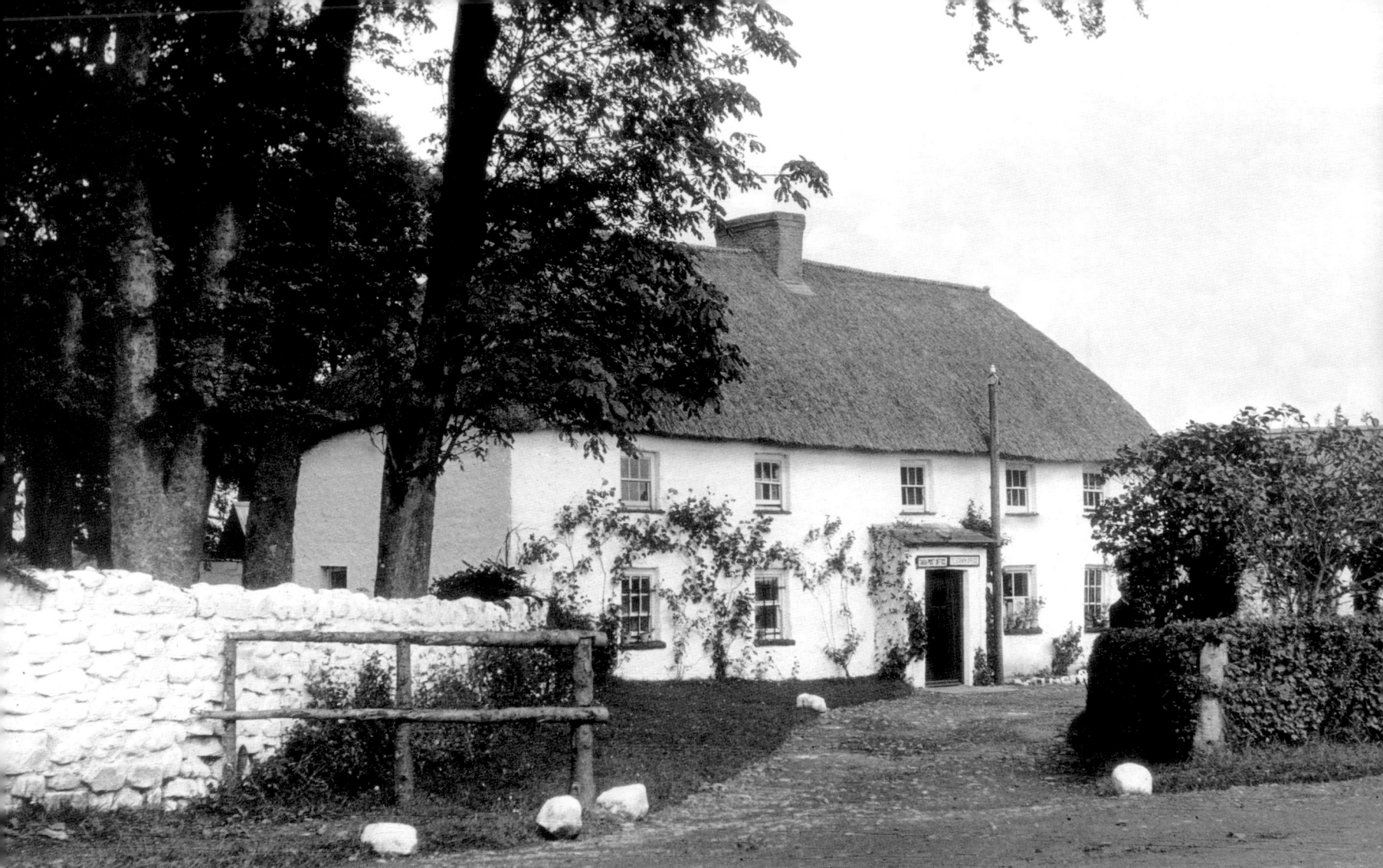

The Post Office, Tara, County Meath (E 646)

9.30 a.m., 18 July 1920

Primo Film, f16, 1/5 sec

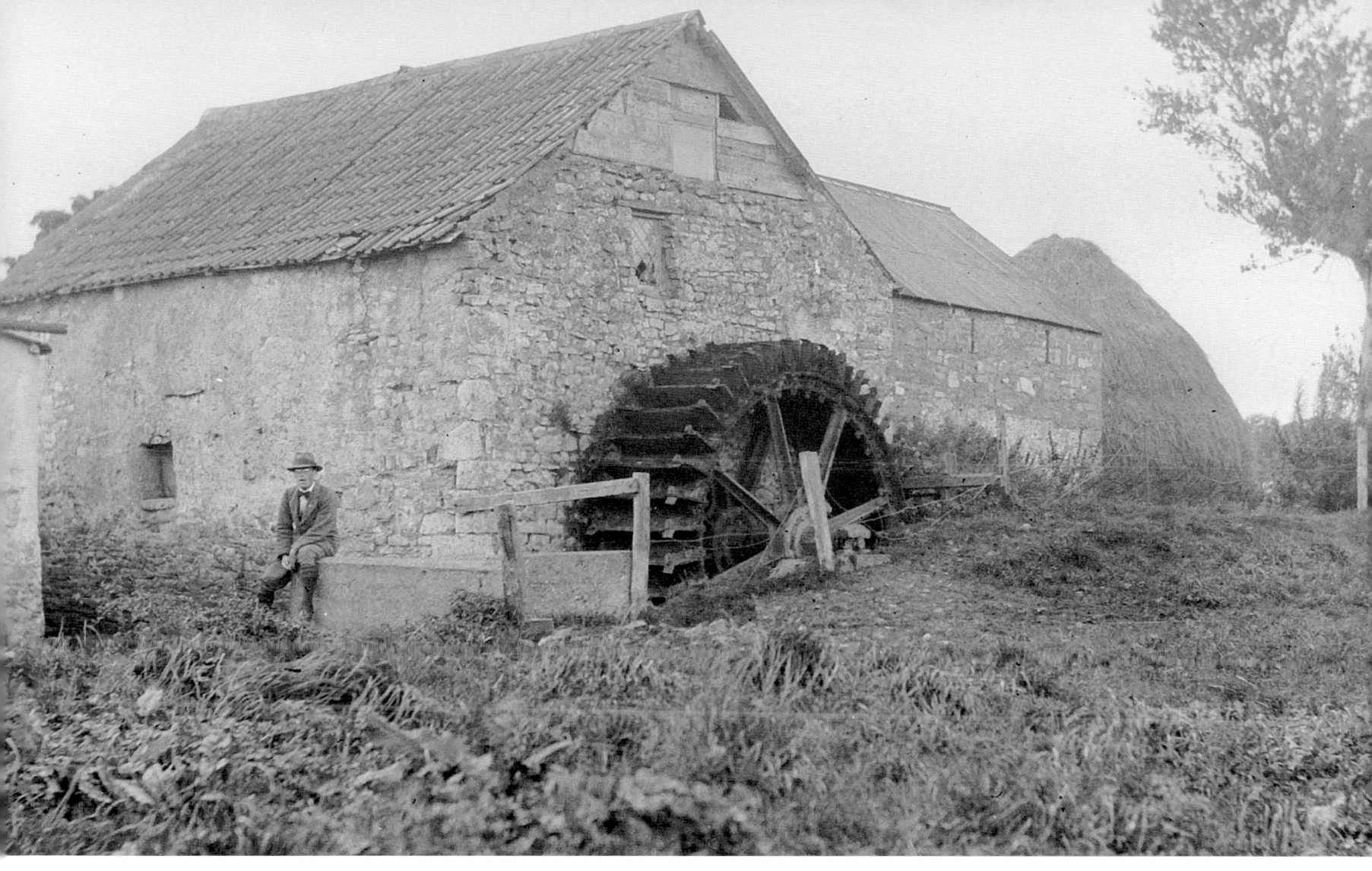

Old Mill, Clonee, [near Dunboyne] County Meath (E 889)

12 noon, 17 September 1922

Primo Film, f11, 1/5 sec

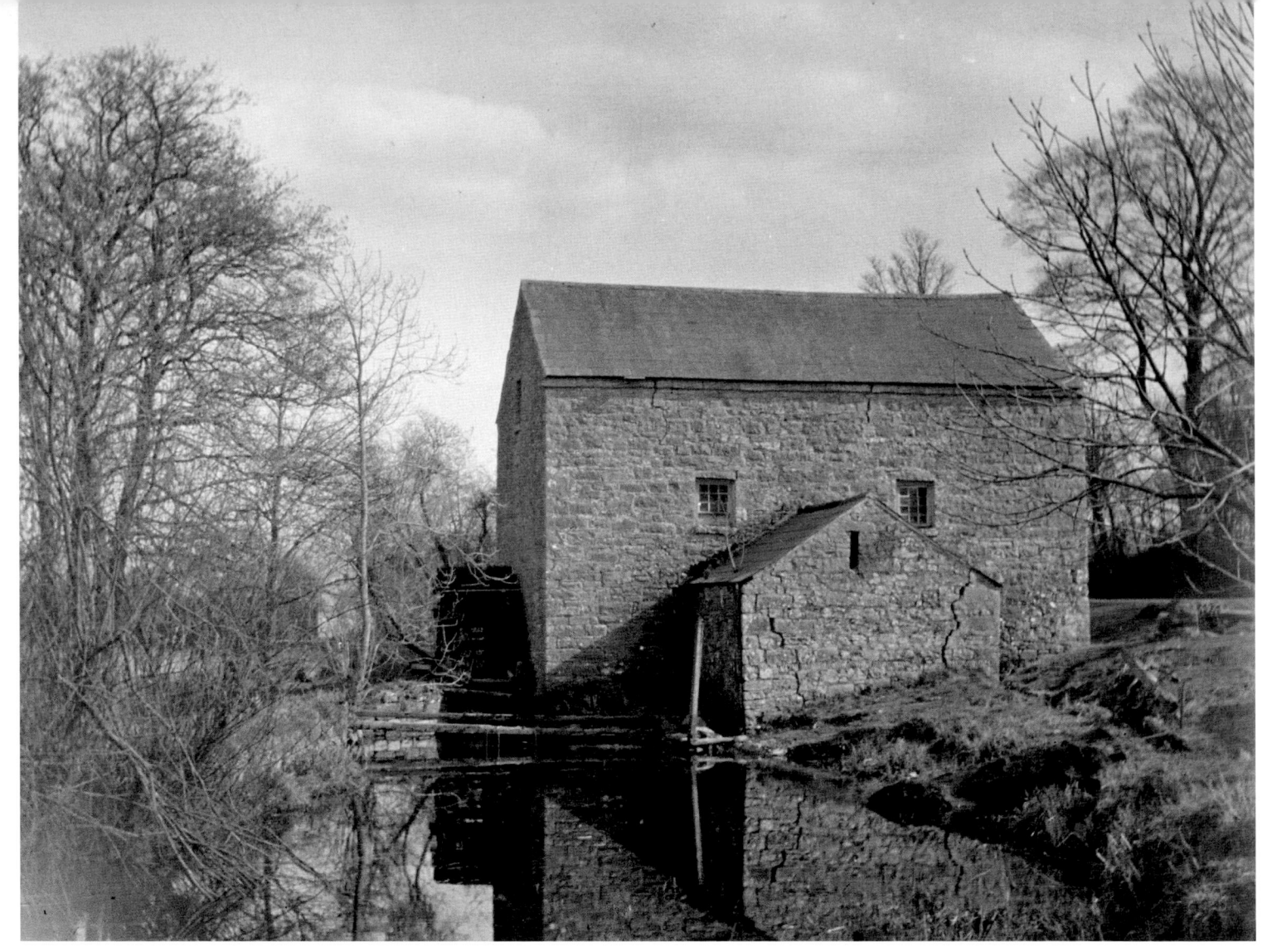

Watermill, River Blackwater, near Kells, County Meath (E 1037)

2 p.m., 17 March 1924

Agfa Film, f6.8, 1/50 sec

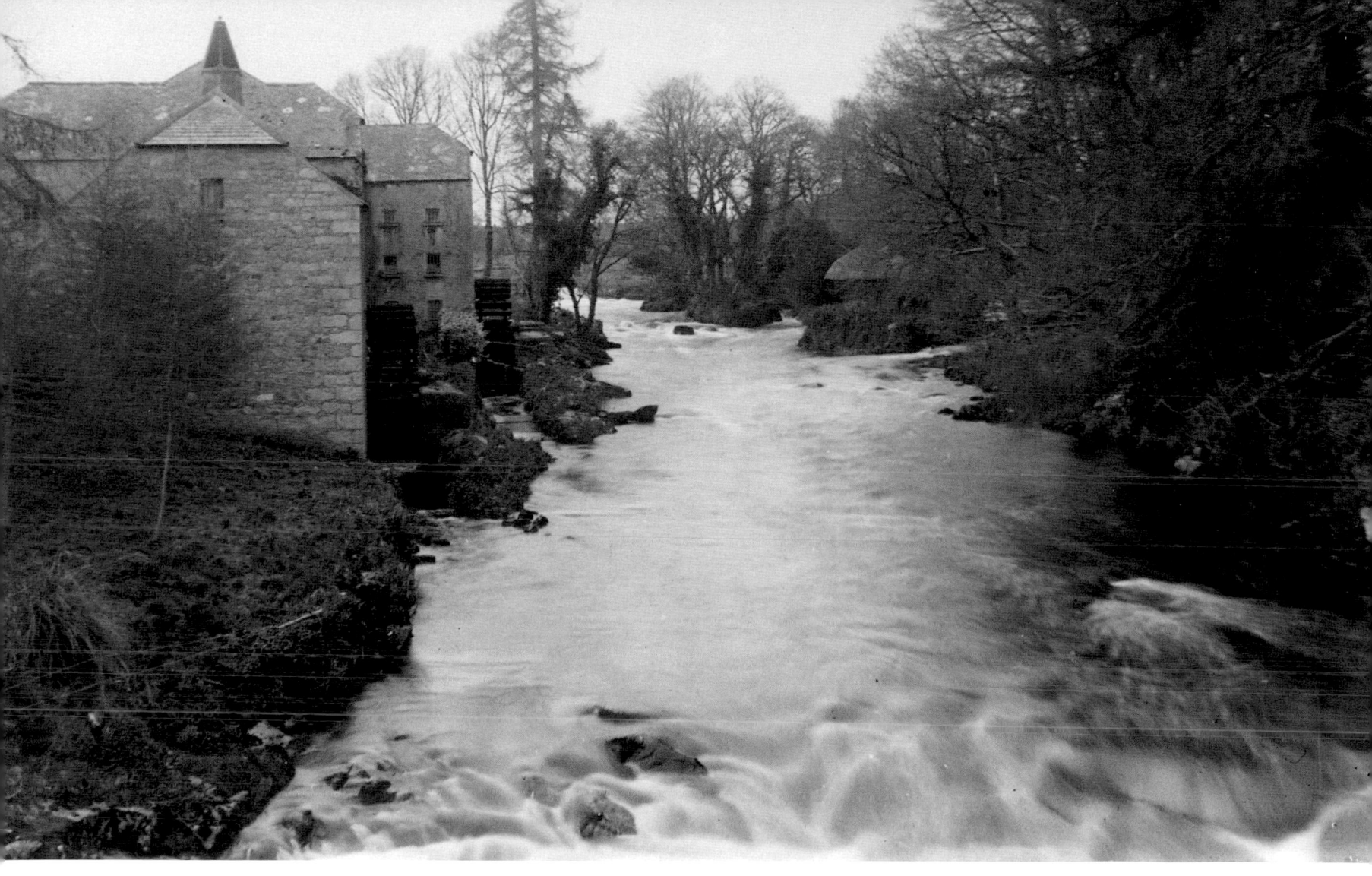

Oldmill, Aghade Bridge, Tullow, County Carlow (E 1361)

5 p.m., 11 April 1937

Wellington Anti Screen, f18, ½ sec

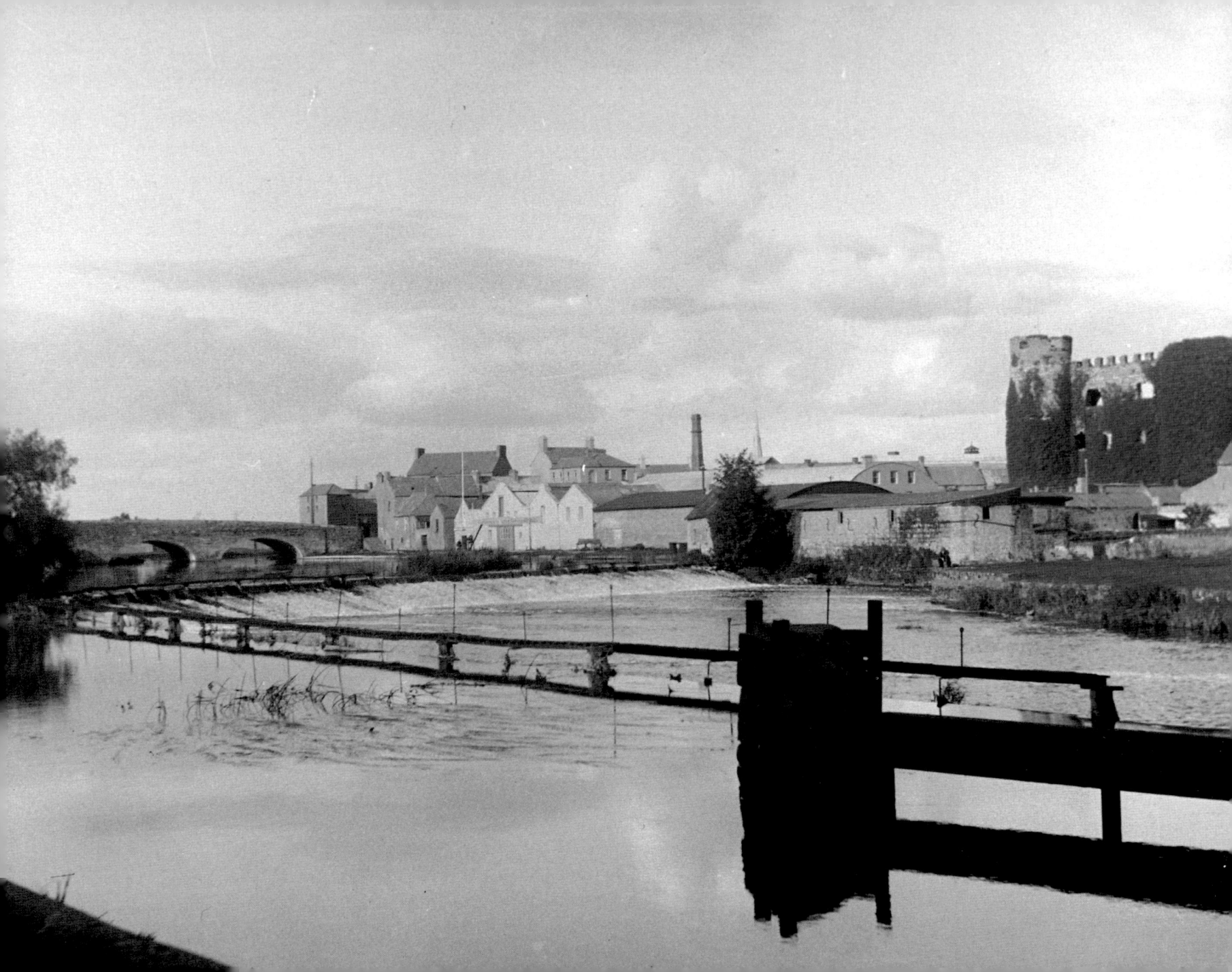

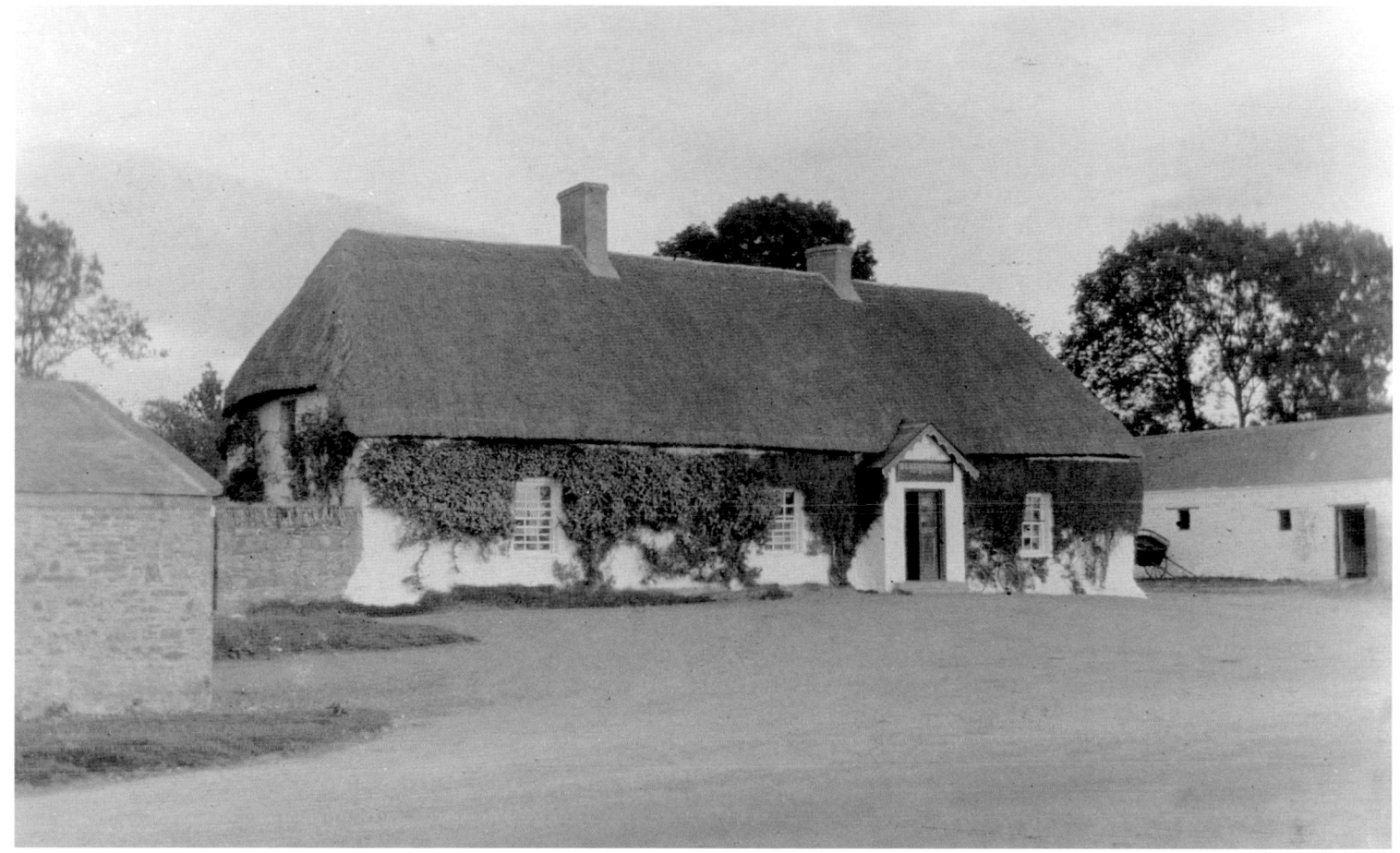

Above: Blackchurch Inn, Naas Road, County Kildare (E 867)

9.30 p.m., 20 June 1922

Primo Film, f8, 1 sec

Facing page: River Barrow and Carlow Castle, County Carlow (E 961)

4.30 p.m., 16 September 1923

Wellington Anti Screen, f10, 1/50 sec

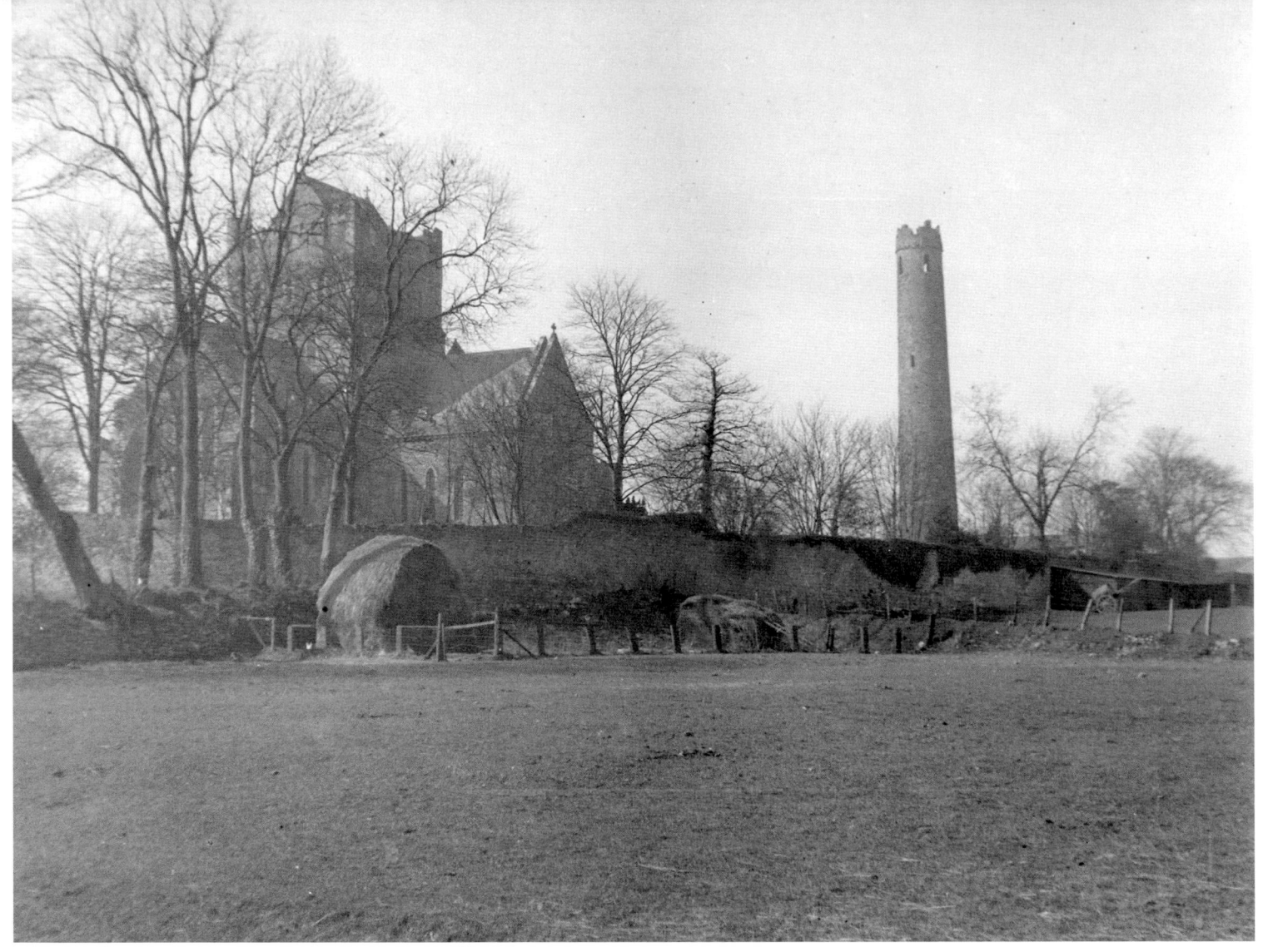

Cathedral and Round Tower, County Kildare (E 68)

11 a.m., 10 April 1910

Imperial Non-filter Orthochromatic, f32, ½ sec

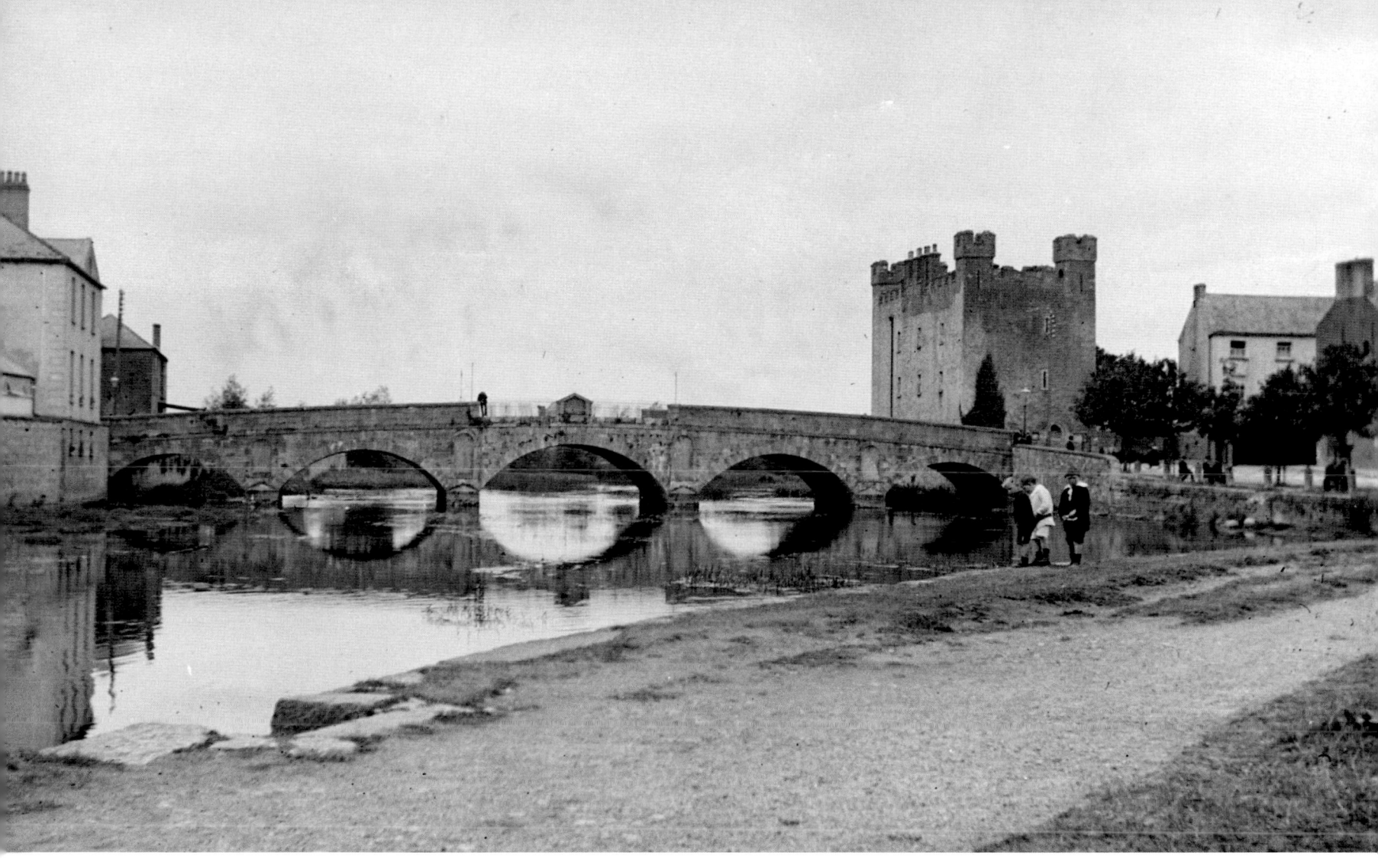

Athy Bridge, River Barrow, and White Castle, County Kildare (E 617)

2.15 p.m., 24 August 1919

Imperial Non-filter Orthochromatic, f11, 1/25 sec

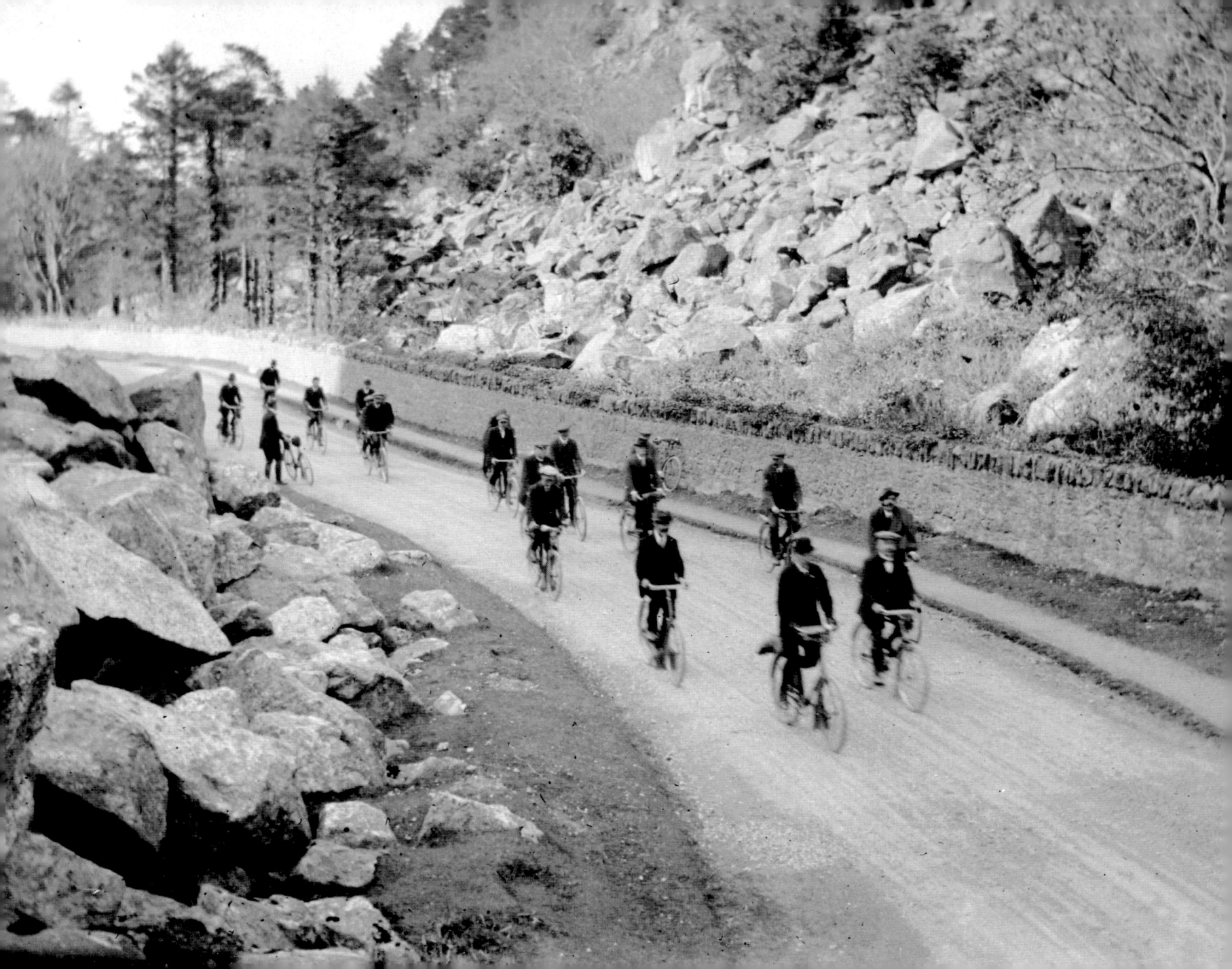

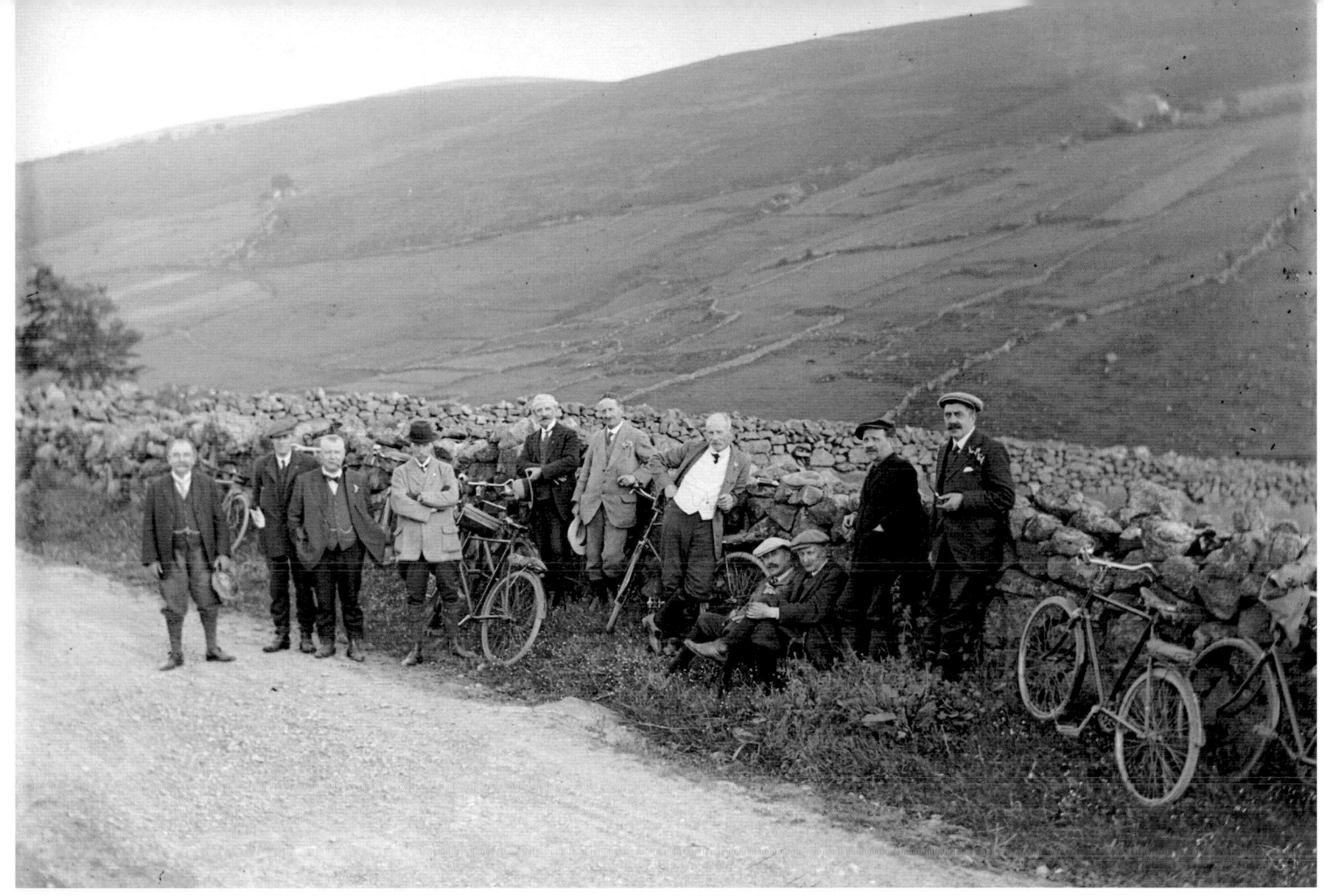

Above: Irish Cyclists Old Timers Fellowship in Glencullen, County Dublin (F 103)

8.15 p.m., 14 June 1919

Imperial Non-filter Orthochromatic, f9, 1/10 sec

Facing page: Irish Cyclists Old Timers Fellowship cycling through the Scalp, County Wicklow (F 99)

5 p.m., 3 May 1919

Imperial Non-filter Orthochromatic, f6.3, 1/50 sec

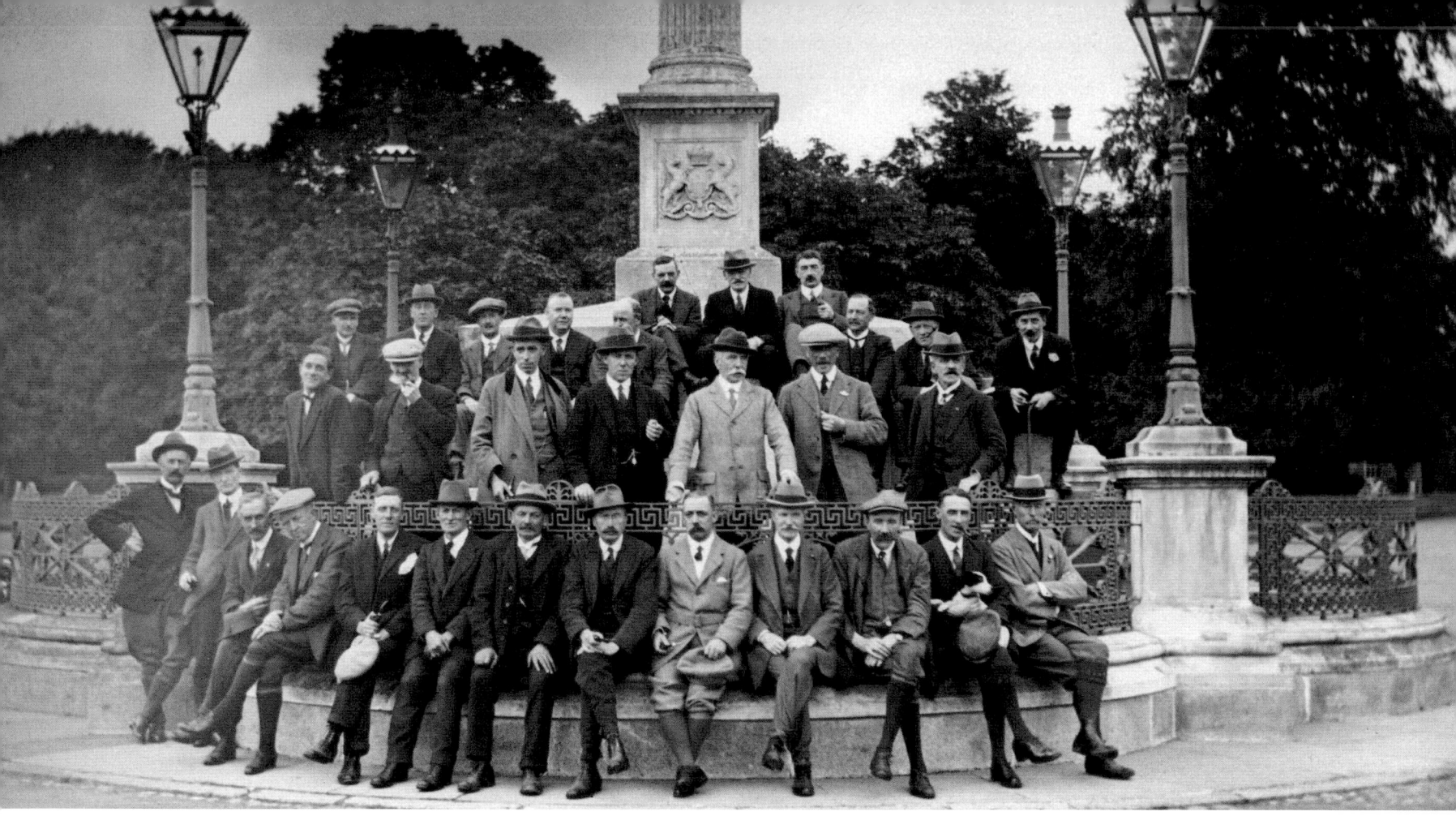

Irish Cyclists Old Timers Fellowship at the Phoenix Park, Dublin (F 156)

3 p.m., 3 September 1921

Imperial Non-filter Orthochromatic, f8, 1/50 sec

RLC RECORDED THIS SCENE IN HIS DIARY:

Old Timers Meet in Park. Turned up at about 3 p.m. to take the place of the Official Photographer who had last been seen heading Galway-wards loaded with fishing implements … After doing the needful in the photographic line, majority of party made for Lucan with of course a halt at Mrs Williams at the Strawberry Beds but not for strawberries.

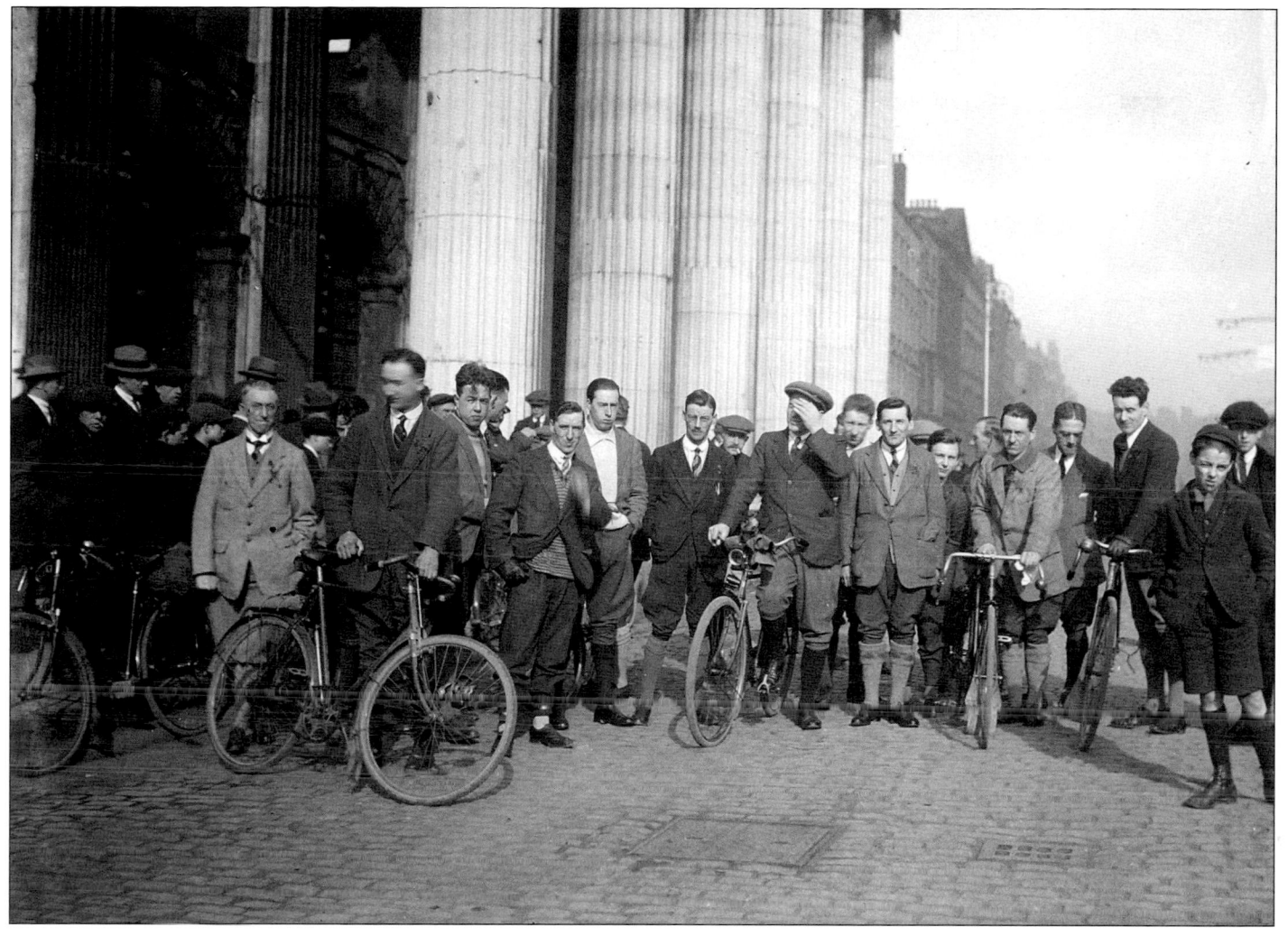

Irish Road Club members at the GPO in Dublin, at the start of St Patrick's Day Run to Ashford, County Wicklow (F 203)

10.30 a.m., 17 March 1925

Barnet Matt Screen, f6.8, 1/25 sec

117

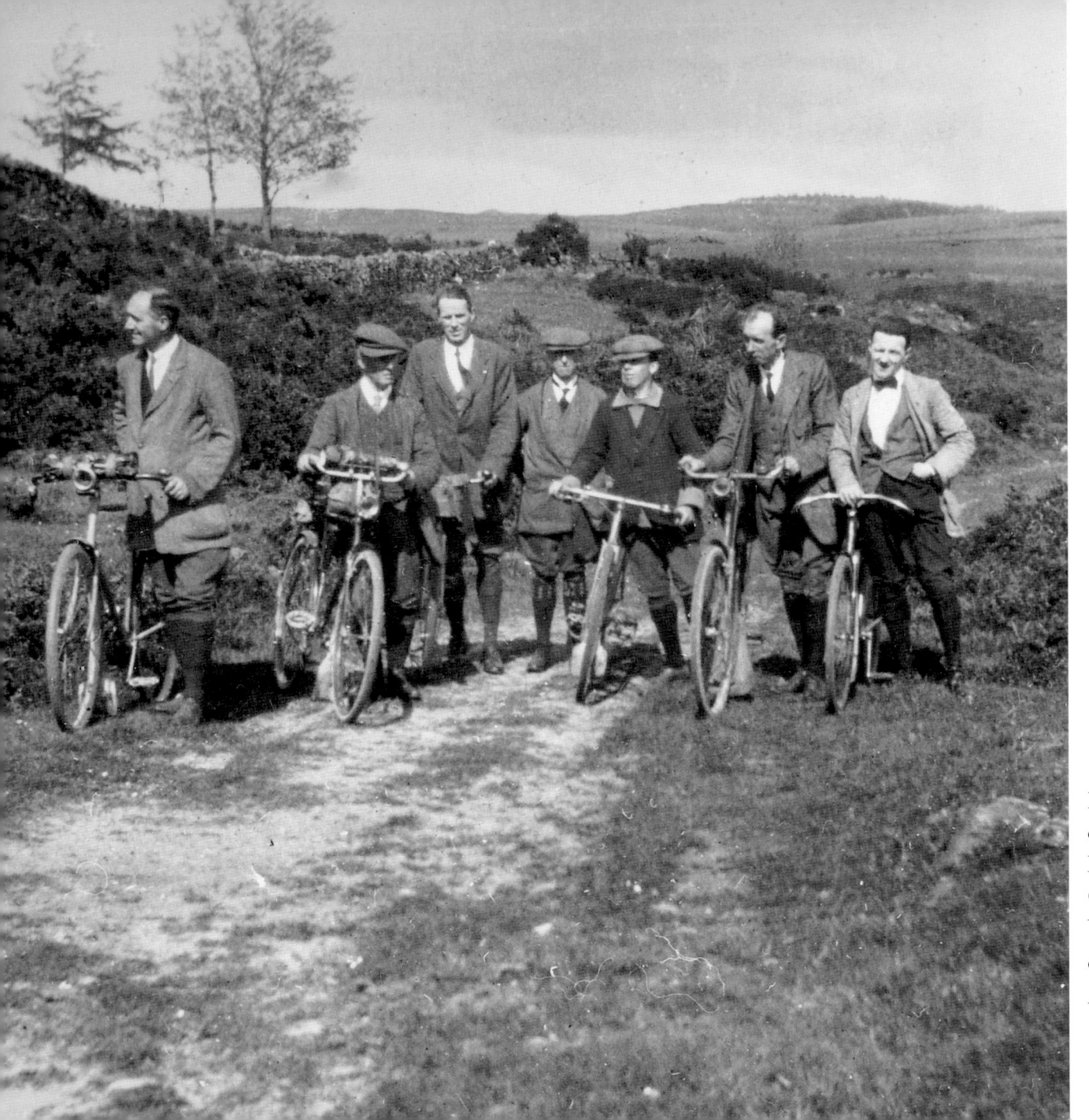

Irish Road Club
on the road near
Little Slaney Ford,
Glen of Imaal, County
Wicklow (E 1052)

6 p.m., 29 June 1924

Agfa Film, f11, 1/5 sec

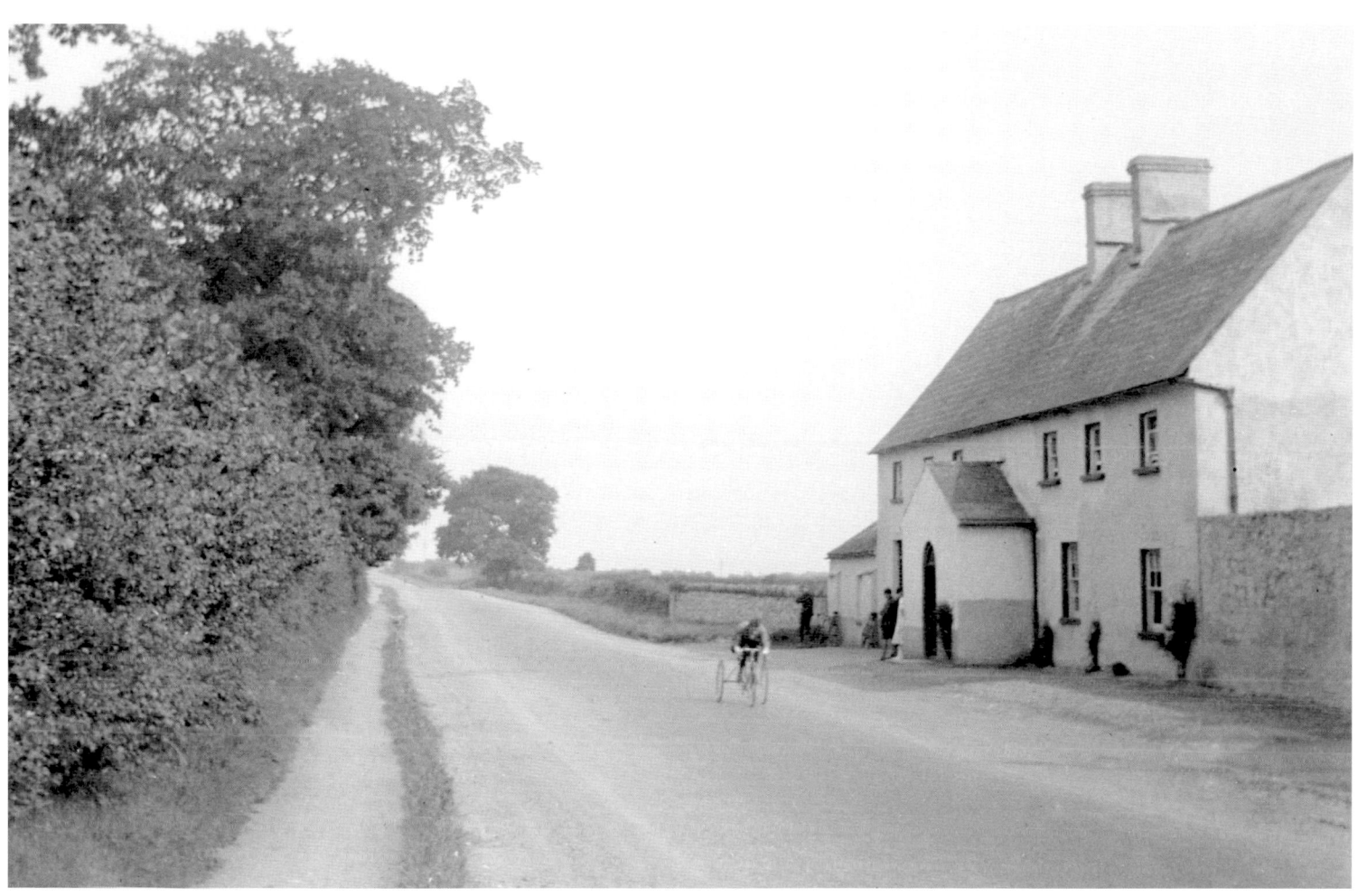

W.J. Taaffe on tricycle outside the Covered Coat public house near Leixlip, County Kildare, during Irish Road Club 50-mile race (E 1251)

5 p.m., 9 July 1927

Barnet Matt Screen, f11, 1/50 sec

Irish Road Club, 50-mile time trial, T. Brangan starting at Ashtown, County Dublin (F 190)

4 p.m., 1 September 1923

Wellington Anti Screen, f6.8, 1/50 sec

Owing to the cold weather on the day only six riders took part in the 50-mile time trial; P. Green, J. Whelan and T. Brangan were the fastest in that order, and the others who rode were D.J. Galavan, R. Oates and W. O'Brien. According to RLC the 'result of trial no use for selection of team'. The 50-mile trial was used for the selection of the Dublin team to face a team from Belfast in the Whitworth Inter City Cup Race held on Saturday 29 of that month:

Held usual 50 mile course. Ashtown, Dunshaughlin, Ratoath, Cloghran Quarry & back. On duty with stove for tea at Ratoath … Reached Ratoath barely in time. Big crowd of Belfast helpers there, but not many of our men. Not having enough to go round, had to leave corners in village unwatched, with result Walker & Belfast man crashed on herd of cows. Priest came hurrying up saying the men were killed so Walker hopped it & managed to finish race. Up to this had made fastest time. Saw whole of 6 of each team through in both directions, then hiked back. Met big crowd of our helpers near railway bridge beyond Clonee. Went on to finish which was very close. Dublin won on placings by 2 & time by 7 mins 30 secs, but Fastest Time went to Belfast.

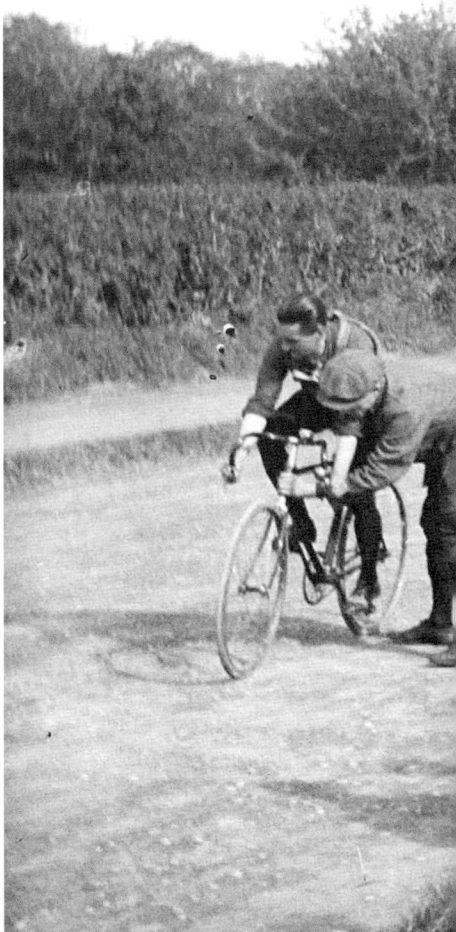

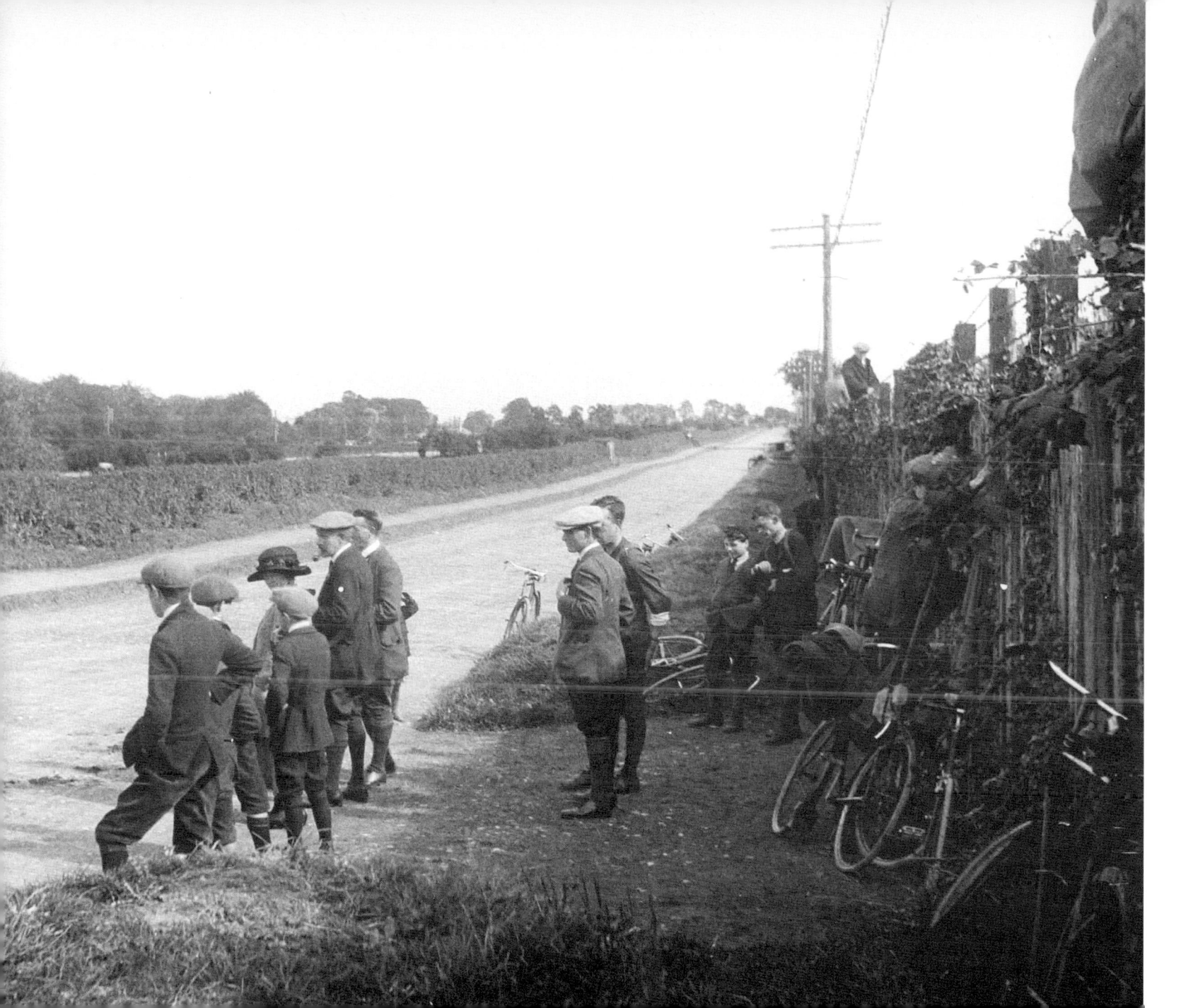

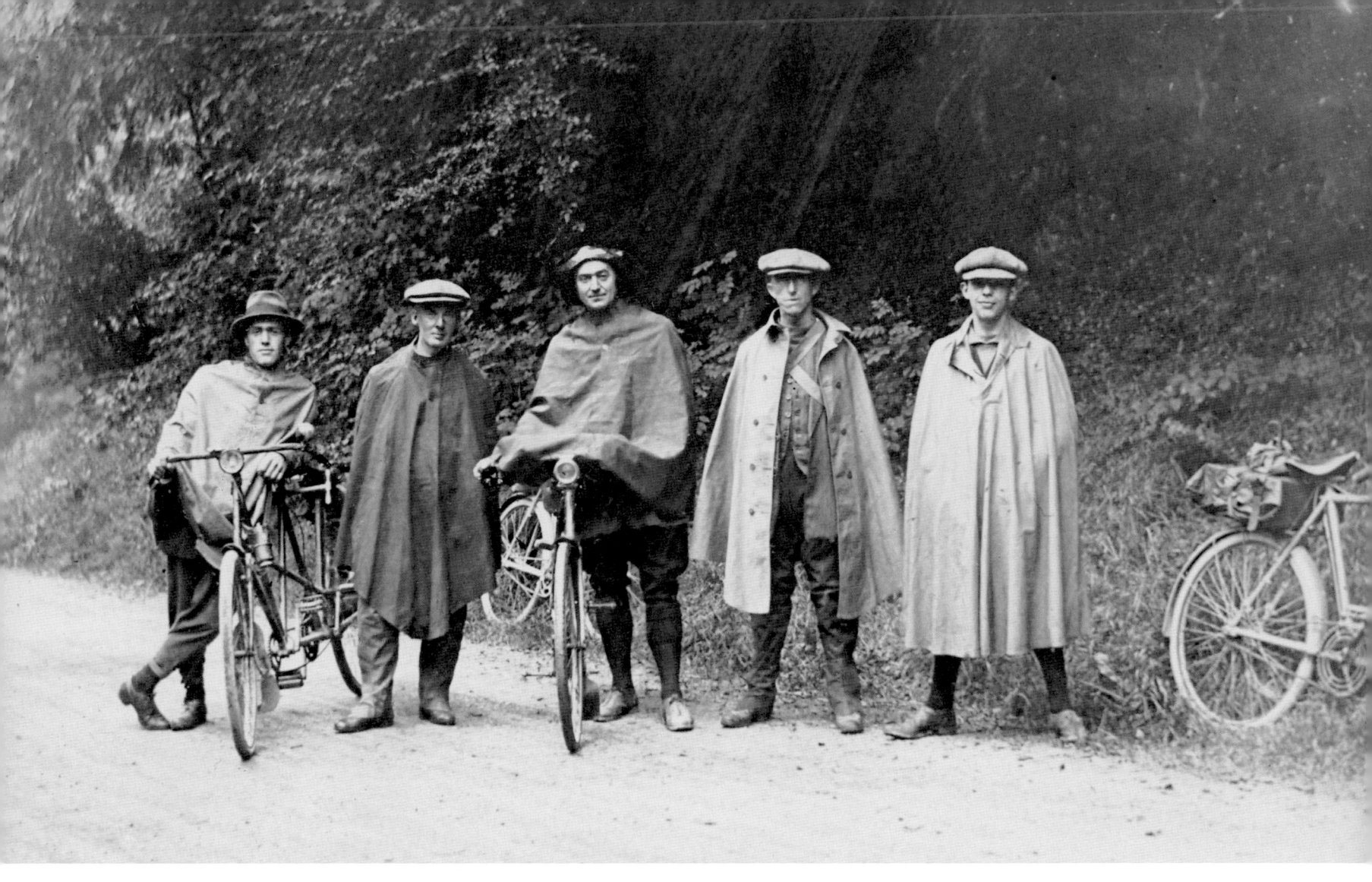

Irish Road Club in King William's Glen, [near Drogheda] County Louth (F 126)

8 p.m., 22 August 1920

Imperial Non-filter Orthochromatic, f8, 2 sec

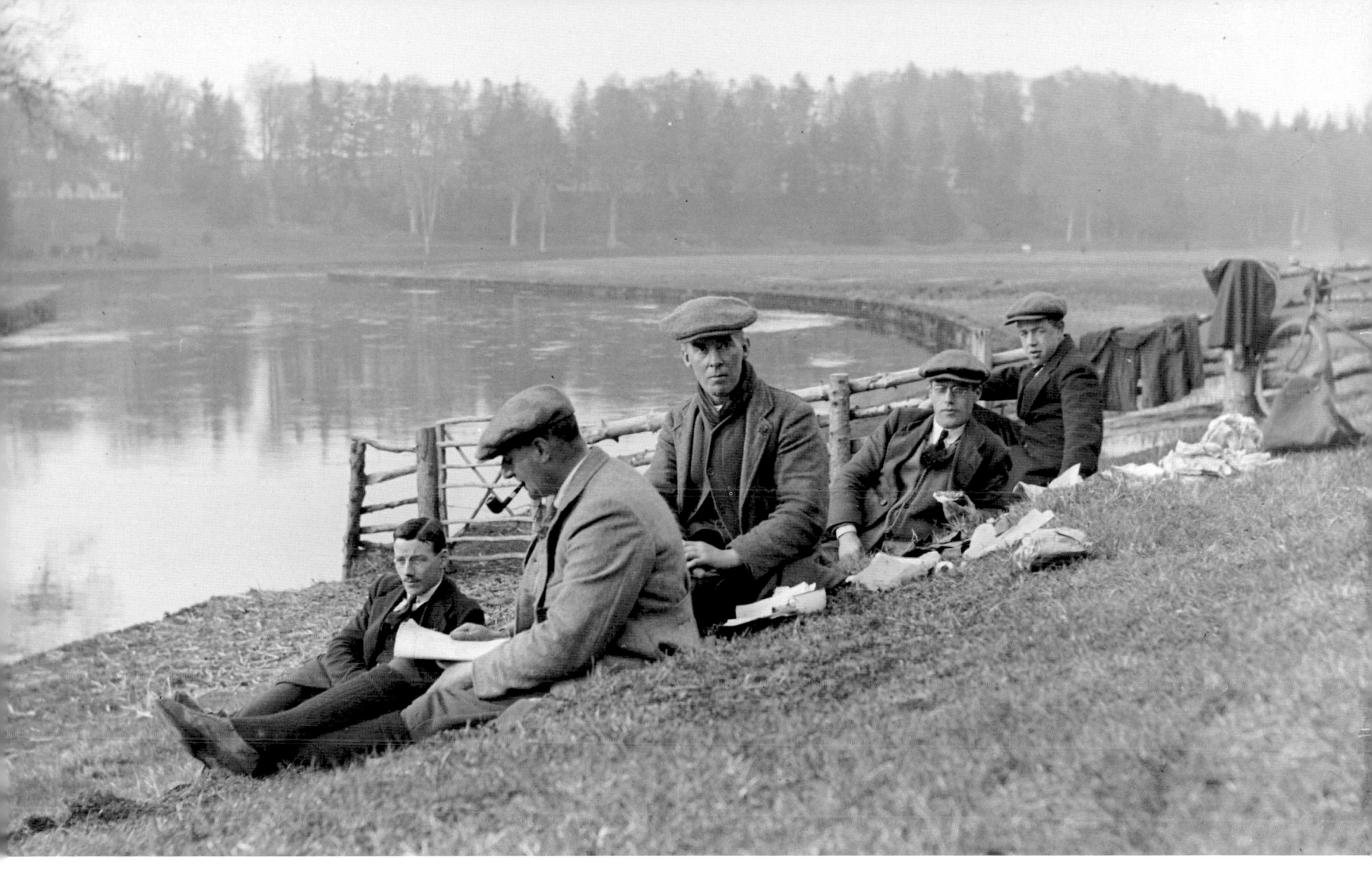

Irish Road Club – an evening meal on the banks of the Boyne, Navan, County Meath (F 162)

6 p.m., 9 April 1922

Imperial Non-filter Orthochromatic, f14, 1/5 sec

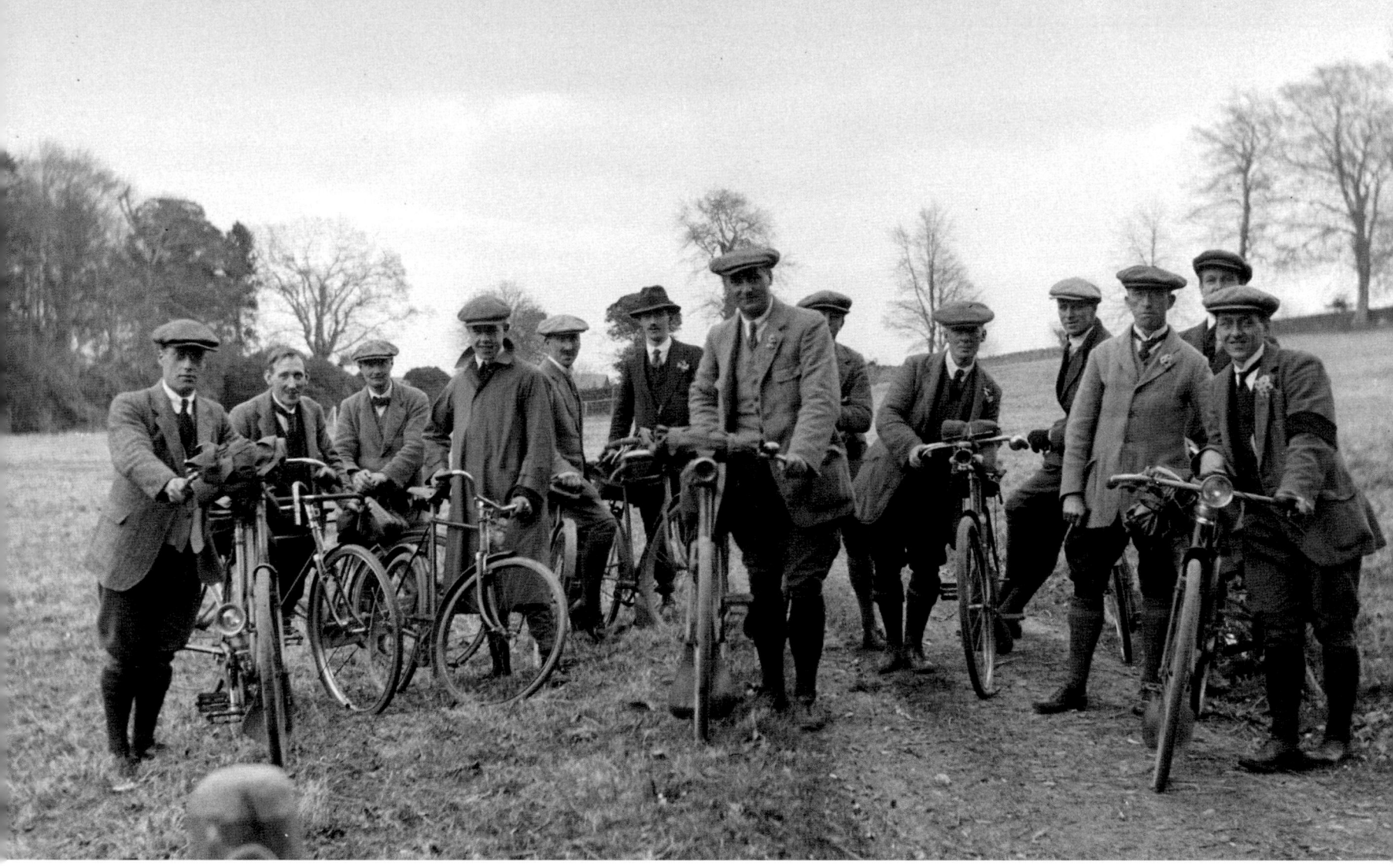

Irish Road Club at Dunran, [near Newtownmountkennedy] County Wicklow (F 164)

8 p.m., 23 April 1922

Wellington Anti Screen, f9, 1 sec

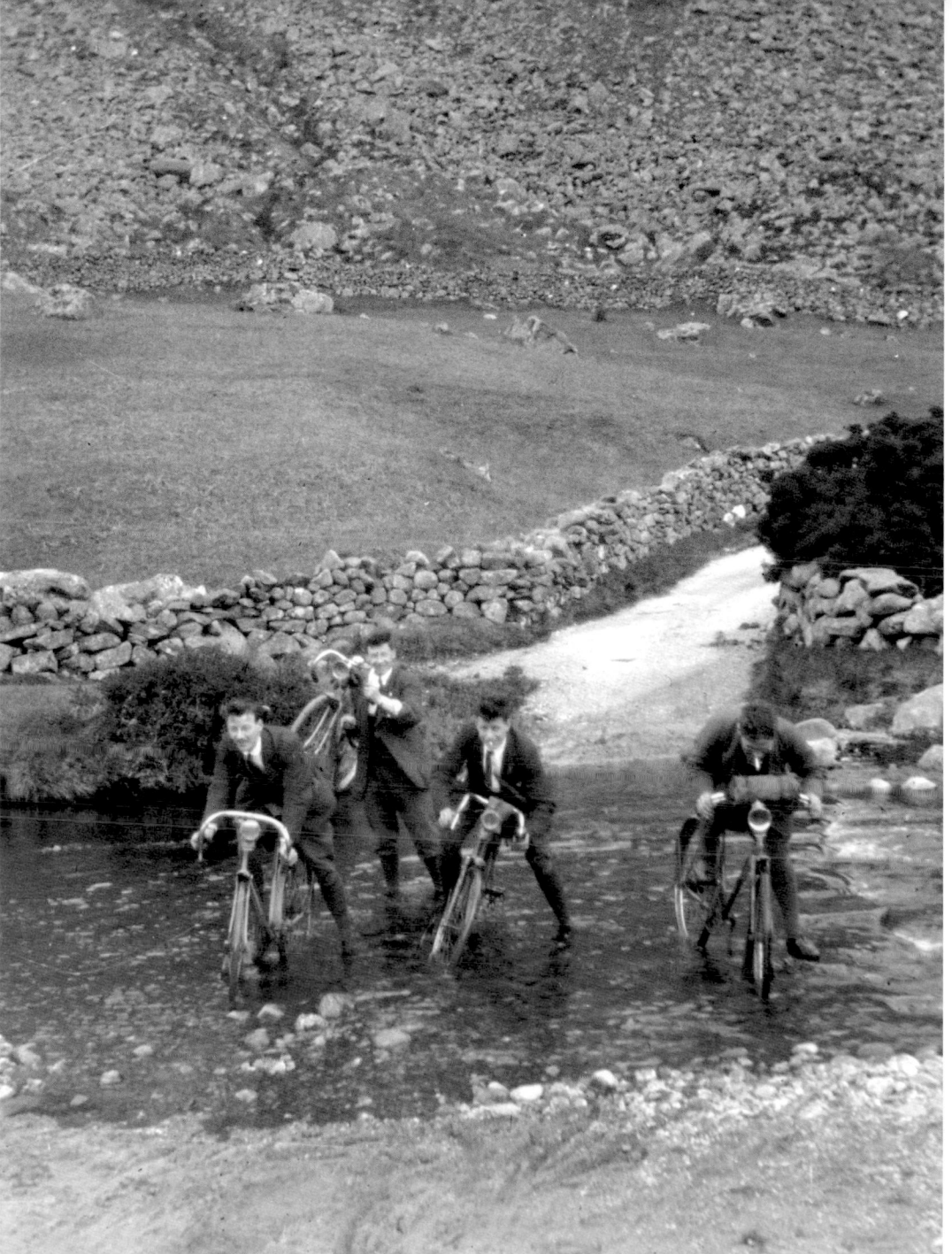

Irish Road Club 'Over the Top Run', crossing the ford at Barravore, Glenmalure, County Wicklow
(F 176)

2 p.m., 25 March 1923

Ilford Screened Chromatic, f6.8, 1/50 sec

RLC RECORDED THIS SCENE IN HIS DIARY:

R. Oates went ahead to take snap going through Ford. Knew something of it from previous experience so let others go in front, Water 1 ft deep. Stones rough. 3 glorious splashes. Photographer was so surprised forgot to press button. However they were so keen on having their photo taken at ford that they stood in river for 5 mins while I got camera out.

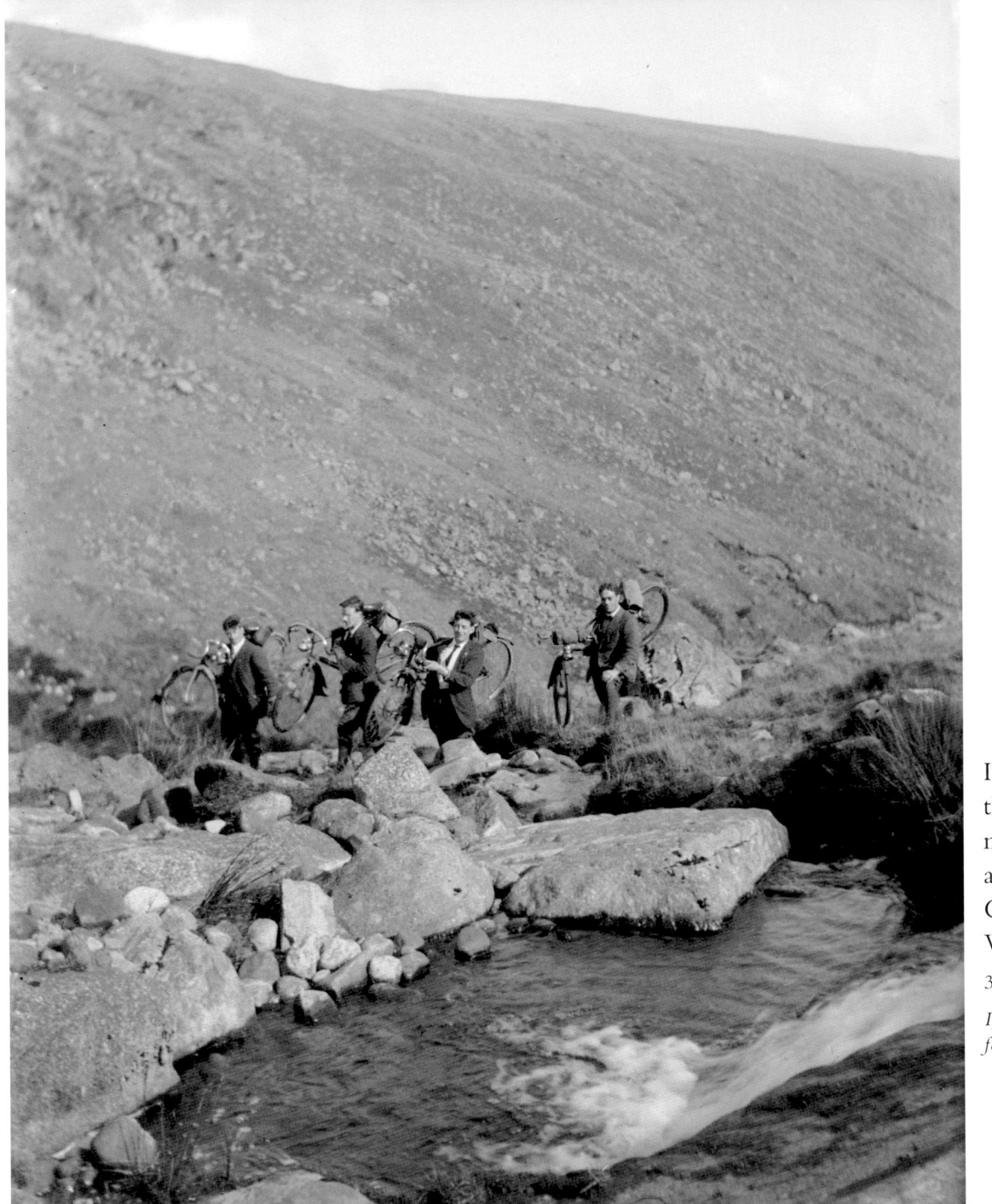

Irish Road Club 'Over
the Top Run', crossing a
mountain stream on the
ascent to the top of
Glenmalure, County
Wicklow (F 177)

3 p.m., 25 March 1923

*Ilford Screened Chromatic,
f8, 1/50 sec*

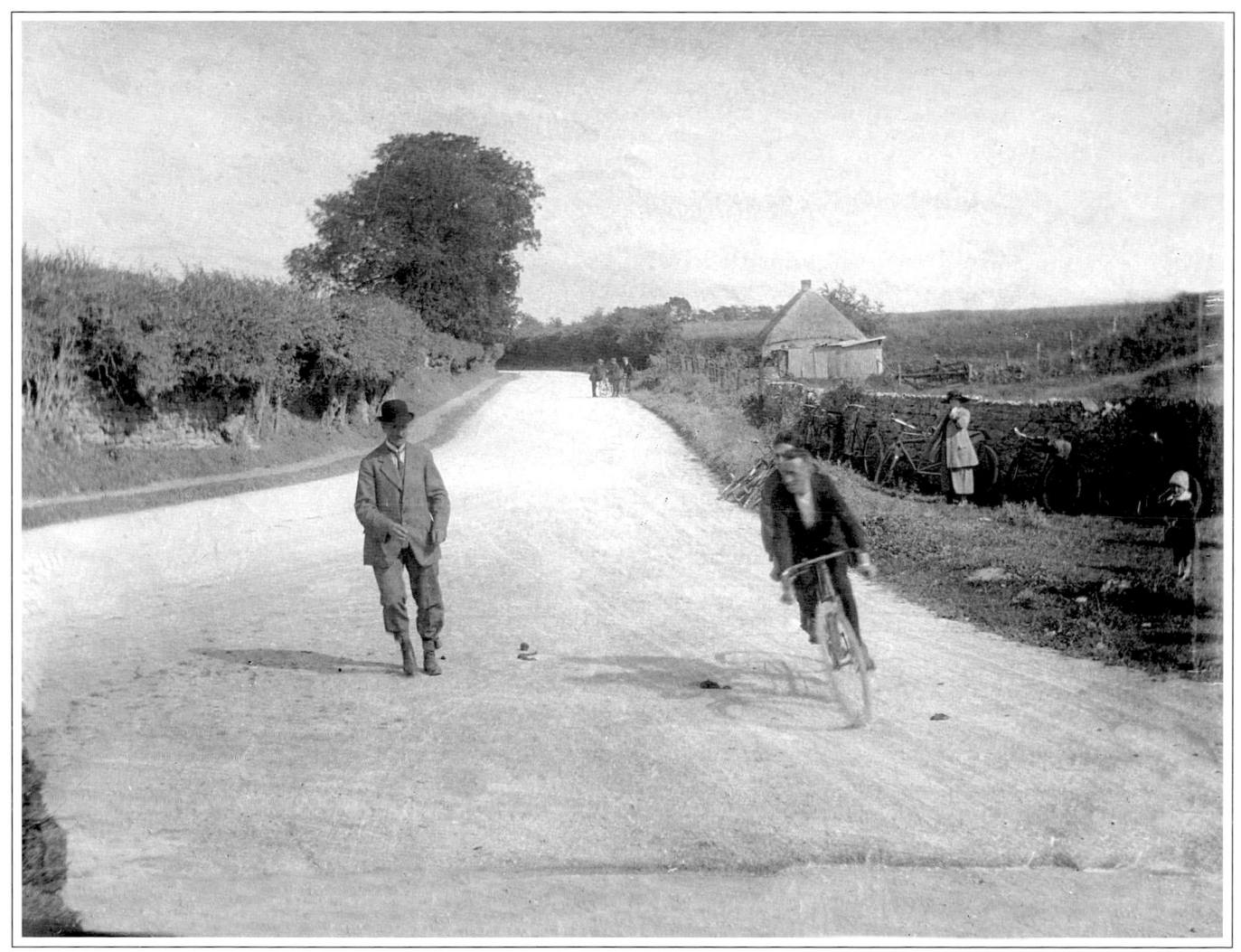

Irish Road Club, 50-mile (handicap) race, M.J. Healy and T.D. Brangan on tandem turning at
Cloghran Quarry, County Dublin (F 182)

4.45 p.m., 21 July 1923

Ilford Special Rapid, f6.8, 1/100 sec

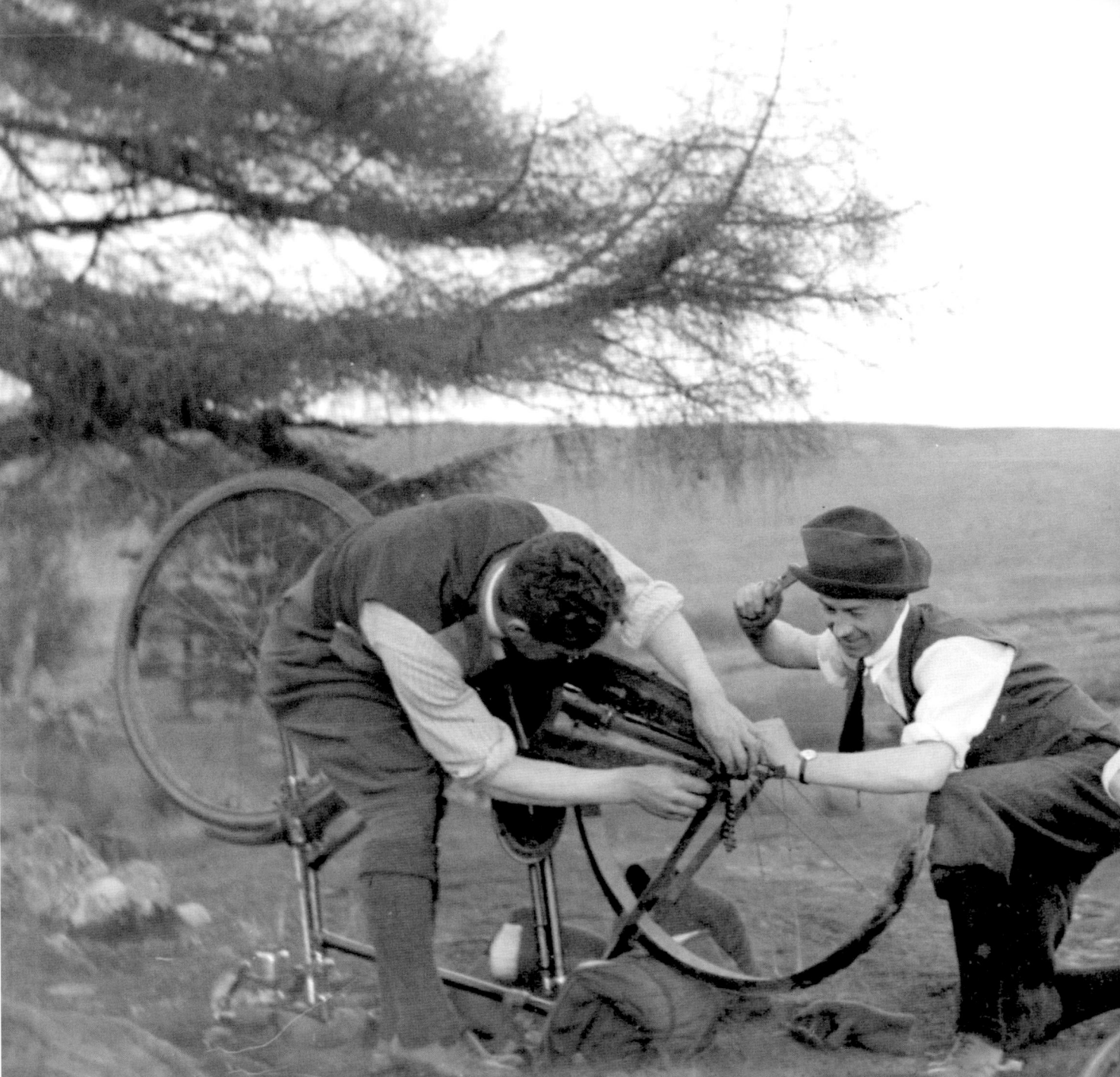

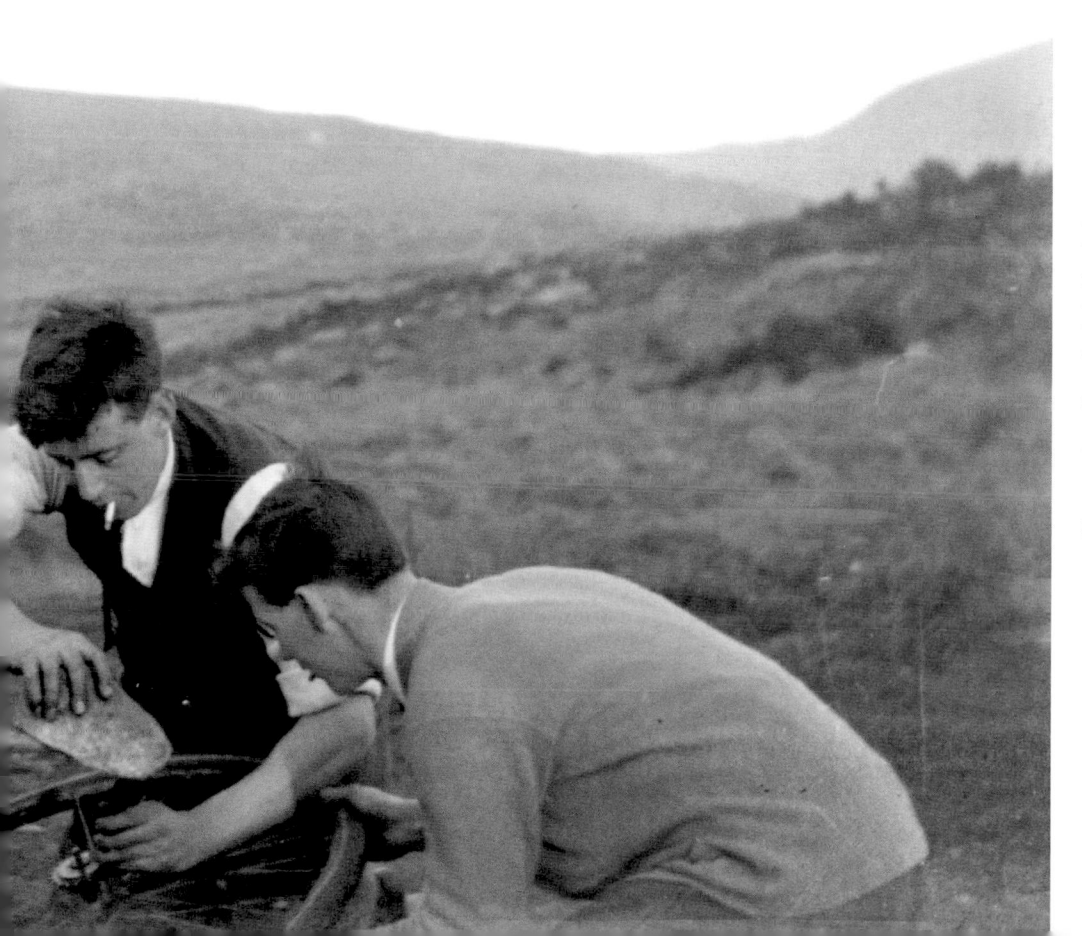

Irish Road Club 'Over the Top Run',
mending a broken freewheel near
Knocknamunnion, Glen of Imaal,
County Wicklow (F 178)

6 p.m., 25 March 1923

Ilford Screened Chromatic, f11, 1/5 sec

RLC RECORDED THIS SCENE IN HIS DIARY:

> *Freewheel having gone out of action all helped
> at investigation. Springs out of action so jambed
> it up with bits of paper fastener from R. Oates
> repair outfit. Wonderful things Oates has in his
> repair outfit. Machine now propellable as semi
> fixed wheel.*

Facing page:

Terenure Motor Club at Newcastle, County Down (F 64)

5 p.m., 23 May 1915

Primo Film, f11, 1/25 sec

This photograph was taken during a trip of the Terenure Motor Club to County Down. On reaching Newcastle, RLC found the members sitting on the harbour wall:

> *One of them had a camera so we both took a photograph of the group & were immediately tackled by two very irate RIC Constables, who charged us with taking photographs of the harbour. Got over this little difficulty by mentioning someone in Dublin Castle, whom we did not know, & were allowed to proceed after being warned against any further photographing.*

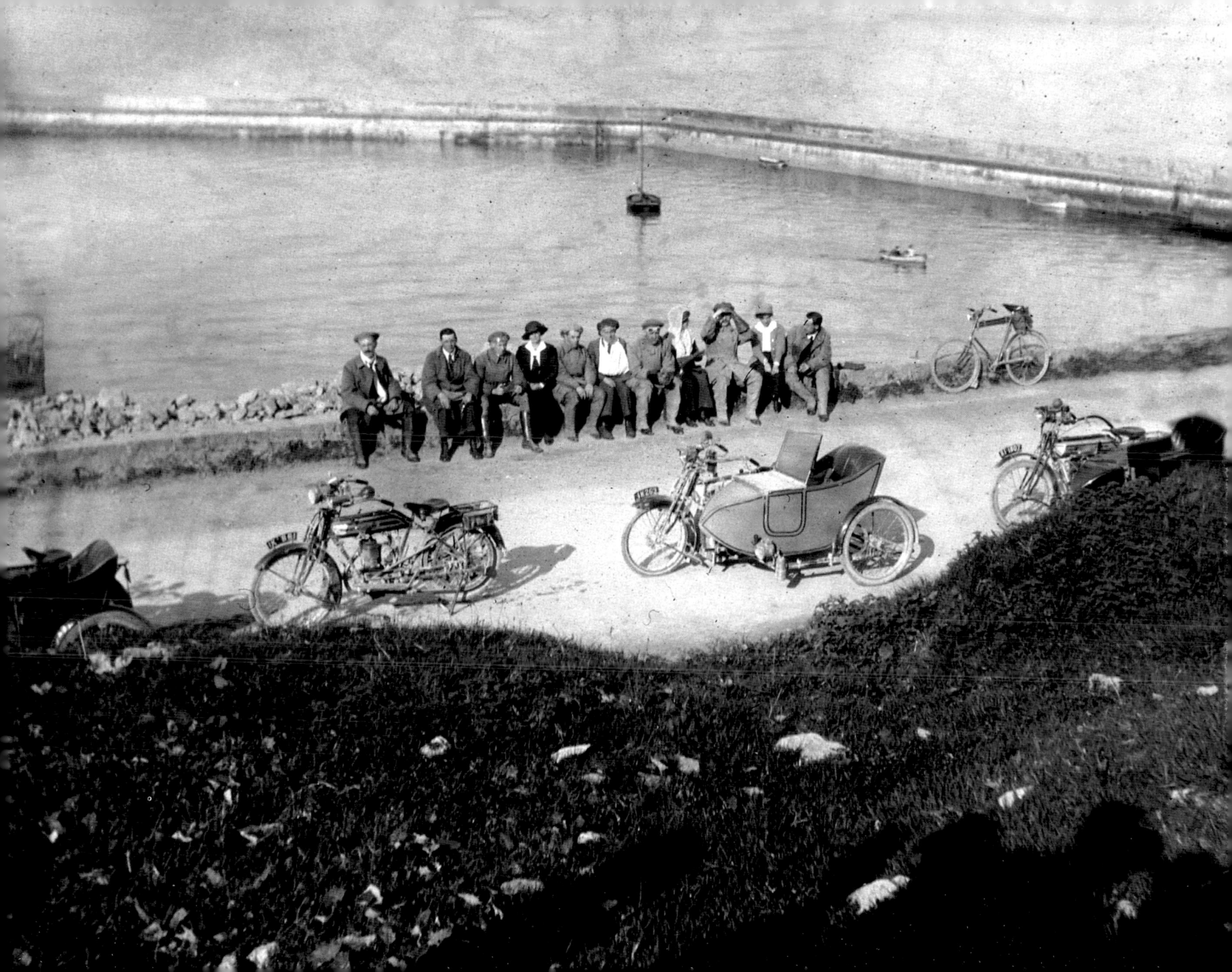

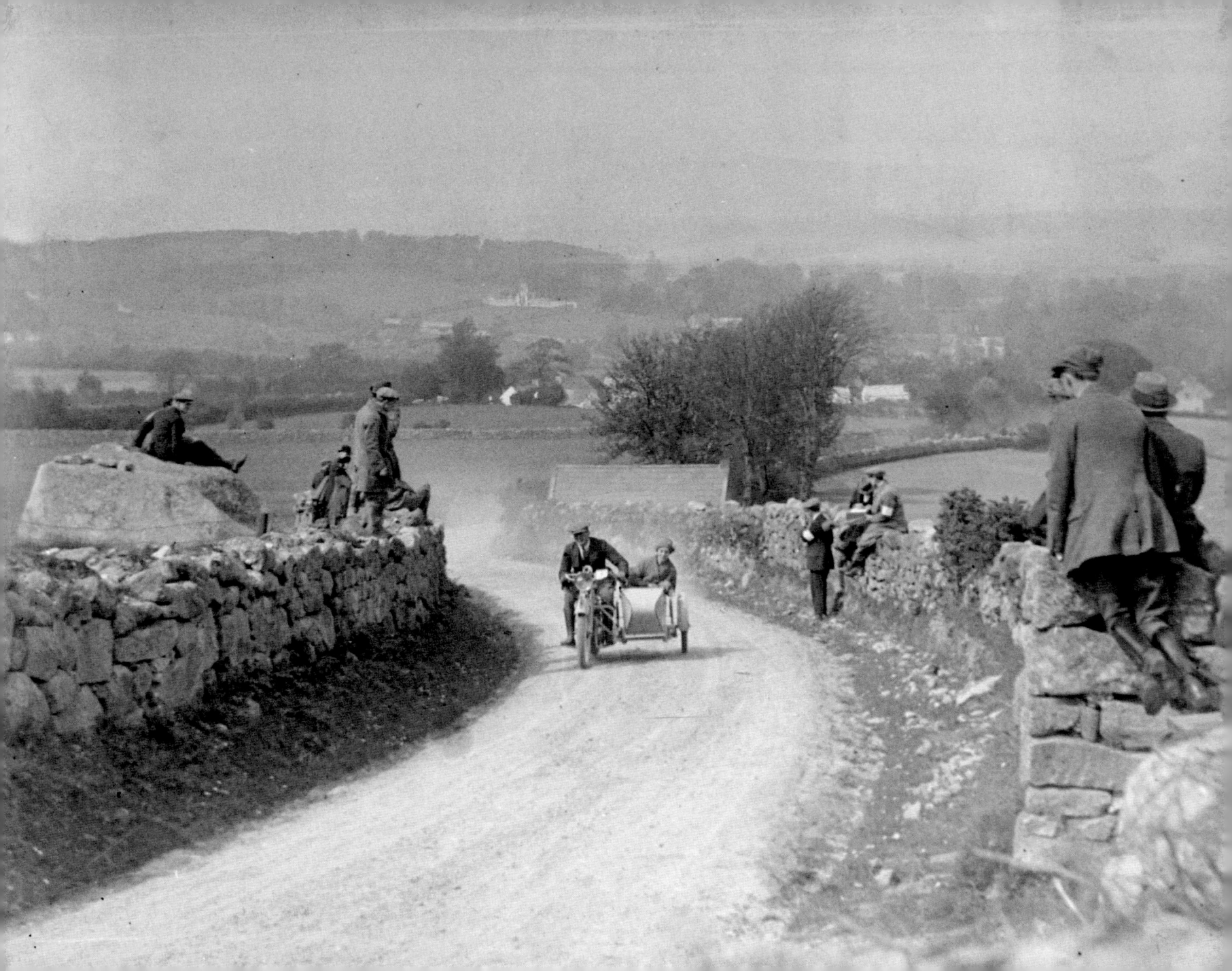

Facing page:

Dublin & District Motor Cycle Club Hill Climb near Glencullen, County Dublin, sidecar machine passing timekeeper (E 637)

3.30 p.m., 15 May 1920

Imperial Non-filter Orthochromatic, f8, 1/100 sec

RLC RECORDED THIS SCENE IN HIS DIARY:

Great crowd of motor-bikes at foot of hill. Climb finished before reaching Roe's Gate, where watched performances. Sidecars came up first, most appeared to have plenty of power in hand. First solo rider came up at a fearful pace, developed a wobble & finally fell a few yards from the finish, getting off with a much scratched face. The front of the machine however was wrecked. This accident put the Wind Up both competitors and officials. The latter shifted the finish a few yards lower down, while the former came up very gingerly. One machine failed altogether. A good climb was put up by an ancient machine made up of scraps.